HISTORY
The Last Things Before the Last

HISTORY
The Last Things Before the Last

SIEGFRIED KRACAUER

Completed after the Death of the Author by
PAUL OSKAR KRISTELLER

 Markus Wiener Publishers
Princeton

For information write to: Markus Wiener Publishers
114 Jefferson Road, Princeton, NJ 08540

Library of Congress Cataloging-in-Publication Data

Kracauer, Siegfried, 1889-1966.
     History: the last things before the last/Siegfried Kracauer.
     Completed after the author's death by Paul Oskar Kristeller.
     Originally published: New York: Oxford University Press, 1969.
     Includes bibliographical references and indexes.
     ISBN 1-55876-080-6
     1. History—Methodology. I. Kristeller, Paul Oskar, 1905–
II. Title
D16.K87   1994   94-12623
907'.2—dc20   CIP

Cover design by Cheryl Mirkin
Collage Background: Print of the Pantheon in the 18th century
Foreground left: Hitler at the *Reichsparteitag* in Nuremburg
Foreground right: Roman statue of Clio, muse of history (Glyptothek, Munich)

Printed in the United States of America on acid-free paper.

Preface
to the first American paperback edition
by Paul Oskar Kristeller

Siegfried Kracauer (1889-1966) was without question one of the most gifted, productive, and original writers and thinkers of our time. Each of his major publications offered diverse perspectives and methods and thus appealed to a broad spectrum of readers.

Kracauer attended school in his native Frankfurt, and studied architecture, philosophy, and sociology. In 1920 he began to write for the Frankfurter Zeitung, then the leading liberal newspaper in Germany. From 1924-1933 he was in charge of the *Feuilleton* section in Frankfurt and then in Berlin. His innovations included reviews of cinema, and photographic materials. Kracauer subsequently wrote and published, first in German and later in English, groundbreaking studies of cinema, a novel, and a monograph on white-collar workers, a previously ignored social class with its own interests, tastes and political inclinations. This analysis of the white-collar worker was a marked advance over Marxist sociology, which recognized only the manual laborer and the capitalist as social classes worthy of emphasis. At the same time Kracauer was an active, but often critical, member of the Institute for Social Research of Frankfurt University and a close personal friend of its directors, Max Horkheimer and Theodor W. Adorno, who analysed and taught sociology and other social sciences from a Marxist point of view.

In 1933 Kracauer and his wife Lili emigrated to France, where they spent eight years before moving permanently to the United States in April, 1941. Many fellow refugees with backgrounds similar to his pursued academic careers, but Kracauer was hampered by a speech defect that precluded lecturing activities. Kracauer worked for the State Department and later for the Museum of Modern Art, the Bollingen Foundation, and the Institute for Social Research.

I met Kracauer for the first time rather casually in his office of the Frankfurter Zeitung when I was a doctoral student of the history of philosophy at the University of Heidelberg. On the same occasion I visited the Institute for Social Research and briefly met its directors, Max Horkheimer and Theodor Adorno. I became much better acquainted with Kracauer when I joined the Columbia faculty during the academic year 1939-40. The Institute for Social Research, still directed by Max Horkheimer and Theodor Adorno, had relocated from Frankfurt to New York and become associated with Columbia University, where it occupied an office from 1933 to 1945 maintaining close relationships with other Columbia departments and with institutes as well as the Union Theological Seminary. During this entire period Kracauer was a faculty member of the Institute. The Institute's meetings, at which papers on a variety of subjects were read and discussed, were attended by many Columbia faculty members. I was invited to attend the weekly meetings and presented one paper myself in due time. Here Kracauer met the sociologists Paul Lazarsfeld and Robert Merton, and it was here that I renewed my acquaintance with Kracauer and it became a close personal friendship.

In 1960 Kracauer began to work as a reviewer and consultant for the Bollingen Foundation, an endowed institution whose directors were influenced by the psychoanalyst Carl C. Jung, and also by Western cultural traditions of classical, medieval, and early modern philosophy, history, philology, and auxiliary disciplines. I have good reason to assume that Kracauer, in his capacity as a consultant of the Bollingen Foundation, was instrumental in giving approval for a 1960 grant application I made to the

Bollingen Foundation to publish the first volume of my *Iter Italicum: A Finding List of Uncatalogued or Incompletely Catalogued Humanistic Manuscripts of the Renaissance in Italian and Other Libraries* (1963). Later that year, Kracauer himself began to work on a book on history, and frequently consulted with me on this project. He kept in close touch with me until his death in 1966. There was hardly a week during which we did not engage in lengthy scholarly conversations, at his or my home or at some coffeehouse or restaurant nearby, or by telephone. I did this gladly because I had the highest respect for him as a writer and thinker.

Kracauer fully realized that this book was uncharted territory for him, concerned with historical research rather than with the social, sociological, literary or art historical problems that he had treated in his earlier works. He told me repeatedly of his concern that his close friendship with Theodor Adorno might be adversely affected by the new turn taken in this book and because he had abandoned issues that were of major interest to Adorno.

When Kracauer died on November 26, 1966, the book about history was unfinished. Of the projected eight chapters, chapters one to four, seven, and the first half of chapter five were practically complete in manuscript form and required only few minor changes. For the second half of chapter five, and for chapters six and eight, Kracauer had written some drafts or synopses that were quite readable but in need of careful editing.

At the request of Lili Kracauer and the editors of Oxford University Press, I agreed to edit the manuscript for publication. I went over the completed chapters and made only minor changes. The unfinished chapters required far more extensive editorial intervention. I added a brief foreword and an epilogue and revised the footnotes and bibliography. The book was published by Oxford University Press in New York in 1969, three years after Kracauer's death.

After his death, Kracauer's friends, disciples, and admirers donated his papers and correspondence to the *Deutsches Literaturarchiv* in Marbach, where they have been readily accessible to interested scholars.

During the following decades, Kracauer's reputation and fame as writer and thinker steadily grew, both in Germany and in this country. On the occasion of the centenary of his birth, in 1989, the *Literaturarchiv* in Marbach mounted a documentary exhibition of his publications, personal papers, and photographs, thus illustrating and celebrating his life, work, and thought. The exhibition attracted many visitors and traveled to other German cities. At the initiative of Professors Mark M. Anderson and Andreas Huyssen the exhibition also came to Columbia University in March 1990, and a symposium on Kracauer's life and work was organized in conjunction with this exhibition. The speakers included Leo Loewenthal, who had known Kracauer personally. The papers of the speeches were printed in a special issue on Siegfried Kracauer of the *New German Critique,* No. 54, Fall 1991, which contains also a selective bibliography by Thomas Y. Levin.

While I am pleased with the rediscovery of Kracauer by a new generation of scholars, I see a series of problems in their attempts to adjust the thinking, writing, and character of Kracauer to their own theories. Especially dismaying to this new generation of scholars is the notion that Kracauer adopted some of his ideas from outside the Frankfurt School. His last work showed a particularly clear divergence from the sociological approach of the Frankfurt School.

Two papers which deal specifically with Kracauer's last book on history are included in the Special Issue on Siegfried Kracauer of the *New German Critique,* No. 54, Fall 1991: Gertrud Koch's "Exile, Memory, and Image in Kracauer's Conception of History" (pp. 95-109) and Inka Mülder-Bach's "History as Autobiography, The Last Things before the Last" (pp.139-157). They neither summarize the book nor indicate that its content fundamentally differs from his earlier writings. Their footnotes cite only books and articles unknown to Kracauer and refer to Kracauer's earlier books as if the book on history were in complete agreement with them. They also fail to indicate that Kracauer, in the footnotes and bibliography of this book, cites for the most part historical, philological, and

philosophical sources, never mentions his earlier writings, and very sel-
dom refers to the sociologists that predominate in his earlier works. And
worst of all, they imply and even state that history was not his major concern. An adequate scholarly interpretation of Kracauer's last work is yet
to be written.

This new edition of Kracauer's important last book which has been
inaccessible for many years, will make the work available for a new generation of readers, and serve as a basis for a new and more adequate interpretation.

Columbia University   Paul Oskar Kristeller
June 1994

Foreword
to the first edition

When Siegfried Kracauer died on November 26, 1966, his
friends were not only grieved by his sudden disappearance, but
also concerned about the fate of the book on history that had
been his main preoccupation during his last years and that he
left unfinished at the time of his death. It was evident from his
conversations and from the sections of the manuscript which
he presented to selected readers and to discussion groups
or published as separate articles that Kracauer had important things to say on the subject of history; and since he
came to the subject rather late in life and did not deal much
with it in his earlier writings, the book on history represents
a new facet of Kracauer's thought, and without it our appreciation and understanding of the man and the thinker would
remain incomplete. Hence it has been a great relief for his
friends and associates when they learned that most of the
chapters of the book had been written by Kracauer before he
died, and that for those sections that were still unfinished he
had left detailed synopses that are sufficient to fill the
gaps and to understand the direction of his thought. We
are all most grateful to Mrs. Lili Kracauer, and to the
Oxford University Press, for the care they have taken to pre-

serve this important work and to present it to us and to its other readers in a form in which it can speak to us.

The name of Siegfried Kracauer has been known to me ever since the time when I was a student at Heidelberg in the 1920's and read admiringly many of the articles he published in the *Frankfurter Zeitung*. I met him only during his later years in New York, but our acquaintance developed into a close friendship of a kind that does not easily or frequently occur among older persons. We had very frequent conversations, personally and over the telephone, and the chief topic of these conversations was the subject that occupied him mostly in these years and that has also been one of my own chief concerns: history.

Kracauer did not teach or lecture very much, but he was an active participant in many colloquia and discussion groups, including the Seminar on Interpretation at Columbia University. Well trained in more than one academic discipline, Kracauer did not belong to any one discipline or profession, let alone to any particular school of thought. He was a philosopher, sociologist, and historian, and above all, a critic and a writer. In drawing on many diverse sources, he was able to assimilate them into his own original way of thinking, and to make important contributions to a number of different fields. He was unconcerned with, and distrustful of, rigid systems and methods, and remarkably immune to fashions and to compromises. Steeped in a genuine experience that comprised many facets of human reality, he impresses both with the richness of his insights and with the firmness and lucidity of his verbal expression. The strength of his style reflects that of his thought, and the less he cared to adapt his words to the passing fashions of his day, the more he will have to say to future readers.

Kracauer's distrust of fixed and definitive systems of thought is deep seated and conscious. He avoids theology altogether, and his attitude towards technical philosophy is ambivalent. He admires Husserl, but mainly for his appeal to the *Lebens-welt*. He admires Erasmus precisely because he refuses to formulate or endorse any fixed theological or philosophical positions. Kracauer's insistence on what is concrete and personal makes him feel closer to writers like Proust or Kafka than to the classical philosophers. It is because he does not believe in our ability to grasp "the last things" through philosophical or theological systems that Kracauer is so much concerned with a "provisional insight into the last things before the last." If history attracts Kracauer for its provisional character, it also does for another reason. As a scholar and moralist, Kracauer has a profound desire "to bring out the significance of areas whose claim to be acknowledged in their own right has not yet been recognized," and to achieve "the rehabilitation of objectives and modes of being which still lack a name and hence are overlooked or misjudged." This concern, as Kracauer knew himself, links his later work on history with his earlier works that had been dedicated to seemingly so diverse problems, and especially with his studies of photography and of the film. Thus he could insist that history is not quite a science, just as photography is not quite an art, and would derive some remarkable insights from a comparison between history and photography.

In accordance with Kracauer's general attitude, the present book does not attempt to provide a philosophy or methodology of history in the form of a systematic exposition. We may rather consider it as a series of meditations on some of the basic problems involved in the writing and understanding of history. He tends to criticize the general theories of history formulated by Hegel and Nietzsche, Spengler and Toynbee, Croce and Collingwood, and to disregard the theories of Heidegger and of the analytical philosophers. Kracauer is more

inclined, and I tend to agree with him, to listen to the practicing historians, to Ranke and Huizinga and especially to
Burckhardt, to Droysen and Marrou, Pirenne and Bloch, to
Butterfield, Kaegi, Hexter, and Kubler. Kracauer is a keen
critic and a good quoter, but in both criticism and approval he
is guided by his own insight. His masterly critique of Croce's
"present interest theory" of history has become once more timely,
as is his critique of Nietzsche, or of "the current infatuation
with social history." And some of his striking insights should
give rise to much further thought and study. "The history of
ideas is a history of misunderstandings." ". . . the assumption
shared by Marxists and non-Marxists alike, that the establishment of a state of freedom from material want will in due time
benefit the human condition as such is much in the nature of
wishful thinking." "The effects of social arrangements on cultural trends are rather opaque." When Kracauer compares the
historian to a sightseer, or speaks of the exterritoriality of the
exile, he benefits from his own personal experience. And when
he states that truth is both in time and above time, he provides
a key for understanding the history of philosophy, and intellectual history, as a valid undertaking.

On several important issues, Kracauer hesitates to give a
definitive solution, but rather formulates a problem and thus
lays the ground for further thought. The discrepancy between
general and special history, or as he calls it, macro and micro
history, represents a serious dilemma. Kracauer seems to think
that the results of special research are so complicated and so
resistant to generalization that most of them must be ignored
by the general historian. I tend to be slightly more hopeful, and
to believe that the results of special research, after some lapse
of time, will penetrate the general histories, and that the diver-

sity of contradictory details can be handled in terms of comparative and qualified statements.

Another basic dilemma that Kracauer forcefully presents but does not resolve is that between chronological time and "shaped" time, or between the general sequence of all events occurring at a given period, and the specific sequences peculiar to one particular area or tradition. Again I should be inclined to be more optimistic, and try to lay the stress on the pluralism of cultural history, while maintaining the concept of universal cultural history at least as a regulative idea in the Kantian sense.

Kracauer's refusal to formulate a system also has the welcome result that his book is far less fragmentary than might have been expected from the state in which he left it. Each chapter, each paragraph, and even each sentence have a substance and bearing of their own, quite apart from the place they occupy in the book as a whole. His introduction states how Kracauer became interested in the subject of history, and the place this book occupies in relation to his earlier works. The first and second chapter deal with the status of history as compared with the natural sciences. The third chapter contains a critique of the "present interest" theory of history. Chapter 4, "The Historian's Journey," stresses the concreteness of historical events, and discusses the question to what extent the historian can overcome his own subjective approach. Chapter 5, "The Structure of the Historical Universe," discusses the dilemma between general and special history. Chapter 6, "Ahasuerus, or the Riddle of Time," is primarily devoted to the dilemma of chronological and "shaped" time. Chapter 7, "General History and the Aesthetic Approach," has been published and deals with the relation between history and the arts. The last chapter, "The Anteroom," discusses the relation between history and philosophy, stressing the intermediary character of history.

I am grateful for having been asked to add a few lines to a book that hardly needs them. For the book embodies much of what I have admired most in Kracauer as a man, thinker and writer. Kracauer was one of the most civilized persons I have ever known, endowed with an unfailing sense of what is genuine and what is false in the world in which we live and in the traditions that lie behind it. He has been able to build his own world by selecting from these traditions what he found valid and congenial. I profoundly agree with the spirit out of which all of his work was written. I admire his experience and insight, and the expression he was able to give to it. I feel that everything Kracauer says refers to a world that is real, to his world which is partly my own, and which I should like to become my own. Everything he says and writes is a precious testimony of his thought and of his life, and of a world, anything but perfect, that he experienced, suffered, and mastered. He carries a message which I hope will not be drowned by the shrill slogans of our day, but will continue to be heard as long as the wisdom and wealth of our civilization, old and always new, will retain its meaning for those willing to read and to think, and to live and act in accordance with their thinking.

New York, Columbia University   Paul Oskar Kristeller
August 1968

Note

When the author of this book died in 1966 he had already completed in virtually final form Chapters One, Two, Three, Four, the first half of Chapter Five, and Chapter Seven. The last-mentioned was published in *Poetik und Hermeneutik III*, Muenchen, 1968. For the second half of Chapter Five he had left a synopsis and an outline. For Chapter Six there exist a synopsis and the essay *Time and History*, published in: *Zeugnisse. Theodor W. Adorno zum sechzigsten Geburtstag*, Frankfurt a.M., 1963; and in: *History and Theory*, Beiheft 6, Middletown, Conn., 1966. Synopsis and essay had to be merged. For Chapter Eight the author left a synopsis that was less detailed in some places.

The author's synopses for the uncompleted chapters contained the basic ideas as well as indications of quotations to be inserted into the text. The final choice regarding the content of the quotations and the exact place of their insertion still had to be made. A large number of file cards exists with important material containing thoughts and comments of the author that to a certain extent have been woven into the text. In preparing the synopses of the un-

finished chapters and related material for publication, it was
necessary to provide connecting words and phrases, to fill in
and often to translate quotations from other sources as well
as to decide between different versions of the same passages.
Besides these editorial decisions, the text remains as the author
left it.

Contents

Introduction

The ancient historians used to preface their histories by a short autobiographical statement—as if they wanted immediately to inform the reader of their location in time and society, that Archimedean point from which they would subsequently set out to roam the past. Following their example, I might as well mention that recently I suddenly discovered that my interest in history—which began to assert itself about a year ago and which I had hitherto believed to be kindled by the impact of our contemporary situation on my mind—actually grew out of the ideas I tried to implement in my *Theory of Film*. In turning to history, I just continued to think along the lines manifest in that book. And all the time I had not been aware of this but, rather, assumed that I was moving on new ground and thus escaping preoccupations which had kept me under their spell for too long a time. Once I had discovered that I actually became absorbed in history not because it was extraneous to my drawn-out previous concerns but because it enabled me to apply to a much wider field what I had thought before. I realized in a flash the many existing parallels between history and the photographic media, historical reality and

The Introduction was written from January 1961 to February 1962.

3

camera-reality. Lately I came across my piece on "Photography" and was completely amazed at noticing that I had compared historism with photography already in this article of the 'twenties. Had I been struck with blindness up to this moment? Strange power of the subconscious which keeps hidden from you what is so obvious and crystal-clear when it eventually reveals itself. This discovery made me feel happy for two reasons: it unexpectedly confirmed the legitimacy and inner necessity of my historical pursuits; and by the same token it justified, in my own eyes and after the event, the years I had spent on *Theory of Film*. This book of which I had always conceived as an aesthetics of the photographic media, not less and not more, now that I have penetrated the veil that envelops one's most intimate endeavors, appears to me in its true light: as another attempt of mine to bring out the significance of areas whose claim to be acknowledged in their own right has not yet been recognized. I say "another attempt" because this was what I had tried to do throughout my life—in *Die Angestellten*, perhaps in *Ginster*, and certainly in the *Offenbach*. So at long last all my main efforts, so incoherent on the surface, fall into line—they all have served, and continue to serve, a single purpose: the rehabilitation of objectives and modes of being which still lack a name and hence are overlooked or misjudged. Perhaps this is less true of history than of photography; yet history too marks a bent of the mind and defines a region of reality which despite all that has been written about them are still largely *terra incognita*.

I might refer to two or three reasons which have increasingly prompted me to make history the center of my preoccupations. There is, first, the desire to arrive at a better understanding of the issues with which we are faced by studying such periods of the past as have undergone roughly similar experiences. True, the knowledge of what has happened then does not tell us any-thing about our own prospects, but it will at least enable us to look at the contemporary scene from a distance. History re-sembles photography in that it is, among other things, a means of alienation.

To exemplify this, take an issue that literally pervades the air we breathe—the enormous expansion of our physical and men-tal environment. It becomes difficult not to think in global terms; and the vision of the whole of humanity has ceased to be a lofty vision. But as the world is shrinking—are we not virtually ubiquitous?—it also extends beyond control. Evicted from our familiar surroundings, we are thrust into open space where many traditional views and customary procedures no longer apply. The ensuing uncertainty about the shape of things and the courses to follow is still increased by the crumbling of part of our idea-system: I am thinking in particular of the loss of confidence in the inherently progressive nature of science, which has come as a blow to the cheerful supporters of the idea of progress. Hence a widespread feeling of powerlessness or aban-donment. And as in the Hellenistic era when parochial security yielded to cosmopolitan confusion, this feeling of being lost in uncharted and inimical expanses seems to work two ways. It breeds distrust of ideologies in general, thus lessening the spell they cast over us; and, conversely, it stirs many, presumably the majority of people, to scramble for the shelter of a unifying and comforting belief.

Religious imagination and theological speculation in the Hel-lenized universe opened up spiritual dimensions which are all but inaccessible to modern man. Do we even aspire to them? Rather, we are confronted with a task which late antiquity could not yet envision; due to our technological know-how, we are equipped, and therefore committed, to try to improve the material conditions under which most of mankind is still living. Incidentally, the assumption shared by Marxists and non-Marxists alike that the establishment of a state of freedom from material want will in due time benefit the human condition as such is much in the nature of wishful thinking. Cultural demands and spiritual leanings may evaporate if they are temporarily put in brackets or taken care of in a facile way to suit the masses. (Perhaps the flatness of modern thought which shows in this assumption is the price we have to pay for our inescapable absorption in the socioeconomic aspects of human affairs?)

The second reason for my preoccupation with history is about the reverse of the first: far from relating to present-day issues, it must be traced to a compassionate interest—an antiquarian interest, as it were—in certain moments of the past. They are beckoning me like Proust's ghostly trees that seemed to impart a message to him. (I sometimes wonder whether advancing age does not increase our susceptibility to the speechless plea of the dead; the older one grows, the more he is bound to realize that his future is the future of the past—history.)

Roughly speaking, my interest lies with the nascent state of great ideological movements, that period when they were not yet institutionalized but still competed with other ideas for supremacy. And it centers not so much on the course followed by the triumphant ideologies in the process as on the issues in dispute at the time of their emergence. I should even say that it revolves primarily around the disputes themselves, with the emphasis on those possibilities which history did not see fit to explore.

This interest is intimately connected with an experience which Marx once pithily epitomized when he declared that he himself was no Marxist. Is there any influential thinker who would not have to protect his thoughts from what his followers—or his

enemies, for that matter—make of them? Every idea is coars-
ened, flattened, and distorted on its way through the world. The
world which takes possession of it does so according to its own
lights and needs. Once a vision becomes an institution, clouds of
dust gather about it, blurring its contours and contents. The
history of ideas is a history of misunderstandings. Otherwise
expressed, an idea preserves its integrity and fullness only as
long as it lacks the firmness of a widely sanctioned belief. Perhaps the period of its inception is most transparent to the truths
at which it aims in the midst of doubts.

One might argue here that history does not know such
caesuras; that actually the controversy goes on after an idea, or
what remains of it, has gained ascendancy. As a matter of fact,
the tradition of any ruling doctrine is a story of continual attempts to adjust it, however precariously, to contemporary demands, ever-changing situations. And these attempts at reinter-
pretation may lead far away from it; no dogma is immune
against heresy and corrosion. But even so the initial phase of an
accepted idea appears to have a significance of its own which
distinguishes it from all subsequent phases. Were it otherwise,
the history of many a powerful belief would not comprise efforts
which tend to justify the concern with the time of its birth. They
invariably spring from the conviction that the dominant creed of
the epoch has been corrupted by accretions, misconceptions,
and abuses which altogether obscure its precious core. And it is
logical that this view should kindle a desire to undo the injurious
work of tradition and rehabilitate that creed in its virgin purity.
From its corrupted state in which it is all but unrecognizable the
eyes turn back toward its yet unspoiled origins. A case in point
is Luther. His development also shows that the return to the
sources is sometimes tantamount to a fresh departure, the re-
storer revealing himself as an innovator.

Be this as it may, I feel immensely attracted by the eras which preceded the final establishment of Christianity in the Graeco-Roman world, the Reformation, the Communist movement. The fascination they exert on me must be laid to my hunch that they carry a message as important and elusive as that of the trees which aroused Proust's compassion. And what would the message be? One thing is certain: it does not figure among the contending causes of those eras but is hidden away in their interstices; it lurks, for instance, behind the debate between Celsus and Origen, or the religious disputes between Catholics and reformers. Its location is suggestive of its content. The message I have in mind concerns the possibility that none of the contending causes is the last word on the last issues at stake; that there is, on the contrary, a way of thinking and living which, if we could only follow it, would permit us to burn through the causes and thus to dispose of them—a way which, for lack of a better word, or a word at all, may be called humane. Werner Jaeger alludes to it when discussing the desire for mutual penetration between Greek culture and Christian faith in the second century A.D.: "Both sides must finally have come to recognize that . . . an ultimate unity existed between them, and a common core of ideas, which so sensitive a thinker as Santayana did not hesitate to call 'humanistic' . . ." Actually both sides failed to achieve that ultimate "humanistic" unity. Need I expressly mention that the possibility of it presents itself at every juncture of the controversy which threads the historical process? There are always holes in the wall for us to evade and the improbable to slip in. Yet even though the message of the humane is virtually omnipresent, it certainly does not claim attention with equal urgency all the time. No doubt this message, whether received or not, is particularly pressing and definite in the eras which reverberate with the birth pangs of a momentous idea. It is they in which the mingling antagonists are challenged to ask the fundamental questions instead of having to tackle this or that sham problem handed down by tradition.

The figure of Erasmus, who lived among the antagonists of such an era without belonging to them, illustrates most of what has been said just now in so striking a manner that I cannot resist the temptation to insert a few remarks about him. They are based on the assumption that he came as close as was possible in his situation to delineating a way of living free from ideological constraints; that in effect all that he did and was had a bearing on the humane.

Erasmus never tired of spreading the message of it. His editions of the Greek New Testament and the Fathers as well as his *Adagia* and *Colloquia* with their constant recourse to Greek and Latin authors clearly tesified to his desire to revive the original simplicity of the Christian doctrine and to accept the ancients he admired into the company of the saints. His satires on monasticism and the corruption of the clergy were no less public property than his demands for Church reform in the spirit of Christian humanism. Nor did he easily miss an opportunity to publicize his ideas about the pitiable condition of the poor, the greed of the princes, and other secular affairs; his tracts and letters teem with references to topical issues, conveying views whose often far-sighted modernism owed much to his de-dogmatized Christian outlook. He abhorred violence and sympathized with the common man, the simple soul. All this the contemporaries knew. They also knew that he was loath to take sides and shunned clear-cut decisions. And they could not help noticing that he invariably rejected the positions offered him by popes and kings. (The stock opinion that he did so out of his sense of independence is a model case of sloppy thinking.)

The conclusion that Erasmus stood out like a monument for

everybody to see would seem to be unavoidable. However, the strange thing is that in spite of his outspokenness he was the most elusive of men. "Nobody has been privileged," a friend of his formulated, "to look into the heart of Erasmus, and yet it is full of eloquent content."

Secrets mean a challenge to the interpreter. Judging from the evidence, the psychological make-up of Erasmus related to the build of his mind in a significant way. It should therefore be possible to trace the diverse aspects of this figure to a hypothetical common source. Such an attempt may not afford insight into the heart of Erasmus but it will at least reveal something about the forces that shaped its contents. Now both the personal leanings and the intellectual pursuits of Erasmus coincide in suggesting that he was possessed with the fear of all that is definitely fixed. To state the same in terms involving his spiritual self, he was essentially motivated by the conviction that the truth ceases to be true as soon as it becomes a dogma, thus forfeiting the ambiguity which marks it as truth. His fear—or should I say, his nostalgia for perfect immediacy?—reflected this conviction; a spiritual rather than a psychological fear, it was largely identical with the mystical strain in him which has been repeatedly emphasized in the literature.

Everything falls into a pattern once you think of this fear as the prime mover behind the scenes. For one thing, various seemingly unrelated personality traits of Erasmus find their natural explanation in its stirrings. It makes one understand his distrust of philosophical speculation and his unwillingness to participate in theological disputations, bound as they were to run into a medley of categorical assertions. It accounts for his ingrained repugnance to any binding commitments and his skeptical attitude toward alleged solutions of certain religious problems which, he observed on some occasion, had better be put off till the time when "we shall see God face to face." And it naturally was at the bottom of his hatred of the absolute assuredness in which Luther indulged—Luther whose turn to the Bible and fight against the abuses in the Church Erasmus unswervingly approved at the risk of getting increasingly entangled in polemics which incommoded him greatly.

More decisive, his fear of the fixed also explains the position which his Christian humanism was to occupy among the competing ideologies of the period. To be sure, Erasmus championed a cause in the sense that he aimed at religious regeneration and social improvements. But since his aversion to formulas and recipes with their congealed contents prompted him to keep his ideas, so to speak, in a fluid state, they did not, and could not, jell into an institutionalized program; from the outset, their true place was in the interstices between the Catholic doctrine, as established by tradition, and the hardening creeds of the reformers. One might even assume that Erasmus would have disavowed, or indeed no longer recognized, his own message had it confronted him in the guise of one of these beliefs; their hold on the masses was bought at a price he was not willing to pay. His cause was precisely to put an end to the historical causes.

This carries all-important implications for the way in which the world responded to Erasmus. The universal fame he rapidly won indicates that at least some of his ideas and endeavors ingratiated themselves with people at large. Not to mention his influence on the Spiritualists, the Spanish mystics, and, in later days, enlightened 18th-century minds—influences partly due to misunderstandings—, he led the theologians back to the sources of Christianity, spread the gospel of humanism, and encouraged fuller literary expression. It cannot be doubted either that his concern for a better society, his belief in perfectibility through knowledge and education, and his insistence on what has time and again been confused with tolerance gave a voice to longings whose existence the soft halo surrounding his public image tends to confirm. Many may have welcomed Erasmus as a liberator redeeming them from narrow-mindedness and prejudice. In the "Erasmus-atmosphere," to use Walther Koehler's term, they could breathe more freely.

But they were scattered in the crowd; they did not rally round Erasmus. His message proper was of little practical consequence; it created a mood rather than a movement, a mood as intangible as a transient glow in the night, a fairy-tale's promise. There were Lutherans, no Erasmians. How could it have been otherwise? True, Erasmus wanted to change institutions, yet he did not want the world to corrupt his inmost cravings by institutionalizing them. Out of his all-pervading fear of the fixed he himself prevented his "cause" from degenerating into a cause, even though he was aware that his reluctance to become "engaged" inevitably spelled defeat. "I am afraid," he wrote seven years before his death, "that the world will ultimately carry the day."

This was exactly what happened: the world, a world split into camps, blurred his intentions and objectives. His wide visibility notwithstanding, Erasmus remained largely invisible. Conservative Catholics and reformers alike lacked the language to comprehend a message which cut across, and transcended, the doctrines to which they adhered. The language they used was geared to their respective causes. So the vision of Erasmus disappeared behind a veil of misinterpretations. Small wonder that he sat between all chairs imaginable. Luther rudely called him an Epicurean, which in a measure he was, and zealous schoolmen accused him of having touched off a religious and social revolution, which was not entirely untrue either. And since he heeded his own counsels in sifting the good from the bad in the conflicting doctrines, the warring antagonists, offended by his refusal to let himself be cast in the role of a partisan, presented him as a weakling who wavered irresponsibly between Rome and Wittenberg and took refuge in unavailing compromises.

From the angle of the world Erasmus was a fickle customer indeed. He defended the uprising of the German peasants as a revolt of misery and despair, but no sooner did they commit excesses than he (sadly) admitted the necessity of repressive countermeasures. He attacked the rigidity of a tradition which opposed the philological revision of sacred texts and yet exhorted the pious to bear with the traditional abuses, arguing that it was impossible to create a new world over night. His evasive attitude toward the cult of the saints and the confession —institutions which he neither criticized nor wholeheartedly endorsed—could not but strengthen the impression of his intrinsic ambiguity. And this ambiguity went hand in hand with his eternally reiterated pleas for peaceful agreements at all costs. "I love concord to such a degree," Erasmus declared in 1522, "that, should a debate develop, I am afraid I would rather forsake part of the truth than trouble the peace."

These words hint of the motives behind his conduct. With Erasmus, the notion of peace was pregnant with Christian meanings; it foreshadowed a fulfillment beyond the reach of the established creeds which, poor substitutes of the unattainable truth, bred only conflict and bloodshed. Hence, what the staunch devotees among Catholics and Protestants stigmatized as undecided wavering on his part was in reality nothing but the deceptive outward appearance of his unwavering determination to move straight ahead toward the peace he envisioned. Fortunately, he was a masterful navigator; for as matters stood, he was obliged to steer his way between the rivalling parties with prudence and much finesse. Yet despite the fact that he pursued a middle course or what looked to the world as such, Erasmus was the opposite of a compromiser. His efforts to bring the dissenters back to the fold and impress upon the Church the need for reforms did not result from opportunistic, basically anti-Utopian considerations but, conversely, amounted to an utterly uncompromising attempt to remove the causes that prevented the arrival of peace. Utopian visionaries condemn those who stick to the middle of the road on the ground that they callously betray mankind by trying to perpetuate a state of imperfection. In the case of Erasmus the middle way was the direct road to Utopia—the way of the humane. It is not by accident that he was the friend of Thomas More.

That most of his contemporaries should ignore an approach which would have lost all its meaning if it had become a cause lay in the nature of things. The question is whether Erasmus himself realized where the way he followed would lead him. His message pointed into an abyss: did he fathom its depths? In one of his *Colloquies* he has Eusebius, its protagonist, extol the divine power moving such ancient authors as Cicero or Plutarch and then propose that "perhaps the spirit of Christ is more widespread than we understand." It is the very thought of Erasmus which Eusebius thus epitomizes. Taking his cue from the apologists and the revered Origen, Erasmus held that the pagan sages too were inspired by divine revelation and that, because of the radiant manifestation of the Logos in Jesus Christ, Christianity was the consummation of the best of antiquity. This extension of Christianity into the virtual goal of all worthy non-Christian strivings permitted him to reconcile his devotion to "Saint Socrates" with his faith in transubstantiation and to protest the Christian quality of his humanistic concerns. He conceived of the humaneness to which he aspired as an outgrowth of Christian liberty.

For all that we know this might well be the whole story. But is it? Note that Erasmus was reportedly as inscrutable as he was outspoken. There must have been things he left unsaid— perhaps things too dangerous to be revealed? To venture a guess at what will forever remain his secret, it is not entirely improbable that, in pondering his road and its destination, Erasmus arrived at conclusions which so filled him with fright that he preferred to lock them away in his heart. He may (or may not) have surmised that in the last analysis he aimed at something beyond the pale of Christianity; that, thought to the end, his true design was once for all to wreck the wall of fixed causes with their dogmas and institutional arrangements for the sake of that "ultimate unity" which the causes mean and thwart.

An old Jewish legend has it that there exist in every genera- tion thirty-six just men who uphold the world. Without their presence the world would be destroyed and perish. Yet nobody knows them; nor do they themselves know that it is because of their presence that the world is saved from doom. The impossi- ble quest for these hidden just ones—are there really as many as thirty-six in every generation?—seems to me one of the most exciting adventures on which history can embark.

Should the reader expect the foregoing observations to be implemented by historical studies proper, I am afraid he will feel disappointed by the sequel. For like the author of *Tristram Shandy*, I am stuck with difficulties and reflections which, meta- phorically speaking, precede the birth of my hero. In fact, per- haps the major reason for my preoccupation with history is an urge to find out more about the constitution and significance of this controversial branch of knowledge. Has history become a science after having emancipated itself, halfheartedly, as it were, from the dominion of metaphysical speculation and theo- logical dogma? Its claim to be a science is by no means uncontested. Nor can it be said to be an art even though it retains traits of a literary genre. And of course, it is not a matter of impressionistic opinions either. History, as we know it today, lies somewhere between the dimensions defined by these pursuits and preferences. It belongs to an intermediary area. However, this area is far from being acknowledged as such. Traditional habits of thought blind us to its existence. Especially the scientific approach and the philosophical obsession with ultimate issues tend to distort the problems involved in historical explorations. In the following, I shall try to set some of these problems —for instance, the characteristics of "historical reality," the relations between the present and the past, the relations between histories on different levels of generality, the question as to whether the underlying subjectivity of historical writings may not transcend itself, etc.—in a perspective which does justice to their peculiar nature. My goal in doing so is to establish the intermediary area of history as an area in its own right—that of provisional insight into the last things before the last.

1
Nature

Modern historiography has in a measure emancipated itself—
with great difficulties and at considerable cost—from the old
philosophico-theological speculations on the (alleged) meaning
of the total historical process. But what about its relations to the
sciences proper? To pose this question means to raise a venerable issue—one which already caused German 19th-century historians to wage war on two fronts: just as they tried hard, if halfheartedly, to rid themselves of Hegelian metaphysics and ingrained theological preconceptions, they turned against Comte's
and Buckle's attempts to "elevate" history to the rank of a science.[1] Remember also Dilthey's persevering, truly heroic efforts
to validate this anti-scientific attitude by attributing to the
Geisteswissenschaften, as he called the family of historical sciences, a different manner of approach from that of the *Natur-
wissenschaften*: the former aspire to "understand" historical
"life," whereas the latter focus on the laws that control natural
processes.[2] He thought of himself as the Kant of history; in a
sense he was the philosopher of historicism. Yet even though his
ideas exerted considerable influence, he did not succeed in settling the issue at stake. Nor of course did Rickert, whose formal

differentiation between the individualizing, value-related historical method and the generalizing, value-free scientific method
faintly echoes Dilthey's more inclusive, more substantive insights.[3] Rather, the debate on whether or not history should be
considered a science continues to fill the professional journals
and is still far from subsiding.[4] The course it is taking suggests
that there is an outspoken tendency today toward bringing historiography into the fold of the exact sciences. Exhortations to
this effect come from strange quarters: Valéry, spellbound by
the transparency and cleanliness of scientific method, blames
the general historians for uncritically proceeding from confused
assumptions and requests them to set forth their axioms and
postulates with a natural scientist's accuracy.[5] That his counsels
fall into line with existing preferences, can be inferred from
much of contemporary theory and practice. Thus Professor
Hans Mommsen in a 1961 statement on historical method declares that Dilthey and Rickert were wrong in placing all the
emphasis on the historian's concern with the individual, the
unique. Their thesis is no longer valid, says he, because it fails to
do justice to certain similarities between historical and scientific
procedures. Historians do set up types, do resort to generalizations; and like the scientists, they too seek to verify some working hypothesis or other.[6] These redefinitions reflect, and acknowledge, an actual change in direction of historical pursuits.
During World War II, Marc Bloch, concerned about the future
of his craft, expressed the hope that history—*"une science dans
l'enfance"*—would outgrow *"la forme embryonnaire du récit,"*
leave behind legend and rhetoric, and become an *"entreprise
raisonnée d'analyse."* [7] Is history going his way? At any rate, the
time-honored genre of the narrative is losing its attractiveness,
while analytical accounts assume a prominent role—a shift of
interest which conceivably benefits the upsurge of studies in

social history. Whatever its reasons, this turn from narration to argument, from description to heuristic inquiry takes place in an intellectual climate conducive to it. The prestige of science is such that it cannot but strengthen the trend envisioned by Bloch and Valéry; indeed, I imagine many a historian to suffer from guilt feelings because of the hybrid nature of his medium. To round out the picture, I might as well mention that some dedicated social scientists and anthropologists basking in that prestige frown on traditional historiography with a mixture of contempt and condescension which is outright hilarious. One of them calls the "writing of history . . . as it has been practiced up to the present . . . a semi-rational activity" and unhesitatingly compares those engaged in it with the "bards of less-developed peoples." [8] It would be difficult to be more ignorant of what makes historians tick. There you have Snow's "two cultures": the literary may miss the fine points of nuclear physics, but their opposite numbers fully match them on this score.

Obviously the chances for bards to develop into scientists would appreciably increase if it could be shown that human affairs are governed by laws that bear on the relationships between repeatable elements of historical reality. Note that the term "law" is used here in a loose sense; it covers both the natural-science laws which enable us to make predictions and the "laws" aspired to by sciences, such as psychology, economics, the social sciences, and anthropology, which altogether inquire into various aspects of human nature, human conduct. The "laws" of these so-called "behavioral sciences"—a generic name which is rather misleading—are at most approximations to the natural laws proper. They apply to patterns of events which may or may not perpetuate themselves; and their inherent claim that they hold sway over the future is hardly more than a pretense. But from the angle of historiography the natural and behavioral sciences can nevertheless be lumped together because the latter, too, search for, and construct, (seemingly) invariant similarities.* Now the behavioral sciences, whose material overlaps that of history, undeniably yield a wealth of "laws" involving historically significant data—a fact frequently illustrated by reference to the statistical regularities in social life.[9] Small wonder that their findings should be put to good use in historical writings. Gilbert Murray was already extolling the importance of anthropology for the history of Greek religion at a time when many of his colleagues still refused to look beyond the pale of traditional classical scholarship.[10] In the more recent past depth psychology asserts itself as a major provider. Namier insists that human conduct can be adequately interpreted only in psychoanalytical terms; [11] E. R. Dodds suggests that the Greeks of the Hellenistic era embraced astral determinism out of an unconscious "fear of freedom" haunting them after the loss of the polis.[12] Nor should it be forgotten that since the days of Max Weber the boundaries that separate history from sociology have become more fluid. It is not only the historians who borrow from the social sciences, but the social scientists on their part occasionally raid the historians' territory, as if prompted by a desire to make it a dependency of theirs.

To all appearances, then, historical reality abounds with regularities similar to those that make up the universe of the natural sciences. Accordingly, human affairs must be assumed to fall

---

* It is understood that scientific laws have a double origin: in the material observed and in the observer's mind. They are both discoveries and constructs. But the share of the subject in their formation need not be considered here. Rather, the interest lies with the problem of whether the worlds of nature and history are equally amenable to the establishment of natural, or quasi-natural, laws. And since this problem mainly involves the peculiar character of given reality, the intervening subjective factor can be kept constant.

largely into the realm of nature or to be an extension of it. On principle, such a fusion may also materialize the other way round; nature may be imagined to partake of man's historicity. This possibility has found a powerful supporter in Marx. He conceives of man as a product and force of nature; and he identifies history as a dialectical process in the course of which man through his labors not only domesticates nature outside him but, in adjusting it to his purposes, changes his own nature, the what and how of his existence.[13] Thus nature is set moving, its sameness giving way to its becoming in time. Of late, an attempt has been made to underpin this idea scientifically. Professor von Weizsaecker, the German theoretical physicist and philosopher, argues that it follows conclusively from the "second law" of thermodynamics [14]—an argument, though, which I suspect to exceed the potential range of a strictly physical law. But be this as it may, the proposition of nature's historicity is practically negligible anyway. Marx himself endorses it only partially; while he is confident that nature, as manifest in man, is subject to historical change, he seems to assign to external nature, nature about us, a nondialectical, independent status and, in consequence, (relative) unchangeability.[15] And since v. Weizsaecker estimates the life expectancy of the historized cosmos at over a hundred billion years,[16] we may rest assured that natural causes will continue to produce their predicted effects for an indeterminate time.

The upshot is that nature, if it changes at all, does so at an incredibly slow pace. And indeed, is man not deeply embedded in it? Geography and climate, physiological make-up and animal drives combine to determine his conduct.* The impact of these

* It is understood that man's conduct is also regulated and canalized by the decisions of the powers that be and by the initiative of individuals, groups, or parties intervening in the social process. Thus a man-made nature is being continually superimposed upon primeval nature. But within the

familiar factors is considerably strengthened by the fact, less
noticed so far, that the life of the mind is ruled by a principle
which bears on the quantity and distribution of the energies at
an individual's disposal. It may be called the "principle of mental economy" and formulated as follows: If an individual works
intensively in one area of human endeavors he will most likely
be merely receptive in others; productivity here entails laxity
there; practically nobody is able to proceed with the same *élan*
on all fronts, in all directions. Einstein's performance as a political thinker lags far behind his unique achievement as a physicist. Inner life, that is, comprises a "zone of inertia" in which
criticism yields to uncritical acceptance and fierce groping to
sluggish *laissez faire*. In this zone we surrender to convention
and prejudice, become creatures of habit, and act in foreseeable
ways. It is to all intents and purposes the dimension of natural
phenomena. The mind cannot help lapsing into it.[17]

What holds true of the individual all the more applies to the
numerous groups which aim at realizing an idea or attaining
some goal. According to the liberal point of view, such groups—
a political party, a religious sect, or, say, an organization for the
defense of civil rights—must be thought of as just the sum of the
individuals comprising them. However, this view is no less untenable than the romantic conception of the collective as a superpersonal entity with a spirit of its own. Actually the basic
unit of a group is not the complete human person but only a
portion of him—that portion which conforms to the common
aspirations. To the extent that an individual "belongs" much of
him drops out of the picture. This is not disproved by the fact
that many a party member devotes himself body and soul to the
Cause; the impassioned partisan expunges part of his possibili-

present context I believe it to be justified to consider only such influences
as originate with the latter.

ties to play his part wholly. The group, then, consists of reduced individuals, compounds of personality fragments selected or even created by the idea which it is to implement. Thus a magnet gathers scattered iron particles from among a mass of material. For this reason group behavior is more rigid, more calculable than individual behavior. To exemplify, under the pressure of the goals defining and limiting its alternatives, a group does not respond to the gradual changes of the social environment but, as if ignoring them, moves straight ahead for a stretch of time—until a point is reached where it, so to speak, formally changes its course, so as to adjust itself to the new situation. At this point it sometimes splits into a conservative and a progressive faction because its members' divergent views of how best to fulfill the group goals—views smoldering under the surface so far—cannot longer be kept subdued and reconciled. While the sequence of an individual's adjustments and reactions may be imagined to unfold in the form of a curve, the way of the group through social reality is tantamount to a succession of straight lines, each pointing in another direction, in keeping with the requirements of the moment; and their junction often marks a crisis. As compared with individuals, groups behave clumsily like mammoths. Their movements show regularities which make them in a measure predictable. They come close to being natural processes.[18]

Groups and individuals are the major components of society at large. Now society is not just the arena for the multiple competing interests they embody, but something in its own right—an entity with specific properties. Conspicuous among them is a peculiar quality of the materials from which it is built: they largely fall into that zone of inertia in which the mind resides absent-mindedly. Many of these materials, such as customs, rites, certain institutions, ever-recurrent routine activities, and the like, coincide in forming the background of our social existence. Whether leftovers from bygone days of excitement and inspiration, sediments, or arrangements prerequisite to ongoing pursuits, they are taken for granted rather than focused upon and treated as controversial issues. In addition, theirs is an enormous survival capacity which owes much to the little attention paid to them and to the conditioning power they develop in the process.[19] These relatively solid fixtures linger on in a more liquid substance: the wash and flow of opinions. Constantly bandied about, the opinions that fill the air should not be expected rigidly to reflect the dominant interests and ideologies of the moment. They are based on hearsay and lack coherence—inevitably so at a time like ours when authentic knowledge is increasingly difficult to obtain and affluence favors a larger margin for choice. The run of them conveys impressions arising from unconscious preferences and shifting moods (which have been frequently manipulated, though). The term "climate of opinion" happily connotes the instability of opinions and their resemblance to the weather. In periods of crisis they may coalesce, gather strength, and generate movements and decisions of consequence—historical change thus being brought about by a medley of sentiments and resentments and the din of confused notions. Plato, afraid of these gales, advised philosophers to stand aside "under shelter of a wall in a storm and blast of dust and sleet." [20] (But are there not storms which clear the air of clouds and dust?)

In sum, society is full of events which defy control because they happen to occur in the dimly lit region where mental intensity is reduced to zero. This is confirmed by the commonplace experience that society, as if moving under its own power, metamorphoses everything that gets enmeshed in its nets. It swallows up all ideas fed into it and, in adapting them to its inarticulate needs, often completely distorts their original meanings. Similarly, all actions designed to alter the given state of affairs are so redirected by the complex forces operative in society that their actual results have little in common with their intended effects. Tocqueville compares their course through the social world with the path of a "kite that travels by the opposite actions of the wind and the cord" [21]—the wind blowing from society, the cord denoting the vision behind those actions. Drawn from our contacts with physical reality, the metaphors of wind and storm suggest that the mind is powerless to interfere with social processes and that, accordingly, these processes obey laws which cannot be tampered with. The social universe with its near-stable customs and volatile opinions, its small groups and masses, would seem to fall under the rule of nature. In other words, it is possible, and legitimate, to break down the phenomena that make up this universe into repeatable elements and analyze their interrelationships and interactions for regularities.[22] In studying social structure and social change, the historian's concerns to a large extent coincide with the preoccupations of the social scientist. Society is a second nature—like the big cities in which it literally engulfs us. Incidentally, the social sciences today avail themselves increasingly of computers to establish formal theories covering various social processes, especially in the area of mass dynamics.[23] May I submit in passing that this tendency toward mathematization corresponds to the character of the material subjected to computer treatment? It appears that, for its perpetuation, modern mass society depends on the predictability—i.e., manipulation—of all individual responses and behavior patterns which are socially significant. We have already gone far in preconditioning people's attitudes; should society carry on this way, the so-called "personality" would dwindle to a mathematical point—man, that is, would be-

come a statistician's dream. (Under the present circumstances
the question as to who is manipulating whom raises problems
of the first magnitude.)

The awareness of the impact of social mechanisms cannot but
undermine the belief in the perfectibility of human society. All
speculative attempts to reconcile this belief with the evidence
discrediting it resort to one and the same argument, paradigmat-
ically exemplified by Goethe's definition of Mephistopheles as
"A part of that power which always wants the evil and always
produces the good." The argument, whose indebtedness to
Christian theology is rather obvious, consists of the following
two interlinked propositions: First, the forces swaying that immense live mass called society are indifferent to man's higher
aspirations, or indeed evil. Second, thanks to the intervention of
a mysterious power acting above our heads, these forces are
coaxed to serve the ends of humanity in spite of their inborn
wickedness—or perhaps precisely because of it. Whether the
power pulling the strings is reason, or an anonymous built-in
device, or some other substitute for good old providence, does
not matter much. Mandeville equates private vices with public
virtues; and even though Adam Smith is reluctant to think of
self-interest in terms of a vice, yet he needs an "invisible hand"
to have the marketers' egoistic pursuits result in the general
good. And of course, here belongs Kant's regulative idea of a
providential nature which utilizes man's vanity, greed, and
selfishness to advance the human race as well as Hegel's World
Spirit or Reason which cunningly sets blind passions to work for
itself. The idea of a power guiding our destinies by remote
control seems to be imperishable. Ranke suspects the existence
of such an "occult force"; [24] the Hegelian in Marx adopts the
scheme of reasoning at the bottom of this idea; and even Burckhardt is not immune from toying with it on occasion.[25]

The lasting appeal it exerts must be traced to a couple of reasons. For one thing, the stereotyped motif of a superpersonal power finds a modicum of support in everyday experience: seeming misfortunes may turn out to be blessings in disguise; the victory of a worthy cause may be due to the efforts of people who, in promoting it, only wish to further their own career, etc. More important, the motif is made to appear as compelling by being tied to the concomitant proposition that human society is definitely corrupt. Kant has it that, seen from without, history looks as if it were a single record of folly and the frenzy of destruction. Once this proposition, which echoes the doctrine of original sin, is accepted, a behind-the-scenes agency, such as Hegel's crafty Reason or Kant's own plotting nature, is indeed needed to wrest good from evil and thus to achieve what, according to premise, man alone would never be able to accomplish. The whole argument stands and falls with the assumption of his blindness or corruptness. Now this assumption is virtually identical with the view that human affairs have all the traits of natural events and that history should therefore be ranged among the sciences. It is the view to which I have tried to do justice in the preceding pages. However, this conception of social, or historical, reality requires qualification.

Among modern statements on the experience of human freedom, Ranke's still stands out as a classical testimony, if only for the reason that it palpably stems from his intense absorption in the spectacle of history: "At every moment again something new may begin . . . ; no thing merely exists for the sake of the other outside of itself; there is none that resolves entirely into the reality of the other." This acknowledgment of freedom's disruptive power is coupled with an awareness of its limitations. It is not absolute. Whatever we do, Ranke continues, is conditioned

by that which has already been done, so that the resultant succession of events—history—presents itself as a coherent fabric
woven of freedom and necessity.[26] Except, perhaps, for its
emphasis on coherence, this statement can be assumed to convey a valid experience. Man is a relatively free agent. (Of
course, an individual's actual freedom varies with the given social conditions. There is no freedom under totalitarian regimes;
and one would vainly seek for it in a society manipulating its
members into complacent conformity.* But this does not impinge on the truth value of that experience. For the rest, have
not at all times rebels risen and martyrs died under torture?)
Interestingly, today's theoretical physicists, weaned from the
mechanistic notions of the 19th century as they are, seem to be
disinclined to follow Tolstoy in characterizing the consciousness
of freedom as just a psychological illusion. Mr. v. Weizsaecker for
one not only considers the freedom of will a fundamental experience but has it that this experience carries at least as much
weight as the doctrine of determinism, which after all is a "theory" not an experience, a program for future empirical research
rather than an established fact. And even though he admits that
the deterministic principle cannot be upset by any inner certainty to the contrary, he is nevertheless disposed, it appears, to
question the range of validity of that principle; in a defiant mood
he challenges its defenders to try to verify their theory: "The
determinative factors of our actions should be shown, then we
will believe in them." [27] His challenge calls to mind an experiment by Eisenstein. Eisenstein planned to insert in his prospective screen adaptation of Theodore Dreiser's novel, *An American Tragedy*—a film which never materialized—a "montage"
sequence designed to externalize Clyde's *monologue intérieur* at

---

* The only people put before a genuine choice in such a society are those
who run it.

the crucial moment when Clyde decides to drown Roberta and make his crime look like an accident. That the sequence was to picture the various factors which then determined Clyde to act as he did clearly follows from the "montage lists" which Eisenstein drew up for it. They consist of a great deal of possibly relevant elements, scattered words before a black screen mingling with a rush of silent images or "polyphonic" sounds, impressions of the actual environment with projections of motives and splinters of thought.[28] Eisenstein's objective in preparing these lists was quite obviously to sensitize the audience to the infinity of factors involved in Clyde's ultimate decision. But in suggesting (and thus aesthetically presenting) infinity, the sequence demonstrates something very important—that we would have to engage in truly endless pursuits to live up to v. Weizsaecker's rhetorical demand for an exposition of the causes which allegedly account for our decisions and actions. On theoretical grounds it is impossible to meet his challenge. The deterministic principle is unverifiable. Why then overburden its significance for interpretation? In many a concrete case this general principle may turn out to be a sheer mirage tempting us to embark on a wild goose chase. There are actions and emergent situations which so stubbornly resist a breakdown into repeatable elements or a satisfactory explanation from preceding or simultaneous circumstances that they had better be treated as irreducible entities.[29] My hunch is that even a Laplacean Demon would be hard put to incorporate them into the chain of causes and effects.

Human affairs, that is, transcend the dimension of natural forces and causally determined patterns. In consequence, any approach to history which claims to be scientific in a stricter sense of the word will sooner or later come across unsurmountable obstacles. If history is a science it is a science with a differ-

ence. This can be nicely illustrated by reference to the devious
ways in which some sociologists try to scientize history. Here is
a random example of recent date, recommending itself by its
very crudeness: Charles Tilly's attempt to interpret the 1793
Vendée revolt from a social scientist's point of view.[30] To summarize Tilly's main conclusions, he infers from the evidence
which his working hypotheses led him to collect that the revolt
culminated in those districts of the Vendée where traditional
farming economy collided with world-open trade and market
economy; that the collision of interests touched off conflicts between the revolutionary mercantile bourgeoisie, already well-
established in the region, and diverse, originally heterogeneous
opposition groups; and that ideological watchwords began to
emerge and to assume a vital function only later on when, with
the hardening of the conflict, the rebels felt urged to close the
ranks. Tilly thus implements his interpretative intentions by
summoning, and arraying, certain regularities of behavior, frequently observed features of social life—e.g., the inevitability of
frictions between groups whose economic interests antagonize
each other; the likelihood of an increasing polarization of the
issues at stake if no compromise seems to be possible; the ensuing need for collective action on the part of groups which,
however divided among themselves, oppose a common enemy,
etc. And what does Tilly achieve this way? Even granted that his
sociological analysis may prove useful to historians of the period, his belief in its value as a historical interpretation is hardly
warranted. With all its generalities combined, this analysis
yields, at best, a shadowy general idea of *a* counterrevolution
located in some no-man's land but does certainly not add up to a
custom-made explanation of *the* Counterrevolution which took
place in the Vendée in 1793. In order really to close in on it, he
would have to supplement his standard regularities by determin-

ing factors more intimately connected with the developments of
his concern; there was a revolution going on at the time, the air
was filled with agitation and battle cries, and all things were in
flux. In sum, he would have to conceive of the Vendée revolt as
a historical phenomenon.

History is also the realm of contingencies, of new beginnings.
All regularities discovered in it, or read into it, are of limited
range. Indeed, the past offers enough examples of the mind's
power to penetrate even the crust of habit and overcome the
inertia inherent in social arrangements. But if man is in a measure free to will and act—committed only to what he has willed
—no phantom puppeteer is needed to set things right (provided
they can be set right). Nor do we have to assume, against all
everyday experience, that it is precisely the adverse spirits and
animal drives which, owing to the artifices of a hypostatized
wire-puller, prompt mankind to achieve humanly desirable
ends. Mephistopheles should create the good by aspiring to evil?
The blessing of religious tolerance should in a miraculous way
have resulted from the horrors of the religious wars? This intrinsically theological proposition reveals itself as a sham paradox in
the light of mundane reasoning; it instances the fallacy of
monism, or rather, the fallacy of the ingrained belief that the
monistic principle—or any other universal idea for that matter—
automatically applies to the concrete cases it logically covers.
Whatever the validity of such high abstractions in their own
dimension, the way down from them to the region of particulars
is by no means a straight line. It sounds awfully prosaic—and
Heaven knows how many intervening social mechanisms blur
the picture—but even so the assumption that evil often breeds
evil and good usually comes from the exertions of the good
deserves more credit than the recourse to a providential agency.
(Were it otherwise, we would in the final analysis be obliged to

acknowledge Hitler as the involuntary redeemer of mankind.)
Burckhardt affirms this view with its pragmatic overtones. He
categorically declares that "no later good will ever excuse an
earlier evil" and attributes any alleviation of the sufferings
which the (inherently evil) state inflicts on its citizens to the
deliberate efforts of the "just and well-meaning" among them.[31]

At this point it becomes possible to supplement the negative
characterization of history as a nonscience, or a science with a
difference, by a first positive, if still incomplete, definition: the
historian must tell a story. Note that the term "story" is being
used here in a loose sense, covering all kinds of narrative statements, including description. And why must the historian tell a
story? Because he invariably comes across irreducible entities—
units which, besides resulting from the junction of otherwise
unconnected series of happenings, mark the emergence of something new, something beyond the jurisdiction of nature. Assuredly, they best respond to a treatment which does not misrepresent them as inevitable effects of an inexhaustible multitude
of causes but pays tribute to their factualness. In our dealings
with these events, ideas, or situations determinism no longer
serves as a reliable guide. The most suitable way of accounting for them consists in narrating them. In telling a story
the historian conforms to a necessity founded on a peculiar
quality of historical reality. This is not generally recognized
today. In their eagerness to identify history as a science contemporary historians, as if loath to be called "bards," tend to place
all the emphasis on scientific procedures and explanations, while
playing down the need for narration. Significantly, a brilliant
American historian has in the recent past found it worth his
while to caution his fellow historians against this trend. "Many
of us," says Professor J. H. Hexter, "have got so preoccupied
with analysis and argumentation that we are in danger of for-

getting how to tell a story and even of forgetting that telling a story is the historian's real business after all." [32] Hexter judiciously adds that especially the "convulsions of a world in upheaval" call for the narrative rather than the analytical historian.[33] In full accordance with this claim, Marc Bloch at the beginning of his *La Société féodale*—a work in which morphological description and analysis by far prevail over story-telling —reviews the 9th-10th-century Arab, Hungarian, and Scandinavian invasions of Europe in the form of a narrative pure and simple. It is in such troubled epochs indeed that the unaccountable asserts itself most vigorously.

However, the fact that historiography must in varying degrees resort to narration does not distinguish it from all the sciences: the natural histories of the earth and the cosmos are in a sense narratives also. Now the stories they tell have a palpably provisional character. The inherent objective of these "histories" is, indeed, to substitute universal laws for all that they are obliged to relate in a merely narrative mode—an objective rooted in the belief that nature, the reduced nature of science, is amenable throughout to the establishment of such laws. And what kinds of laws are fit to replace the narrative? Clearly, they will have to differ from those which have been considered so far in that they do not just involve repeatable component parts of the story told but account for the whole temporal sequence it covers. Darwin's theory of the evolution of living organisms by way of natural selection is representative of these "longitudinal" laws, as they may be called. They supersede sheer story-telling by explaining why that which has occurred actually must have occurred.

Are we entitled to assume that longitudinal laws of this type also apply to the whole of human history? I mean laws which do not grow out of theologico-metaphysical speculations as in

Hegel's case but have a more or less scientific character. At any rate, the quest for them threads the modern age since its beginnings. That this quest was stimulated, if not touched off, by the Christian conception of a divine plan regulating the destinies of mankind can be inferred from Vico's *Scienza nuova,* which marks the divide between theological and secular ideas about history, with the latter already tipping the balance. Vico was both a staunch Christian believer and a thinker steeped in the intellectual climate of the rising age of science and man's emancipation from supernatural authority. So his great and bizarre work (which, incidentally, goes far in anticipating modern methods of historical research) represents, among other things, a sustained effort to reconcile the transcendental rule of providence with the immanent necessity of the total historical process. His goal is not to dispose of the traditional Christian outlook but to fit it into the scientific scheme of things. To achieve his ends, he postulates a historical law according to which it lies in the nature of all nations to pass from a "divine" stage via the "heroic" period to a "human" stage; and at the same time he has it that this "natural law of nations," of which those obeying it are entirely unaware, is established, or administered, by divine providence in order to prevent human society from relapsing into savagery. (Note that his insistence on a benevolent providence acting above our heads is true to type; like all other monistic-oriented thinkers perplexed by the seeming discrepancy between "private vices" and "public virtues" he cannot help tracing the virtues to the operations of a superior agency.) Thus the divine power in charge of world affairs turns into a natural law that without any supernatural intervention governs "ideal eternal history" with its *corsi* and *ricorsi.* This law can be identified as a connecting link between the era of Christian theology and that of mundane reason; even though it is thought of as completely immanent, it receives its justification from the faith in a divine regime.

To nineteenth-century minds any such justification must have seemed to be gratuitous. Both Comte and Marx radically sever the umbilical cord between Christian tenets and universal historical laws. The laws proposed by them have a purely immanent character and lay claim to scientific validity. This is not to imply that the time-honored question as to the meaning of history would have left the two thinkers indifferent. On the contrary, their laws are also attempts to grapple with it. To be sure, in an era determined to put man on his own feet this question no longer admits of solutions involving divine supervision or interference. But the issue lingers on and calls for response. In consequence, the secular ideas of progress and evolution are increasingly burdened—or should I say, overburdened?—with the task of replacing the theological interpretation of history. And under the impact of the connotations which thus accrue to them, the upward movement toward the Beyond is projected onto the horizontal plane, and temporal goals come to supplant the eschatological expectations.[34] Marx and Comte seize on these ideas, if in different ways; and with their aid, they not only assess the significance of the historical process but try to precipitate what they believe to be its fulfillment. The laws they proclaim also serve as levers for political reform; they assume the surplus function of action programs.

Now these laws—which are of interest here only in their capacity as scientific statements—share a basic characteristic: They are conceived of as natural laws; they rest on the assumption that human history is identical with the history of nature, a nature imagined to be capable of evolution. Comte's famous "law of the three stages," which governs the progressive development of the diverse sciences and by extension the whole of (Euro-

pean) history, has all the earmarks of such a general natural
law. Marx too holds that nature and history cannot be separated
from each other and, accordingly, denies any methodological
differences between the science of history and the natural sciences.[35] His so-called historical materialism bears witness to
this. In tending to equate recorded history with a progressive
succession of class conflicts traceable to the inevitable contradictions, at each consecutive stage, between the onward pushing
forces of production and the existing economic structure of society, Marx subjects the historical process to the very kind of
necessity which we are accustomed to attribute to the workings
of nature.*

Once again, what about the validity of these laws? Many
objections raised against them bear on the rather high-handed
manner in which they deal with the given data. It has been
judiciously remarked, for instance, that pre-modern history does
not fit into the Marxist scheme; that Marx actually overstretches
his concepts of "class" and "class conflict" in applying them to all
of the past.[36] And nothing could be more legitimate than
Dilthey's verdict on the inappropriate abstractness of Comte's
doctrine: "All these abstract images of the philosophers of history do is to represent the real course of history again and again
in different fore-shortenings." [37] But in thus lending a voice to
the historian's ingrained suspicion of general philosophical state-

---

* I hasten to add that he does not do so all the time. On more than one
occasion he admits of the possible impact of human actions on historical
change; thus he seems to hold that mankind today is faced with the
alternative of achieving socialism or lapsing into barbarism. There is cur-
rently a tendency toward featuring this nonnaturalistic aspect of Marxian
dialectics. Is it the decisive aspect? Without denying the importance of
such inconsistencies, I still believe the Marx who thought he had discovered the law that controls "prehistory" to be of greater philosophical and
historical significance than, the almost existentialist Marx whom some of his
present-day exegetes—e.g., Sartre—distil from his writings.

ments, Dilthey also intimates that the factual errors of Comte and Marx—or of Buckle, for that matter—must partly be laid to the universal character of their respective laws. Because of their enormous distance from historical reality, such universal laws cannot possibly avoid setting the material in a perspective apt to distort and/or omit large portions of it.* Their more or less inevitable inadequacy to the facts is an accessory shortcoming.

And this leads to their really essential defects. Spellbound by the triumphant natural sciences, those 19th-century law-givers build from two premises which are very vulnerable indeed. The first—the identification of history with nature—has already been indicated. It necessarily yields laws which, by definition, not only unduly minimize the role of contingencies in history but, more important, preclude man's freedom of choice, his ability to create new situations. They acknowledge instead a sort of natural evolution, so as to make allowances for the idea of progress without having to break away from strict determinism. When Marx, the deterministic-minded scientist and Hegel-inspired dialectician, exhorts the workers to unite and shake off their chains, he concedes a freedom to them which is in effect a sham; its sole function is to accelerate a process that would run its preordained course anyway. With him, this process is a necessity as binding as any physical law. So he draws on it to make predictions in natural-science fashion, which in turn bolster his exhortations. In this respect, too, his attitude is of a piece with Comte's. Yet the very freedom which both of them throw overboard subsequently raises its head and gives the lie to their forecasts. Comte was a failure as a prophet. And Marx has proved abysmally wrong in predicting that under industrial cap-

* I am touching here on the momentous problem of the relationships between the general and the particular. Some aspects of this problem will be discussed in Chapters 5 and 8.

italism pauperism is bound to grow and that its growth will
increasingly revolutionize the proletariat. The very economic
and technological evolution he foresaw gave rise, in advanced
capitalistic countries, to political changes which effectively
altered its predicted course. Most certainly, these changes—
strong labor unions, democratization of governments, etc.—also
owed something to the widespread apprehensions called forth
by Marxist augury itself. It was "self-frustrating," to use a term
of Carr's.[38]

The other premise at the bottom of these laws involves the
issue of historical time. Since Comte and Marx think of human
history in terms of natural history, they take it all the more for
granted that, like any physical process, history unfolds in measurable chronological time. With them, the historical process is
tantamount to a linear movement—a necessary and meaningful
succession of periods along a time continuum indefinitely extending into the temporal future. In other words, they unquestioningly confide in the magic of chronology.[39] But what if their
confidence turns out to be unwarranted? If calendric time is
not the all-powerful medium they suppose it to be but also an
empty, indifferent flow which takes along with it a conglomerate
of unconnected events? If, paradoxically, that one-dimensional
flow must be imagined as being both the carrier and not the
carrier of all significant historical forces and developments?
Then the historical process evolving in chronological time
assumes an ambiguous character; it is not least a phantom process; and its ambiguity infallibly reflects upon the laws which
allegedly govern it. In anticipating here questions which can be
broached only later on,* I merely wish to suggest that Marx's
and Comte's conception of historical time, far from being self-
evident, poses problems not even perceived by them. And this

* See Chapter 6.

further discredits their pronouncements about the course of human history.

Spengler marks an advance over nineteenth-century thought in as much as he repudiates "that empty figment of *one* linear history." [40] Indeed, his foremost merit consists in what he himself terms his turn from the Ptolemaic to the Copernican system of history; he takes his diverse cultures out of the common medium of chronological time which points to the present—our present—and assigns to each a time of its own. (That he has all of them gyrate in an unaccountable temporal limbo is rather awkward, though.) Need I elaborate on the rest of the Spenglerian tenets? It will suffice to call to mind the fact that he defines those cultures as plant-like organisms which, rooted in their respective mother regions, pass through invariably the same stages of youth, maturity, and old age. Moreover, he insists that they stick to their set course without ever influencing one another. Each is born, and possessed, with a particular idea and realizes itself in the form of works and actions peculiar to it; even the sciences of these giant monads resist being brought onto a common denominator. Conceivably, such views are incompatible with the idea of a progressive historical process. Yet what counts here is this: that in spite of all that separates Spengler from his predecessors, his basic attitudes toward history do not differ from theirs. He too equates history with nature and in doing so, even goes behind Marx and Comte; as the reactionary he is, he refrains from contaminating nature by evolutionary tendencies. It is a static nature to which his biological metaphors refer. And he too is so completely captivated by science that he does not in the least hesitate to bring the whole of history under the rule of a law—a natural law which, more rigid than all previous ones, not only obliterates human freedom at the outset but ruthlessly smothers the dream of it. In conse-

quence, his doctrine is exposed to the same criticism as the 19th-
century historical laws; like them, it unduly extends the realm of
necessity. (By the way, a secondary weakness of Spengler's system may be found in its inherent affinity for methodologically
questionable procedures. His array of cultural units tempts him
to compare with each other such accomplishments of different
cultures as can be attributed to identical stages of their development; but as a rule, these comparisons are suggested by his
general conceptual scheme rather than derived from a close analysis of all the pertinent circumstances. The inevitable result is
irrelevant analogies. It is this abuse of comparative method
which Henri Frankfort has in mind when he warns against an
"emphasis on similarities, torn from the cultural context which
holds the secret of their significance." [41]

When Spengler appears, Toynbee is not far away. Things are
a bit difficult with him because there are at least two Toynbees:
the scientific-minded historian and the "engaged" spiritual
leader. As for the historian Toynbee, he takes his cue from
Spengler, the only (negligible) difference between them being
that he replaces the latter's cultures by twenty or more less
strictly self-contained civilizations—nonbiological entities permitted to commune with each other and to figure on the general
chronological scale. That he believes to proceed empirically
where Spengler decrees from on high is sheer self-deception.
Actually, he capitalizes on his familiarity with the Graeco-
Roman civilization to construct a model accounting for its
growth and especially its decay, and then uses this "Hellenic
model" to explain goings-on in the other civilizations of his
acquaintance.[42] In the end, it looks as if all of them disinte-
grated according to the same pattern. Thus his civilizations turn
into comparable units whose similarities, contrived rather than
found, prompt him to indulge in ready-made isomorphic analo-

gies after the manner of Spengler. It is inevitable that his concern with the stereotyped life cycle implemented by these units
should confer upon it the status of a universal natural law.
Fortunately, Toynbee himself saves me the trouble of dwelling
on the fallacy of his panoramic vision. The spiritual leader he
also is rejects it wholesale. He not only declares the future to be
unpredictable,[43] but admits the possibility for Western mankind to carry on indefinitely and pleads for its renewal in a
Christian spirit. There is something schizophrenic about Toynbee; while the historian in him features analogies and regularities favoring prediction, Toynbee the prophet refuses to acknowledge their import. Nevertheless the twain are made to meet by
means of constant modifications. The Spenglerian Toynbee, who
promotes the cyclical theory, adds new models to the Hellenic
one, so as to refine his scheme; and the other Toynbee exempts
the so-called "higher religions" from the preordained course of
the multiple civilizations for the purpose of sustaining Christianity, all cycles notwithstanding. Also, the image of a chariot
moving onward as its wheels—the civilizations—are turning
around is called upon to illustrate, and justify, the impossible
fusion of the two opposite views. Nice as the image is, it hardly
fits the case. In short, eager for integration, Toynbee twists and
bends his system in about the same way as Dali does the
watches in his famous painting, "Persistence of Memory"—until
the whole, following the example of the civilizations, disintegrates into a soft mass of incoherent pieces.

Of course, there is more to it than meets the eye. While it is
true that all these historical "laws" crumble upon closer inspection, it is equally true that all of them comprise a hard core of
substantive observations and experiences, some growing out
of an intimate contact with historical reality. The flimsiness of
Comte's philosophy of history does not affect the vitality of one

of its main incentives and ingredients—his idea of a science of
social statics and dynamics. Nor is Spengler's and Toynbee's
refusal to identify history as a flow of events in linear time
discredited by the illusory panoramas they develop from their
notion of multiple historical times. And Marx's substructure-
superstructure theory carries much more weight than his Hegel-
inspired scheme of the historical process which it helps implement. Let alone that his theory sheds light on previously unknown historical motivations, it provides an invaluable criterion
by which soberly to assess and, if need be, debunk idealistic
claims and lofty arguments. All these truths are relatively independent of the systems to which they belong. Theoretically,
they might as well have been established without any speculative trimmings. Yet the universal historical laws into which they
willy-nilly expand are perhaps needed to pry them loose from
their moorings. Besides thus acting as a sort of catalytic agent,
these "laws"—strange mixtures of scientific pretenses and theological leftovers—are, moreover, apt to yield insight of consequence. Consider that they aspire to cover the past in its entirety. So they must, in a manner of speaking, view its expanses
from an extremely high altitude. They resemble aerial photographs; exactly like them, they are bound to bring normally
unseen patterns and configurations into focus. This explains
their potential revealing power. From his elevated position
Spengler, for instance, discovers the phenomenon of "pseudo-
morphosis"—a new culture, born into the orbit of a powerful
older culture, being obliged to express its peculiar strivings and
visions in the language of the older, whose meanings then tend
to overshadow theirs. (He thinks of the obscuring effect of Hel-
lenism on what he labels "Arabic" culture.) [44] For the rest, this
would not be the first time that notoriously devious conceptions
breed genuine knowledge.[45]

To draw the balance, human history irrevocably differs from

natural history in that it proves impervious to longitudinal historical laws—laws which, by implication, mistake the historical process for a natural process. Unlike natural history, whose narrative components may, on principle, be superseded by such laws, the history of human affairs must retain an epic quality. Its irreducible share of freedom ultimately defies any treatment in natural-science fashion which shuts out that freedom.

And here, at the end, a property of history comes into view which complements its definition as a story-telling medium. While the scientist, in narrating, say, the history of the earth, will record the given facts as facts—as possible elements of general laws, that is—the historian on his part is not satisfied with merely relating past events (although he may have to do so also) but feels it incumbent upon him to explore their specific shapes and qualities. He deals with humans after all. And the interest we take in them requires him to seize on the events he summons in their concreteness, or indeed uniqueness, no matter whether and how he will be able to link them together. When the assassination of President Kennedy became known in New York, people spontaneously formed little groups in the streets and, under the impact of the shock they suffered, talked and talked to each other. Many wept. Did they in their anguish talk about the crime, grope for the motives behind it? They did and did not. From this natural topic they invariably reverted to the victim himself—his youth, his way of living, his unfulfilled goals. No doubt a primitive instinct impelled them thus to evoke a past which had been the present a moment ago and to picture to themselves, and try to appraise, the full scope of what they—we —had thoughtlessly possessed and abruptly lost. In doing so, they followed a desire which is at the bottom of all history writing: they wanted to "understand."

One cannot speak of this desire without recalling Dilthey's

persistent efforts to feature "understanding"—the German
Verstehen—as the main concern of the *Geisteswissenschaften.*
"Understanding" is a pivotal concept with him. Dilthey inter-
prets it in terms which hold their own, despite their being
grounded in a psychologizing and somewhat foggy philosophy
of life. He conceives of history as a life process which, passing
through us, involves our entire existence; and he argues that, in
order to "understand" the phenomena comprising that process,
we must experience them with the whole of our being, so that
the life that we are communes with theirs.[46] From Ranke to
Huizinga or Isaiah Berlin many a practicing historian similarly
insists on the need for the historian's total involvement.* [47]

For the rest, imbued with the spirit of historicism, Dilthey
tends to stress the role of *Verstehen* at the expense of scientific
knowledge—a fact already mentioned at the beginning of this
chapter. In his view, historical understanding has nothing to do
with scientific explanations; rather, unconcerned for laws and
regularities, it exhausts itself in penetrating individual entities
of, perhaps, untraceable origins. Quite so. Yet Dilthey thus unduly limits the territory to be explored. Since "the freedom of
history rises on the ground of nature-necessity," [48] historical reality contains uniformities and, indeed, causal relationships
which call for the historian's attention also. A historian confining
himself to "understanding" in Dilthey's sense would miss a good
deal of the "components, factors, aspects" [49] that lay claim to
his understanding. History is a double-edged proposition. To be
sure, it does not belong among the sciences, but it is a science
deserving the name only if it assimilates to itself all that they
may have to offer and, in general, behaves toward them in a
comrade-like way.

* This preliminary discussion of the concepts of story-telling and understanding will be carried on in Chapter 4: see esp. pages 95–97.

2
The Historical Approach

Modern historiography would seem to come into its own if it manages to elude not only the Scylla of philosophical speculations with their wholesale meanings but also the Charybdis of the sciences with their nature laws and regularities. What then enters the historian's field of vision is a conglomerate of "particular events, developments, and situations of the human past" [1]— successive and/or coexistent phenomena which altogether make up historical reality. In the light of mundane reasoning this universe shows the following (minimum) characteristics: It is full of intrinsic contingencies which obstruct its calculability, its subsumption under the deterministic principle. (True, things may change under a unified global management of human affairs, but then the question arises to what extent can the living forces which produce the contingencies be subjected to worldwide control without either revolting or withering. If anarchy calls for order, order tends to beget anarchy.) In addition, historical reality is virtually endless, issuing from a dark which is increasingly receding and extending into an open-ended future. And finally, it is indeterminate as to meaning. Its characteristics conform to the materials of which it is woven. The historian's

universe is of much the same stuff as our everyday world—the
very world which Husserl was the first to endow with philosophical dignity. At any rate, this world is the nearest approximation
to what he calls the *Lebenswelt* and identifies as the source and
ultimate justification of all human sciences. The sciences, says
he, idealize the experiences we make in that common intersub-
jective world; they "hover, as if in empty space, above the
Lebenswelt." [2] But actually history differs from the natural sciences in that it "hovers" there at a much lower altitude than
they, for it directly deals with the kind of life which falls into
the orbit of everyday experience. To think of this life as a continuous process would be rather venturesome. Burckhardt not
only features periods of crisis and extreme change but believes
certain ideas and movements to emerge from "hidden depths" [3]
(which, however, does not prevent him from coveting historical
continuity); * and Marx turns the spotlight not so much on the
over-all significance of history as on the radical breaks in it [4]
(without, however, abandoning the notion of a dialectical historical process). This is not to imply that the historical universe
should be imagined as being unstructured. At least in the modern age many developments are traceable to socioeconomic
influences. Art forms have a way of unfolding and subsiding
according to a sort of immanent logic. Controversial issues cast-
ing their spell over the population at large—e.g., Church reform
in the Renaissance—are likely to touch off a series of interrelated events. And there are periods which impress us as having
an outspoken physiognomy of their own.[5] But these given patterns, strands, and sequences thread a material which is for long
stretches inchoate, heterogeneous, obscure. Much of it is an
opaque mass of facts.

It is up to the historian to chart a course through these ex-

* Cf. Chapter 6, pages 150–52.

panses. Now whatever questions he brings to bear on some portion or aspect of historical reality, he is invariably confronted with two tasks: (1) He must establish the relevant evidence as impartially as possible; and (2) he must try to render intelligible the material thus secured. I am aware, of course, that fact-finding and exegesis are two sides of one and the same indivisible process. The historian cannot assemble the evidence needed unless he is guided by an idea, however vague, of what he wants to recover of the past and why he wants to recover it; and reversely, the evidence he gathers may in turn oblige him to modify his original hunches. So it goes on, spontaneity constantly alternating with receptivity. Yet for the purposes of analysis these two intertwined components of any historical inquiry had better be kept apart. One might also say that the historian follows two tendencies—the realistic tendency which prompts him to get hold of all data of interest, and the formative tendency which requires him to explain the material in hand. He is both passive and active, a recorder and a creator.

No doubt his procedures resemble those of the scientist. Does not the scientist too proceed from hypothesis to experiment and observation and back again to hypothesis in a practically interminable movement? Yet these similarities of conduct should not lead one to confuse history with a science proper. In fact, their unifying effect is largely outweighed by the methodological implications of the differences between human affairs and the events of nature. (The logical positivists, eager to stress the scientific character of historiography, tend to minimize the impact of these material differences, while harping upon the similarities between scientific and historical method. Their argument rests on the assumption that universals substantially cover the areas they define and that the general properties of a class of phenomena—in our case those similarities—take precedence

over the less general qualities of the particular phenomena belonging to that class. Impregnated with the awe of high abstractions, this assumption conforms to ingrained habits of thought; I
wonder, though, whether it is invulnerable. Considerations
along the lines of a material logic may qualify the claim to
unconditional priority of formal logic.)* [6] Remember that, unlike the scientist's nature world, historical reality, this mixture of
natural events and relatively free decisions, resists a breakdown
into repeatable elements which relate to one another in definitely fixable ways. Nor is the whole of it amenable to (longitudinal) laws. This constitution of the historical universe—
which has more in common with the *Lebenswelt* than with the
reduced nature of the scientist's making—poses problems not
found outside it. They bear, for instance, on the establishment
of the evidence, the degree of objectivity attainable to the historian, etc.; and they are decidedly of greater consequence than
all the similarities that obtain between historical and scientific
pursuits.

The beginnings of modern historiography are marked by a
strong concern with the realistic tendency which stood little
chance of asserting itself in the then prevailing moral and philosophical histories. Efforts to expose the past in its nakedness
went hand in hand with attacks on the speculative syntheses
veiling it. The 18th-century Goettingen historians, such as Gat-
terer and Schloezer, condemned the "superficialities of the *phi-
losophes.*" [7] Ranke likewise aimed at protecting historical reality
against its violation by "an abstract system, construction, and
philosophy of history"; [8] he rejected, in Butterfield's words, "a
schematization that did not issue out of the recorded facts." [9] In
the preface to his *Geschichte der romanischen und ger-
manischen Voelker von 1494 bis 1514* he flouted the moralizing

* See Chapter 8.

historians of his time who assigned to history the "office of judging the past, of instructing the present for the benefit of future
ages." [10] Follows the famous statement that he himself only
wants to show *"wie es eigentlich gewesen"*—"how things actually were." [11]

This book, his first, appeared in 1824. Only fifteen years later,
and photography came into being. It seems of great interest to
me that, in the dimension of the representative arts, Daguerre's
invention raised issues and demands similar to those which
played so large a role in contemporary historiography.

It was a conscious connection for Heine, who, in the dedication of *Lutezia* to Prince Pückler-Muskau, which is dated Paris,
August 1854, states the purpose he had in mind with this book
on "politics, art, and popular life," which he arranged from his
journalistic writings. "To brighten the saddening reports," he
writes, "I interwove them with descriptions from the field of the
arts and sciences . . . This was . . . done . . . to give the
genuine picture of the time itself in its smallest nuances. An
honest daguerreotype must render faithfully a fly as much as the
proudest horse, and this is what my reports are: a daguer-
reotypic history book in which each day entered its own picture
and the artist's ordering mind, by assembling such pictures, produced a work in which that which is depicted documents its
faithfulness authentically by itself. But in any case, my book
. . . may serve the later historian as a historical source which,
as I said, carries in itself surety for its daily truth." [12]

Was it the *Zeitgeist* to which this correspondence of historiography and the new invention of daguerreotypy must be laid? I
shall show that they point to significant analogies between history and the two media which portray the world about us with
the aid of a camera—photography itself and photographic film.
For an understanding of history it may therefore prove helpful

to inquire into the nature of these analogies. Of course, one cannot find out about them without taking a look at the relevant characteristics of the photographic media.[13]

Not all the art media can be said to have a peculiar character: the various styles in painting, for instance, are least dependent upon the materials stylized and given technical factors. But photography resembles the diverse branches of knowledge in that it calls certain properties its own which tend to condition work within its confines. As far back as the archaic days of the medium, discerning critics diagnosed them by marvelling at the camera's exceptional ability to record as well as reveal visible, or potentially visible, physical reality. Gay-Lussac for one revelled in the "mathematical exactness" [14] of every detail on photographic plates and insisted that no detail, "even if imperceptible," can escape "the eye and brush of this new painter." [15] (The term "painter," as used here, calls to mind the time when automobiles still looked like carriages without horses.) By the same token, a Paris journalist would, toward the end of the century, praise the first Lumière films for presenting, or indeed being, "nature caught in the act." [16] In short, it was recognized at the outset that photography is uniquely equipped to follow the realistic tendency to an extent unattainable to the related traditional arts.

This led the naïve 19th-century realists to identify photography as a reproduction technique. They were agreed that it records nature with a fidelity "equal to nature itself"; [17] and they extolled prints which, to paraphrase Ranke's dictum, seemed to them to show how things actually are (*wie es eigentlich ist*). Delacroix compared daguerreotypy to a "dictionary" of nature.[18] Photography is in character only, those scientific-

minded realists held, if it is tantamount to an impersonal rendering of external phenomena. Proust in his novel adopted this
view, perhaps because it enabled him effectively to contrast his
involuntary, completely subjective memories with the external
and objective memories deposited in photographic statements.
So he features emotional detachment as the photographer's foremost virtue. With him, the ideal photographer is an indiscrim-
inating mirror, the counterpart of the camera lens.[19]

When meditating about their craft, historians sometimes drag
in photography and then claim that the historian should not be
mistaken for a cameraman. Thus Droysen declared that the historical narrative is not intended to "photograph" past events but
aims at conveying our conceptions of them from this or that
point of view.[20] Modern historians chime in: "The function of
the historian," says Namier, "is akin to that of the painter and
not of the photographic camera: to discover and set forth, to
single out and stress that which is of the nature of the thing, and
not to reproduce indiscriminately all that meets the eye." [21]
Marc Bloch too speaks of the meaninglessness of a "simple photographie" of human reality.[22] Such references to the photographic medium would be entirely uncalled for were not the
historians making them alert to the possibility that history and
photography have something to do with each other after all. On
the other hand, they hint at this possibility only to deny it
categorically. Why do they reject the very comparisons they
themselves care to suggest? All of them want to discredit the
positivistic notion of the historian as a sheer recording instrument, passively (and impassively) registering a mass of unsifted
data and facts. And not only Droysen, the contemporary of the
primitive 19th-century realists, but also Namier and Bloch, who
should have known better, take it for granted that the camera

holds up a mirror to nature. As a result, they must, indeed, imagine the historian deserving of the name to be the antipode of the photographer.

Naïve realism has long since gone; and nobody today would dream of calling the camera a mirror. Actually, there is no mirror at all. Even Proust's ideal photographer is bound to transfer three-dimensional phenomena to the plane and sever their ties with the surroundings. More important, he cannot help structuring the inflowing impressions; the simultaneous perceptions of his other senses, certain perceptual form categories inherent in his nervous system, and not least his general disposition, compel him to organize the visual raw material in the act of seeing. This being so, there is no earthly reason why the photographer should suppress his formative urges in the interest of the necessarily futile attempt to achieve objectivity—that simon-pure objectivity so coveted by Taine that he wanted "to reproduce the objects as they . . . would be even if I did not exist." [23] In any case, all great photographers have felt free to select motif, frame, lens, filter, emulsion, and grain according to their sensibilities. (Was it otherwise with Ranke? His vision of universal history, for instance, did not seem to encroach on his desire to show things as they were. Perhaps it is possible to say of him that his formative strivings joined forces with his realistic designs.) The upshot is that photographs true to type may range from neutral renderings of physical reality to highly subjective statements. Had Namier been aware of this he might have found it advisable to compare the historian to a photographer instead of a painter. Fortunately, at least one distinguished contemporary historian—H.-I. Marrou—is sufficiently conversant with the medium to expose the bias of his confreres. He draws attention to the prints of men like Nadar and Cartier-Bresson; and he judiciously argues that, thanks to the intervention of authentic photographers in the mechanical processes involved, their pictures have something personal about them and are profoundly informed.[24]

Should we conclude, then, that in the final analysis photography does not differ from the established arts? The history of the photographic media tells us of efforts and achievements which seem to bear out this conclusion. Take the 19th-century "artist-photographers": not content with what they believed to be a mere copying of visible reality, they set their mind on pictures which, as an English critic requested, would delineate Beauty instead of solely representing Truth.[25] One of them, the sculptor Adam-Salomon, indulged in portraits which, because of their "Rembrandt-lighting" and velvet drapery, caused Lamartine to recant his initial opinion that photographs were just a "plagiarism of nature." [26] The camera, "this new painter," thus reassumed the function of a painter in the traditional sense. Nor do the experimental photographers of our days care about its specific abilities. Quite the contrary, they often deliberately depart from the realistic point of view, utilizing the techniques at their disposal to produce pictures which might as well be reproductions of abstract paintings.[27] In film, the same longings for emancipation from the outer world, for self-expression, and rounded-out composition, manifest themselves time and again. The *avant-garde* film artists of the 'twenties, for instance, edited otherwise realistic pictorial material according to musical rhythms, freely invented shapes instead of recording and discovering them, and made real-life shots illustrate contents and meanings which were anything but an implication of what the visuals actually showed.[28] That similar intentions also materialize in historiography should all the more be expected since history coincides with the camera crafts in challenging its adepts to capture a given universe. The challenge is strict enough to rouse the urge for discounting it. To remain within the dimension of art, numbers of historical writings impress you as being determined by their authors' inherent form designs rather than the peculiar formation of their material. It goes without saying that I do not think here of romanced lives and the like but of certain works of professional scholarship. They testify to an acute consciousness of organizational arrangements and matters of style; and there is an air of completeness about them which recalls the compact texture of experimental photographs. One wonders, for example, whether Huizinga's *The Waning of the Middle Ages* does not primarily stem from his desire to shape a mood and from a concern with Beauty that limits the scope of his research by stimulating and guiding it.[29]

Even though Pieter Geyl finds fault with the aestheticizing attitude behind this work, he cannot help respecting it as a "masterpiece." [30] True, in my Father's house are many mansions, but is it not equally true that, from a secular point of view, some mansion or other may be preferable to the rest of them? I submit that the products of a medium with specific characteristics are the more satisfactory if they build from these characteristics. To express the same in negative terms, an accomplishment defying the properties, if any, of its medium is likely to offend our sensibilities; the old iron structures with their borrowings from neo-Gothic stone architecture are as irritating as they are venerable. It follows from this principle—which I have called the "basic aesthetic principle" in my *Theory of Film* [31]—that the photographer will not come into his own unless he tries to do what his camera permits him to do better than anybody else; he must go to the limit, that is, in recording and penetrating physical reality. Imagine two photographic portraits, one in the nature of a casual self-revelation, still "instinct with the illusion of life," [32] and the other so stylized in terms of lighting, background, etc., that it no longer suggests life in its flux: there is no question but that the former will strike one as more intrinsically photographic than the latter. The photographer's approach may be said to be "photographic" if his formative aspirations support rather than oppose his realistic intentions. This implies that he resembles not so much the expressive artist as the imaginative reader bent on studying and deciphering an elusive text. His "intensity of vision," one of the guild has it, should be rooted in a "real respect for the thing in front of him." [33] Owing to the camera's revealing power, he has also traits of an explorer who, filled with curiosity, roams yet unconquered spaces. The genuine photographer summons up his being not to discharge it in autonomous creations but to dissolve it into the substances of the real-life phenomena before his lens, so that they are both left intact and made transparent. If photography is an art, it is an art with a difference: unlike the traditional arts, it takes pride in not completely consuming its raw material.

A few lines after having indicated his determination to show "wie es eigentlich gewesen," Ranke makes a remark of similar consequence: "The writing of history cannot be expected to possess the same free development of its subject which, in theory at least, is expected in a work of literature." [34] (Somewhat vague as Ranke's theoretical observations usually are, they have the advantage of resulting not from a pottering about with a set of abstractions but from his undiluted experience as a practicing historian.) What he wants to convey is this: It is the historian's business adequately to render, and account for, human affairs of the past. This in turn means that his craft imposes certain restrictions upon him. He lacks the novelist's or dramatist's freedom to alter or shape his material as he pleases. Ranke thus formulates a principle which delimits the field of historiogra-

phy; its function is that of a "no trespassing" sign warning potential transgressors of the dangers they may incur. Need it be
said that this principle—whose validity for history in the modern sense can hardly be doubted—corresponds to the "basic
aesthetic principle" which serves as a criterion for photographic
activities? In exact analogy to the photographic approach, the
"historical approach" comes true only if the historian's spontaneous intuition does not interfere with his loyalty to the evidence but, conversely, benefits his empathic absorption in it.
One will now better understand why historians are filled with
distrust of philosophical speculations which, like oversized gar-
ments, hang loosely around the body of facts and why they
entertain scruples, legitimate or not, about historical writings
whose literary beauty stands out conspicuously.

The thing that matters in both photography and history is
obviously the "right" balance between the realistic and formative tendencies. The conditions under which that balance materializes can be epitomized by a simple, quasi-mathematical
formula: Realistic Tendency $\geqq$ Formative Tendency. This formula covers a diversity of cases. They may be arranged along a
continuum the one pole of which I propose to assign to statements intended to lay bare some portion of given reality as
faithfully as possible. I am thinking of the many fact-oriented
historical accounts which, often in the form of monographs,
concentrate on the exhibition of a complex of events, developments, or situations, with only the slightest interference of subjective preferences and formative designs. Their equivalents in
the dimension of camera work are straight pictorial records,
such as artless photographs, impersonal newsreel shots, and the
like. Statements in this vein come nearest to being reproductions. But at least they meet the minimum requirement of their
respective media. The opposite pole of the continuum is occu-

pied by readings in which spontaneity and receptivity seem to be in a state of equilibrium, interpretation so perfectly matching the pertinent data that it neither overwhelms them nor leaves an undigested remainder. Alfred Stieglitz's print of a group of huddled trees is a photograph of really existing trees and at the same time a memorable image—or should I say allegory?—of autumnal sadness. Among the parallels I have come across in historiography, Panofsky's "principle of disjunction" is as good an example as any. According to it, in the high and later Middle Ages works of art which borrow their form from a classical model are as a rule invested with Christian significance, whereas works of art which illustrate a classical theme drawn from pagan literary sources invariably represent their topic in a nonclassical, contemporary form.[35] The principle fits the findings of empirical research all the more neatly since Panofsky is at pains to explain the known exceptions to the first alternative. If the equilibrium is strained it becomes very precarious indeed: at first sight, certain photographs—e.g., Moholy-Nagy's *From the Berlin Wireless Tower*—appear to be nonobjective compositions, while upon closer inspection they reveal themselves as renderings of natural objects from an unconventional camera angle. A light shift of emphasis in the same direction and the "right" balance between reproduction and construction is upset. We enter the region where the historian's formative impulses get the better of his realistic intentions . . .

There is, then, a fundamental analogy between historiography and the photographic media: like the photographer, the historian is loath to neglect his recording obligations over his preconceptions and fully to consume the raw material he tries to mould. But this is not the whole story. Another basic analogy bears on the subject matter peculiar to the two fields of endeavor. Provided the still and motion picture cameras acknowl-

edge the "basic aesthetic principle," they customarily focus on a
world which is certainly not the abstract nature of science. Nor
is it a world intimating some well-ordered cosmos, for "there is
no Cosmos on the screen, but an earth, trees, the sky, streets,
and railways . . ." [36] Rather, "camera-reality"—the sort of reality on which the photographer, or film maker, opens his lens—
has all the earmarks of the *Lebenswelt*. It comprises inanimate
objects, faces, crowds, people who intermingle, suffer, and hope;
its grand theme is life in its fullness, life as we commonly experience it.

Small wonder that camera-reality parallels historical reality in
terms of its structure, its general constitution. Exactly as historical reality, it is partly patterned, partly amorphous—a consequence, in both cases, of the half-cooked state of our everyday
world. And it shows features which are of a piece with the
characteristics of the historian's universe. To begin with, photographers seem to be prone to highlight the contingent nature
of their material. Random events are the very meat of snap-
shots; authentic photographs look as if their subjects were
plucked en route. By the same token, film makers have a penchant for rendering transient impressions and unforeseeable
encounters. (That this susceptibility to the accidental rather
than providential may be turned to advantage also by historians,
was recognized already at the beginning of photography. In the
Brockhaus Lexikon of 1840 Friedrich von Raumer's contemporary histories are praised for resembling daguerreotypes in that
they capture the "fleeting shadows of the present" on the
wing.)[37] Chance configurations being fragments, photography
further tends to suggest endlessness. A genuine photograph precludes the notion of completeness. Its frame marks a provisional
limit; its content points beyond that frame, referring to a multitude of real-life phenomena which cannot possibly be encom-

passed in their entirety. And films? It is as if they were animated by the chimerical desire to establish the continuum of physical existence with all its psychological and mental correspondences. To make us aware of it, film directors frequently digress from the action they picture for no reason other than to explore the visible environment in which it comes to pass; thus Olivier in his *Hamlet* has his camera incessantly travel and "pan" through the labyrinthine interiors of, alas, a studio-built Elsinore. Or a seeming *Gestalt* is broken down into virtually innumerable elements; an ideal case in point is Eisenstein's attempt to evoke, in his stillborn screen adaptation of *An American Tragedy*, the infinity of factors and circumstances instrumental in Clyde's decision to murder Roberta.*—There is, in addition, the camera's affinity for the indeterminate. To be sure, the photographer endows his pictures with form and meaning to the extent that he makes deliberate choices. But however selective, his prints still are bound to record nature in the raw. Like the natural objects themselves, they will therefore be surrounded by a fringe of indistinct multiple meanings. The same holds true of motion pictures as a matter of course. Discussing the properties of the film shot, a French critic sagaciously observes that it "delimits without defining" and that it has the quality, "unique among the arts, of offering not much more explanations than reality." [38]

But what is the good of indulging in analogies? Why dote on a subject only to jilt it for a similar subject? So do monkeys swing from branch to branch, tree to tree. Moreover, such comparisons are all too often products of intellectual laziness. They serve to substitute an apparently familiar topic for the unfamiliar one under consideration; and those making them usually capitalize on superficial resemblances to return, as fast as possi-

* See pages 28–29.

ble, to the port from which they ventured forth. However, in the case of the present meditations, analogical procedures are justified, if not required, for two reasons. First, the analogy between historiography and the photographic media is not simply an easy expedient but results from the solid fact that work in the two areas hinges on identical conditions: both crafts are committed to concern themselves with given worlds of comparable structure and therefore canalize the performers' creative possibilities in like ways. Second, the field of history is cluttered up with inherited habits of thought and themes of long standing which altogether render it nearly impenetrable. The ascendancy of abstract reasoning under the auspices of science and traditional philosophy is apt to obstruct all efforts to interpret the experiences and aspirations peculiar to this area in really appropriate terms. Actually, the whole area is pervaded, and overshadowed, by a curious blend of concrete *ad hoc* insights and ill-fitting generalities. Add to this that previous modes of conversing with the past—e.g., the Christian conception of history—stubbornly survive and, camouflaged or not, continue to prove attractive; their presence cannot but create a deceptive semblance of familiarity which further blurs the picture. In contradistinction to this state of things, the photographer's universe is, in a way, more readily accessible. As pictorial media, photography and film speak directly to the senses; and anybody susceptible to aesthetic values is, on principle, in a position to appraise their particular beauties, potentialities, and limitations without much ado. This opens up promising avenues for analysis. Not to mention that the analogy with photography helps defamiliarize habitual aspects in the historical field, the odds are that our understanding of certain issues with which the historian is grappling will greatly profit by recourse to corresponding issues in the photographic crafts. Here implications and solutions hidden from view in the historical dimension stand a fair chance of becoming visible at once. It may be anticipated that especially the cinematic narrative is rich in clues that afford an opportunity for enlightening comparisons.

3
Present Interest

"On the wide ocean on which we shall venture out," says Burckhardt in the opening passage of his *Renaissance*, "the possible
routes and courses are many, and the identical studies made for
this volume could, if dealt with by another man, . . . easily occasion essentially different conclusions." [1] Burckhardt's remark,
made at so important a place, testifies to his intense awareness
of the role which the historian's personal outlook and indeed
temper play in the rendering and understanding of the past.
(The reason why historical knowledge involves subjectivity to a
larger extent than does strictly scientific knowledge lies primarily with the fact that different universes challenge the investigator's formative powers in different ways. While the establishment of the world of science, this web of relationships between
elements abstracted from, or imposed upon, nature, requires
mathematical imagination rather than, say, moral ingenuity, the
penetration of the historian's world which resists easy breakdowns into repeatable units calls for the efforts of a self as rich
in facets as the human affairs reviewed. [2] That these too may in
a measure be subjected to scientific treatment proper is quite
another matter.)

Because of the cognitive functions of the historian's self, a definition of its nature would seem to be all the more desirable. Should it not at least be possible to fasten, so to speak, this elusive entity to the peg of rationally controllable conditions? Here is where a theory comes in which—to express it in the terms of that theory—could not arise but in the wake of historicism. Since historical writings themselves are products of history, the argument runs, the views they convey depend on their authors' position in time and place. This proposition means two things—that the historian's mind is shaped by contemporary influences and that in turn his preoccupation with contemporary issues accounts for the why and how of his devotion to the past. The living present is thus identified as the fountainhead and goal of history. The foremost philosophical exponents of this "present-interest" theory are Croce and Collingwood. Without neglecting the conditioning power of the historian's environment, they pay special attention to the need for his involvement, moral or otherwise, in the problems of his day. One knows Croce's dictum that history is contemporary history;[3] he supplements it by contending that "only an interest in the life of the present can move one to investigate past fact."[4] (As a person and historian, he himself was animated by a magnificent interest in the cause of liberty.) Similarly, Collingwood features the historian as a "son of his time"[5] who "re-enacts" the past out of his immersion in present-day concerns.[6] In addition, both thinkers are alert to the necessity for them to justify their emphasis on the present by endowing it with metaphysical significance. This gets them into deep waters, for both of them refute, or pretend to refute, any principle governing the whole of human history and yet cannot help re-introducing it in order to explain the uniqueness of the present moment. It will suffice to mention that Croce conceives of this moment as a phase—the temporarily ultimate phase—of a dialectical and, all in all, progressive movement. True, Collingwood, who radically reduces history to the (better manageable) history of thought, does not share Croce's belief in total progress,[7] but he too holds that the successive thoughts of the past form a comprehensible chain leading to, and climaxing in, the present. With the two of them, the ideal historian is the mouthpiece of History's last will, or, in Croce's words, of the "spirit" which *is* history and "bears with it all its history." [8] Whenever philosophers speculate on the "idea of history," Hegel's "world spirit" pops up behind the bushes. Finally, both thinkers insist that the historian cannot discover that which is essential in history unless he reconstructs the past in the light of what Collingwood calls his "a priori imagination" —an imagination which, according to premise, is geared to the requirements of the situation in which he finds himself. Indeed, if, as both Collingwood and Croce take for granted, the present moment virtually contains all the moments preceding it, only those who really live in and with the present will be able to get at the core of past life. In this view, historical truth is a variable of present interest. The time whose son the historian is not only transmits to him its preferences and prejudices but rewards his dedication to its peculiar tasks by offering him guidance as he ventures into the dark of times gone by.

No doubt there is something to be said in favor of this proposition. The first of the two assumptions it comprises—the assumption of the impact of the historian's "milieu" on his (unconscious) thought—is actually endorsed by many a practicing historian.[9] In fact, it sounds all but self-evident. On their way through time, nations, societies, and civilizations are usually confronted with problems which, delimiting their horizon, captivate the imagination of all contemporaries. Think of such present-day issues as the struggle for supremacy between the democratic and Communist power blocs, the revolutionary advance of Western technology, the transition from a national to a global frame of reference, the increase of leisure time and the ensuing demand for "mass culture" on a hitherto unheard-of scale, etc.: whatever we hope and fear relates to these issues, whether we know it or not. They literally hypnotize the mind; and arising from the crisscross patterns of divergent opinions, a confused din of them permanently fills the air. Their seeming inescapability lends weight to Carr's advice: "Before you study the historian, study his historical and social environment." [10] Given to studies in this vein, historians of historiography advance many observations to the effect that historical writings tend to reflect responses to the fixed topics of the periods from which they issue. Butterfield, for instance, shrewdly remarks that the stand which German 19th-century historians took in the then raging political dispute between pro-Austrians and pro-Prussians automatically colored their ideas about the beneficial or disastrous consequences of the German medieval monarchy. As a result, "problems of German medieval history were staged against the background of the nineteenth-century struggle between Prussia and Austria, even though this involved a gigantic anachronism." [11] There is no end of such attempts to demonstrate the projective character of historiography. Here are, selected at random, some of the findings they yield: Kant's ethics flows from the moral convictions of German pietism; [12] Niebuhr's Demosthenes is a thinly disguised Stein or Fichte, his Chaeronea the counterpart of Jena; [13] Gibbon's work reveals him as a disciple of Voltaire, a "Européen de l'âge des Lumières"; [14] and of course, nobody can fail to notice that Mommsen's Roman History mirrors the views of the 1848 German liberals.[15] (Mommsen himself was quite conscious of the "modern tone" of his narrative in which he deliberately used contemporary political terms to "bring down the ancients from their fantastic pedestal into the real world.") [16]

Findings of this type immediately strike us as plausible because we are accustomed to credit environmental influences and the like with the power of swaying minds. So it is natural for us to think of the historian as a son of his time. I submit that this apparently self-evident assumption is the outcome of faulty reasoning. It cannot be upheld unless one accepts Croce's doctrine that the historical period is a unit informed by the "spirit" of that period, that any such period is a phase of the historical process, and that the historical process must be imagined as a dialectical movement whose successive phases are meaningfully connected with each other. (It goes without saying that Collingwood's thesis of the all-inclusiveness of "present thought" falls into line with Croce's.) Then it is possible indeed to define the historian's self in terms of its position in time; it fulfills its true nature if it conforms to the spirit of the period to which it belongs. However, the Croce-Collingwood doctrine suffers from two irremediable shortcomings: it rests on the untenable premise that the flow of chronological time is the carrier of all history; and it flagrantly conflicts with a large body of experiences regarding the structure of the period. Since the interrelated concepts of the period and of historical time will be dealt with later on,* I shall confine myself here to a remark, somewhat provisional at that, on the doctrine's inadequacy to these experiences. Contrary to what Croce postulates, the typical period is not so much a unified entity with a spirit of its own as a precarious conglomerate of tendencies, aspirations, and activities which more often than not manifest themselves independently of one another. This is not to deny the existence, at any given moment,

* See Chapter 6.

of certain widespread and even prevailing beliefs, goals, attitudes, etc. I venture to guess that their presence, an empirical fact rather than a metaphysical "must," is in a measure accounted for by the "principle of mental economy," established in Chapter 1; for the rest, would it not be surprising if there were no interaction of a sort between the heterogeneous elements that make up a period? Simultaneity also favors cohesion. But if the period is a unit at all, it is a diffuse, fluid, and essentially intangible unit. Note the admirable caution with which Marc Bloch approaches an issue which Croce settles dogmatically. Bloch, truly a historian's historian, acknowledges the impact which, in the heyday of the feudal age, French culture as a whole exerted on Europe, and then tentatively adds a few reasons for its sweeping success. That he himself does not set great store by them follows from his concluding remark: "But this having been said, we may well ask ourselves if it is not futile to attempt to explain something which, in the present state of our knowledge of man, seems to be beyond our understanding—the ethos of a civilization and its power of attraction." [17]

And here is the point I wish to drive home. If the historian's "historical and social environment" is not a fairly self-contained whole but a fragile compound of frequently inconsistent endeavors in flux, the assumption that it moulds his mind makes little sense. It does make sense only in the contexts of a philosophy which, like Croce's, hypostatizes a period spirit, claims our dependence on it, and thus determines the mind's place in the historical process from above and without. Seen from within, the relations between the mind and its environment are indeterminate. Even supposing that contemporary influences were better definable than they actually are, their binding power would still be limited by the mind's freedom to initiate new situations, new systems of relationships. After having brilliantly deduced the effects of Periclean Athens on the formation of Thucydides' mind, Finley, the Harvard classicist, voices scruples about his own inferences; he declares that "the influence of the contemporary world on any man is of a complexity which defies all but the crudest analysis." [18] His circumspection compares favorably with the kind of observations dear to students of historiography —observations which exhaust themselves in showing that this or that historian unintentionally projects influential contemporary ideas into his accounts of the past. To be sure, such projections do occur but they are by no means inevitable. Maitland, for example, knew how to avoid them, thereby improving on Bishop Stubbs, his contemporary, who unwittingly added Victorian liberalism "to the cargo that the Anglo-Saxons brought with them to England from their North German forests." [19] Nevertheless, at this point an objection suggests itself which seems to confirm the impact of time and place. Are we not usually able to trace documents, literary products, or works of art to the periods of their origin? We undoubtedly are. Upon closer inspection, however, this argument defeats its purpose, for as a rule achievements of the past can be dated only on the basis of characteristics which do not, or at least need not, involve their intrinsic intentions and meanings. Clues may be offered by stylistic peculiarities, references to otherwise familiar events, the recourse to knowledge unobtainable before a particular historical moment, etc. Moreover, as with all circumstantial evidence, the conclusions drawn from these secondary characteristics are anything but irrefutable truths. In sum, the whole assumption examined here stands and falls with the belief that people actually "belong" to their period. This must not be so. Vico is an outstanding instance of chronological exterritoriality; and it would be extremely difficult to derive Burckhardt's complex and ambivalent physiognomy as a historian from the conditions under which he lived and worked. Like great artists or thinkers, great historians are biological freaks: they father the time that has fathered them. Perhaps the same holds true of mass movements, revolutions.[20]

According to the second assumption inherent in the present-interest theory, the historian is not only a son of his time but a son utterly devoted to it. He must be prompted by a deep concern with its problems, sorrows, and objectives, or else the past he wants to resuscitate will never come to life. Croce and Collingwood bring this line of thought to its logical conclusion by contending that present-mindedness is prerequisite to any significant reconstruction of historical reality.

Their radical proposition sheds light on the dangerous implications of the assumption underlying it. I intend to show that this assumption entails a shift of emphasis from the realistic to the formative tendency which threatens to upset the "right" balance between the two of them.* Historians who proceed straight from present interest are apt to obscure, and indeed submerge, the evidence. A nice instance is the following: under the pressure of conventional preferences and, I presume, contemporary reader demands, Cortés biographers have up to now featured only the more dramatic events of his life—the conquest of the Aztec, the expedition to Honduras, etc.—while leaving unused the rich source material in the archives of Mexico and Spain which would have enabled them to shed light on the Conqueror's later career.[21] The investigator's aggressiveness tends to frighten the past back into the past; instead of conversing with the dead, he himself does most of the talking. Remember Butterfield's remark on the "gigantic anachronism" to which 19th-century German medieval histories fell prey because of

* See pages 56–57.

their authors' naïve indulgence in pro-Prussian or pro-Austrian
sentiments.

It pays to take a good look at Collingwood's argument in
support of his position. To be sure, exactly like Croce, he points
to the necessity for the historian to secure the facts, or what we
commonly believe to be facts, with scholarly accuracy; he even
requests him to "re-enact" past experiences—a request which
obviously calls for an effort on the historian's part temporarily to
disregard present-day experiences. Yet at the same time Collingwood characterizes the ideal historian in terms which make it
seem improbable that he should ever be able to live up to these
obligations. A counterpart of the Baconian natural scientist, Collingwood's historian treats history as if it were nature. Instead of
waiting for what the sources may wish to tell him, he questions
his material in accordance with his own hunches and hypotheses
and like a scientific experimenter forces it to answer his questions.[22] How the poor man will manage to get substantial answers from the past—a past which is not merely nature—
without waiting for its possible communications, Collingwood
does not care to reveal to us.

Or rather, he tries to clarify the issue by comparing the historian with the sleuth in detective novels.[23] As he sees it, both
figures coincide in detecting hidden truths by way of active
questioning. It is a particular detective Collingwood has in
mind: Agatha Christie's incomparable Monsieur Hercule Poirot.
This archetypal model of a Collingwoodian historian derides the
police for collecting everything which might eventually turn out
to be a clue and, strictly opposed to their pedestrian methods,
emphatically asserts that the secret of detection consists in using
one's "little grey cells." In Collingwood's words: "You can't collect your evidence before you begin thinking, he [Poirot] meant;
because thinking means asking questions (logicians, please

note), and nothing is evidence, except in relation to some definite question." [24] Now much as I admire Hercule Poirot's miraculous "a priori imagination"—miraculous because it often hits
the mark in the absence of any palpable clue—as an assiduous
reader of detective stories I am bound to admit that he is not
the only detective with a superior record and that some of his
peers are little inclined to agree with him on this score. Superintendent Arnold Pike of Scotland Yard for one, the hero of Philip
MacDonald's delightful yarn *Murder Gone Mad*, refuses to rely
on his "little grey cells" at the beginning of an investigation: "I
just try to collect facts whether they appear to have any bearing
on the case or not. Then, suddenly, when I've been digging
round long enough and hard enough, I maybe dig up something
which seems to click in my mind and become a good starting-off
place for a think." [25] I might as well add that his subsequent
think is very ingenious indeed. There are, then, sleuths and
sleuths. The moral is that Collingwood should have read more
detective novels.

Fortunately, the spell his theory casts over him wears thin at
intervals—which, on some such occasion, permits Collingwood
to realize that his historian is in a predicament; he is faced with
the problem of resurrecting a past whose nature his involvement
in present thought tends to conceal from him. The problem so
posed admits only of one "solution": if the historian does not
seriously reach out for the evidence and get close to it—if he
insists on present-mindedness—the evidence must be made to
move toward him. Collingwood, intent on demonstrating that
pronounced aggressiveness and intimate contact with the given
material may well go together, eagerly seizes on this seeming
possibility. He claims that historians had better concentrate on
events or developments for which they show genuine affinity.[26]
The idea behind his advice is that the attraction which this or

that aspect of historical reality exerts on the historian will be reciprocated in kind—i.e., cause all relevant facts to rush out of their hiding-places, as if drawn to him by a sort of magnetic power. They are his for the asking. Nor need he further look into them; thanks to his sympathy for his subject matter, he knows all that there is to be known about it from within. It is understood that Collingwood's advice—by the way, he is not alone to offer it [27]—fails to dispose of the problem it is meant to solve. Granted for the sake of argument that under certain circumstances the historian following this suggestion succeeds in bridging the gap between his "little grey cells" and the far-distant evidence, what will happen to those portions of the past which do not strike a sympathetic chord in him? Are they doomed to oblivion? More important, the device in which Collingwood takes refuge rests on the belief that love makes you see. Quite so. Yet the reverse holds true also, especially in the case where love is inseparably coupled with present interest. Then in all likelihood a historian's affinity for his topic will blind rather than sensitize him to its specific qualities. Arther Schlesinger, Jr.'s *Age of Jackson*—certainly a product of sympathy for this age—is considered not so much a contribution to original historical scholarship as a "young humanitarian's politically inspired volume that succeeded in creating a popular image of Jackson as a forerunner of F.D.R." [28] Collingwood resorts to an ineffective expedient; and he rejects precisely the kind of love which really serves as an eye-opener: love of the past for its own sake.

But his recourse to eligible affinities plays a marginal role after all. In the final analysis the Croce-Collingwood doctrine is founded on the two thinkers' conviction that history amounts to something like a comprehensible whole, an intelligible arrangement of things. Indeed, they *must* postulate the wholeness of the historical universe in order to justify their identification of history as contemporary history. This equation is meaningful only if the historian's material is thought of as making up a virtually consistent and surveyable "cosmos" of a sort. Only then is he in a position to indulge in present-mindedness and yet have access to the past; only then may he reconstruct past thoughts from present thought without running the risk of misconstruing them. As elements of a, so to speak, closed system all pieces of the evidence he gathers can be expected to fall by themselves alone into place. The present-interest theory hinges on the idea of such a system—on one of the pipe-dreams of unfettered reason, that is. Once this dream is abandoned, it is easy to see that present interest lacks the magic attributed to it by Croce and Collingwood; that the historical facts are stubborn enough not to yield their secret to a historian who just treats them after the manner of a scientific experimenter.

The ultimate consequences of this theory—consequences which Croce and Collingwood would hardly have sanctioned, though—are illustrated by a pseudo-historical genre which lies in the border region between history proper and prophecy. Born out of an existential concern with the present and the future in its womb, the genre I have in mind springs from the experience that the way in which we conceive of the past will help us achieve our goals (or interfere with their attainment). "History feeds on history." [29] I do not wish to suggest, of course, that all histories partial to a cause would fall into that border region. It all is a matter of degree. No doubt the various Catholic and Protestant accounts of the Reformation are to a larger or lesser extent "engaged," but even so numbers of them are true histories inasmuch as they originate in an often admirable effort to render their material with scholarly detachment. This property of theirs makes them differ from what I should like to call "existential" histories. No sooner does the historian's apologetic passion exceed his capacity for detachment than he crosses the threshold which separates the past as a field of study from the past as a means of exhortation, as a whip, a fiery challenge. History, as envisioned by the Jewish Prophets, is a series of partly supernatural transactions, with God's wrath or forgiveness constantly intervening in the course of secular events. By the same token, peoples acquiring statehood or assuming a new existence are prone to invent a past which transforms them into the standard-bearers of significant destinies. A striking case in point is the young Nietzsche, who in his essay *Vom Nutzen und Nachteil der Historie fuer das Leben* champions such uses or abuses of the past. He condemns the historians of his day—this "generation of eunuchs" [30]—for indulging in aimless scholarly pursuits. Historicism, he has it, enlarges our horizon beyond our wants, destroys the instincts of the people, paralyzes vitality, etc.; it is altogether a vain human effort, a science got out of hand. Instead, he pleads for histories which serve "life," the life of the present. Croce's dictum: "History is contemporary history" still reverberates with Nietzsche's determination to make the past meet the needs of the living. But while Croce advocates present-mindedness as a prerequisite of knowledgeable interpretation, Nietzsche holds that the last thing we, the living, do need is knowledge: ". . . each people and in fact each man who is to become *mature,* wants . . . a delusion to be wrapped in, a . . . protective and veiling cloud . . ." [31] Plainly speaking, Nietzsche yearns for historians who surrender their preoccupation with what really happened to such representations of the past as foster the illusions that keep us going. The demands of "life," however deceptive, would thus take precedence over the, in his view, emasculated search for historical truth, much of which he deems unnecessary anyway. As for these demands,

Nietzsche looks forward to a time when we will again disregard the masses and turn the spotlight on the individuals, "who form a kind of bridge over the arid stream of becoming." [32] Here you have the idea of the "superman" in a pupa state. (On the other hand, the phrase of the "arid stream of becoming" with its anti-evolutionary ring—a phrase vaguely reminiscent of the Plato word quoted in Chapter 1 *—is well worth remembering.) The rub in all of this is that Nietzsche, out of his inordinate and rather juvenile infatuation with "life," shuts his eyes to the enormous achievements of historicism; that he just wants to liquidate it instead of uncovering its meanings and then telling us where we should go from there. His essay has traits of an adolescent's inconsequential rebellion . . . . It remains to be mentioned that the existential genre stands the best chance of materializing when the whole of history comes into view. The larger the units a historian is dealing with, the greater the temptation for him to lapse into purposeful constructions with prophetic overtones.

Yet I have no intention of throwing the child out with the bath water. It would be foolish indeed to deny that, like us other mortals, the historian is often moved by present interest. And this justly so; the fact that we live only once involves a moral obligation toward the living. The historian's concern with them —his desire better to understand the present—inspires many of his inquiries into the life of the dead. He may relate, somehow, the past to the present; and he may even wrest this or that secret from the past precisely by probing it in the light of contemporary needs.[33] Burckhardt, anxious to strengthen the awareness of historical continuity, considers it proper for historians to feature all those past facts whose consequences make themselves still felt in our time, our culture.[34] Is there a historian

* See page 24.

who would not see eye to eye with him? To find out how we have become what we are has ever since been one of the grand designs of history.[35]

However, none of these customary practices can be traced to the chimerical assumption that present interest is the master key which opens all the doors to the past, the axis around which everything revolves. Rather, whenever historians—I mean real historians—give the present its due, they do so, as Meinecke puts it, in the conviction that this is a "legitimate and necessary goal, but neither the only nor the highest one." [36] They would not dream of confusing present-mindedness with a methodological requirement. Take Marc Bloch: eager to transform history into a science, he insists, not unlike Collingwood, on the necessity for the historian to proceed with a scientist's aggressiveness from the very beginning; to cross-examine the past, that is, by means of constructs and models which flow from his "a priori imagination," or, by extension, his present-mindedness. Yet, historian that Bloch is, he hastens to add that the models are nothing but provisional scaffoldings: "Naturally, the method of cross-examination must be very elastic. . . . Even when he has settled his itinerary, the explorer is well aware that he will not follow it exactly." [37] (I wonder, though, whether the elastic method suggested by Bloch will always result in adjustments fitting the case. Elastic breaks if overextended.[38])

What counts, then, is the difference between present interest as a starting-point for, or terminus of, historical studies and present interest as defined by Croce et al.[39] Now present interest in the first sense so little precludes "antiquarian interest" that it is entirely consistent with an approach to the past which pays full tribute to the available evidence instead of neglecting, Collingwood fashion, its possible contributions over the allegedly superior constructions of "present thought." It is an approach patterned on Superintendent Arnold Pike's prudent devotion to the facts rather than Hercule Poirot's magisterial indifference to them. (But the contempt in which the little Belgian detective holds material clues makes him all the more an endearing incarnation of paternal omniscience.) The literature abounds with testimony in favor of this mode of treating the given data. Even historians who feel that present-mindedness is of the essence request the student of history to explore the past without regard for our well-being, our calamities. So Burckhardt.[40] His wavering in this respect marks an attitude fairly widespread among contemporary historians.[41] (He himself tried to escape the present, yielding to the "unfulfilled nostalgia for that which has perished." [42]) Others promote, or indulge in, antiquarian pursuits pure and simple. Huizinga has it that true history probes the past also because it is significant in its own right.[43] And Namier never tired of looking for the seemingly irrelevant; "in fact, he spent all his life in byways." [44] Still other historians— e.g., Harnack [45]—make a point of combining their appreciation of disengaged research with critical comment on the tenets of the present-interest school of thought. Thus Lovejoy explicitly attacks Dewey's proposition that "all history is necessarily written from the standpoint of the present . . ." [46] (Dewey and Collingwood are strange bedfellows indeed; but *les extrêmes se touchent,* especially in the near-vacuum filled with sets of sharp-edged abstractions.) The attack is borne out by a statement palpably saturated with personal experience. Lovejoy not only wants the historian to get rid, as best he can, of the preoccupations of his time but argues that such an "effort of self-transcendence" will enrich his knowledge of the present.[47] He will find what he did not seek, precisely for turning his back on it.[48] At the very end of his *Social and Economic History of the Roman Empire,* a work of profound and completely detached scholarship, Rostovtzeff, as if emerging from a long dream, addresses himself to his contemporaries. The evolution of the an-

cient world, says he, has a lesson and a warning for us. Our
civilization will not survive unless it be a civilization not of one
class, but of the masses. But is not every civilization bound to
decay as soon as it begins to penetrate the masses? [49] Unexpected, like a rare flower, this meditation grows out of the soil of
the past.

One cannot discuss the relations between the past and the
present without referring, sometime, to Proust. He is one of the
highest authorities on these matters. Clearly, Proust sides with
Lovejoy and the rest of the anti-Collingwood historians. In his
view the past gives itself up only to those who lean over backward in an attempt to make it speak; and only an "effort of self-
transcendence" in this vein will, perhaps, enable us to arrive at
an understanding of our present condition. Proust's thought is
thrown into relief by that episode in his novel where he tells us
that he was suddenly overwhelmed with happiness when, during a carriage ride, he saw three trees which formed a pattern
strangely familiar to him; he believed them to have surged out
of the forgotten days of his infancy. The sensation of *déjà vu* he
experienced went together with an awareness that the "phan-
toms of the past" were beckoning him. "Like ghosts they seemed
to be appealing to me to take them with me, to bring them back
to life." And why did they so anxiously try to capture his attention? Looking at them, he felt that they wanted to impart a
message which concerned him personally. "I watched the trees
gradually withdraw . . . seeming to say to me: '. . . If you allow us to drop back into the hollow of this road from which we
sought to raise ourselves up to you, a whole part of yourself
which we were bringing to you will fall forever into the abyss.'"
Note that Proust leaves it in the open whether or not the message of the three trees bears on his infancy and through it on his
present self. He asks himself: ". . . were they but an image

freshly extracted from a dream of the night before . . . Or had I indeed never seen them before . . . ? . . . I could not tell." [50] Proust shares Burckhardt's nostalgia for lost causes.

It follows from what I have said so far that there is no peg onto which to fasten the subjective factor, operative in history writing, with any certainty. The historian is not just the son of his time in the sense that his outlook could be defined in terms of contemporary influences. Nor is his conception of the past necessarily an expression of present interest, present thought; or rather, if it is, his aggressiveness may cause the past to withdraw from him. The historian's mind is in a measure capable of moving about at liberty. And to the extent that he makes use of this freedom he may indeed come face to face with things past.

Orpheus descended into Tartarus to fetch back the beloved who had died from the bite of a serpent. His plaintive music "so far soothed the savage heart of Hades that he won leave to restore Eurydice to the upper world. Hades made a single condition: that Orpheus might not look behind him until she was safely back under the light of the sun. Eurydice followed Orpheus up through the dark passage guided by the sounds of his lyre and it was only when he reached the sunlight again that he turned to see whether she were still behind him, and so lost her for ever." [51] Like Orpheus, the historian must descend into the nether world to bring the dead back to life. How far will they follow his allurements and evocations? They are lost to him when, re-emerging in the sunlight of the present, he turns for fear of losing them. But does he not for the first time take possession of them at this very moment—the moment when they forever depart, vanishing in a history of his own making? And what happens to the Pied-Piper himself on his way down and up? Consider that his journey is not simply a return trip.

4
The Historian's Journey

Macaulay compared history to foreign travel.[1] Indeed, historians are much in the same position as ordinary tourists: they too wish to perceive the sights they have come to see. This is by no means an easy job. Actually many people go abroad without seeing anything. Once they have convinced themselves that, say, the Parthenon is at the place assigned to it by the guidebook, they immediately take pictures of their beloved ones before an ancient column. The column serves them as an alibi back home. For the rest, these picture hunters are less fortunate than animal hunters because they cannot even "eat" their prey; in shooting unseen objects, they irretrievably lose sight of them. Something of this kind may also happen to historians. At any rate, Pieter Geyl makes Macaulay look like such a traveler. Macaulay's obsession with Progress and the superiority of the present, says he, caused him to treat "the generations that had gone before with self-righteous condescension." But this mental attitude, Geyl continues, is deeply unhistorical; it "must lead the historian to view the past in terms which may be entirely irrelevant and result in a picture lacking in the truth of intimacy." [2] And how does the historian manage to attain to that "truth of intimacy"?

Certainly not by staying in the present while visiting the past. If he remains the person he is he will hardly be able to penetrate the fog that veils the sights as he arrives on the spot. To get at the core of things he must take advantage of the mind's freedom to alter the cast of the mind. The job of sightseeing requires a mobile self. In the following I shall present a rough scheme of the mental operations in which many a historian engages on his way back to past centuries.

In one of his best known statements Ranke protests his desire to blot out his self so that only the things themselves may do the talking. He wants to suspend his personal leanings and judgments in order to show "wie es eigentlich gewesen." The objectivity at which he aims is of a special kind; it is partly grounded in the belief that God manifests Himself in the unfolding of universal history. Ranke is prompted by religious feelings. Historiography, he also declares, lives up to its ultimate mission if it reveals itself to be in sympathy with the universe and privy to its secrets.[3] The historian, then, would have to blot out his self not just for the purpose of dispassionately rendering the course of past events but with a view to becoming a participant observer engrossed in the uniquely significant spectacle that evolves on the stage of the world. In Ranke's ideal historian the disengaged researcher who aspires to expose the facts as they are, insolubly merges with the worshiper, if not mystic, who purifies his mind to contemplate the wonders of divine wisdom.[4] So the objectivity he achieves is a rather complex product; it results from both a mind reduced to a blank and a mind more substantial and wider in scope than the one voided for its sake. I might as well mention in passing that Dilthey dismisses Ranke's plea for self-extinction as something impossible to fulfill. Contrary to what Ranke suggests, Dilthey argues,

the historian cannot understand the past unless he seizes on it
with his whole being; instead of vainly trying to extinguish his
self, he had therefore better expand it, a universal self making
for universal understanding.[5] Quite so. Yet since the historian,
unlike the poet, is under an obligation to build from given materials, the desirable extension of his subjectivity is contingent on
its previous shrinkage. And why should it be impossible for him
to check the thrust of subjective influences? Actually his self is
much more flexible and manipulable than Dilthey seems to realize. The historian, that is, may go far in putting it in brackets or
indeed effacing it—in any case far enough to respond to many
signals which would otherwise be lost on him. In the intermediary dimension of history, differences in degree and approximations are anything but negligible. Ranke's yearnings point in the
right direction.

In that passage of his novel where he relates the neutral objectivity of photographs to the photographer's emotional detachment, Proust lucidly describes two different states of mind—one
in which a person's self wields full power and the other in which
it has withdrawn from the scene. The passage is devoted to a
visit which Marcel pays to his beloved grandmother after a long
absence. Upon entering her room unannounced, he immediately
feels that it is not he himself who is looking at her: "Of myself
. . . there was present only the witness, the observer with a
hat and traveling coat, the stranger who does not belong to the
house, the photographer who has called to take a photograph of
places which one will never see again. The process that mechani-
cally occurred in my eyes when I caught sight of my grandmother was indeed a photograph." This photograph, a projection
of Marcel's vacant mind, pitilessly exhibits what he, the complete Marcel, had not seen before; for we "never see the people
who are dear to us save in the animated system, the perpetual

motion of our incessant love for them, which before allowing the images that their faces present to reach us catches them in its vortex, flings them back upon the idea that we have always had of them . . ." For the first time Marcel now sees his grandmother as she really is, sees, sitting on the sofa, a "dejected old woman" who bears no resemblance whatever to the picture which he has lovingly formed of her in his soul.[6] His inner picture yields to the photograph at the very moment when the loving person he is shrinks into an impersonal stranger; as a stranger he may indeed perceive anything because nothing he sees is pregnant with memories that would narrow his field of vision. No sooner does Marcel enter his grandmother's room than his mind becomes a palimpsest, with the stranger's observations being superimposed upon the lover's temporarily effaced inscription.

Sometimes life itself produces such palimpsests. I am thinking of the exile who as an adult person has been forced to leave his country or has left it of his own free will. As he settles elsewhere, all those loyalties, expectations, and aspirations that comprise so large a part of his being are automatically cut off from their roots. His life history is disrupted, his "natural" self relegated to the background of his mind. To be sure, his inevitable efforts to meet the challenges of an alien environment will affect his outlook, his whole mental make-up. But since the self he was continues to smolder beneath the person he is about to become, his identity is bound to be in a state of flux; and the odds are that he will never fully belong to the community to which he now in a way belongs. (Nor will its members readily think of him as one of theirs.) In fact, he has ceased to "belong." Where then does he live? In the near-vacuum of extra-territoriality, the very no-man's land which Marcel entered when he first caught sight of his grandmother. The exile's true mode of exis-

tence is that of a stranger.[7] So he may look at his previous
existence with the eyes of one "who does not belong to the
house." And just as he is free to step outside the culture which
was his own, he is sufficiently uncommitted to get inside the
minds of the foreign people in whose midst he is living. There
are great historians who owe much of their greatness to the fact
that they were expatriates. Thucydides expressly states that his
long exile enabled him "to see something of both sides—the
Peloponnesian as well as the Athenian . . ."[8] In our days
Namier's alien background—he hailed from Poland—is held to
be partly responsible for his unprejudiced and novel approach to
English history.[9]

It is only in this state of self-effacement, or homelessness, that
the historian can commune with the material of his concern. I
assume, of course, that he really wants to get the feel of it and
not only aims at verifying his initial hypotheses and hunches
with its aid. A stranger to the world evoked by the sources, he is
faced with the task—the exile's task—of penetrating its outward
appearances, so that he may learn to understand that world
from within.

The most promising way of acquiring such knowledge is presumably for him to heed Schopenhauer's advice to the art student. Anybody looking at a picture, Schopenhauer claims,
should behave as if he were in the presence of a prince and
respectfully wait for what the picture may or may not wish to
tell him; for were he to talk first he would only be listening to
himself.[10] Waiting in this sense amounts to a sort of active
passivity on the historian's part. He must venture on the diverse
routes suggested to him by his intercourse with the evidence, let
himself drift along, and take in, with all his senses strained, the
various messages that happen to reach him. Thus he will more
likely than not hit upon unexpected facts and contexts some of

which perhaps turn out to be incompatible with his original assumptions.[11] But do not his wanderings bring again his self into play, the very self which according to premise should have been put to sleep? They do and do not. Actually the self operative in the process is only part of the self in its fullness—that part of it which functions as a sheer receiving instrument.

For obvious reasons scientific-minded historians tend to disparage this kind of passiveness, contending that it is neither useful nor indeed possible. Marc Bloch, for instance, categorically asserts that "mere passive observation, even supposing such a thing were possible, has never contributed anything productive to any science." And he qualifies his admission that no historian can exactly follow his itinerary as he investigates the sources * by immediately adding that without it the historian "would risk wandering perpetually at random."[12] Fortunately, Bloch's objections need not be taken too seriously. An outcome of his ardent desire to scientize (social and institutional) historiography, they are in a measure invalidated by his own research procedures; as a practicing historian he himself leans over backward in doing justice to the given data, no matter whether they corroborate his scheme of explanation or not. For the rest, not even all scientists are disposed to accept his verdict on "mere passive observation"; the late Wright Mills held that, precisely in the interest of theory-formation, social scientists had better pay attention to the random ideas and fancies that inadvertently cross their minds.[13]

What I have called active passivity is a necessary phase of the historian's work. His behavior during this phase has been characterized to perfection by a remark of Burckhardt which breathes the spirit of Wordsworth's line: "Wisdom oft / is nearer when we stoop than when we soar."[14] Reminiscing about the

* See page 76.

way in which he familiarized himself with the source material
for his *Griechische Kulturgeschichte,* Burckhardt observes that
in any such case violent exertion is least fit to force the desired
result: a gentle pricking up of the ears coupled with steady
industry will carry one further.[15] (It goes without saying that
this does not apply to Collingwood's ideal historian who, were
he ever to prick up his ears, would not hear anything because all
that comes to him from the past is drowned in the din of contemporary noises.)

There are limits to self-effacement and passive observation in
its wake. I have been told about anthropologists who, bent on
comprehending the mentality of some primitive tribe, eventually felt and acted as if they belonged among its members. They
lost their identity and accordingly ceased to be participant ob-
servers. Personality transformation in this direction defeats its
purpose because it annuls the minimum distance that must be
upheld between the researcher and his material. Remember
that, despite his self-extinction, Marcel does not completely
desert Marcel in his grandmother's room. What this implies for
even the most accurate rendering of past events was driven
home to me in a conversation with a young American historian
of German descent who interviewed me in behalf of his research
on German intellectual history under the Weimar Republic. I
had participated in the life of the community whose history he
wanted to tell. The thing that vividly struck me in our discussion
was that everything he had dug up so far was true to fact, while
nothing had happened the way he related it. So I anticipated
that in his account all that was a matter of fluctuating opinions,
agonizing doubts, and spontaneous decisions during the 'twenties would freeze into a more or less rigid pattern of trends,
cross-currents, majority and minority attitudes, and the like. And
since many experiences I had then undergone were obviously

doomed to slip through the net of the concepts and labels he
used to establish this pattern, I wondered at the incommensurable relationship between the picture he was about to draw and
the reality which it was designed to cover. He did not represent
the events as I knew them—events in flux and amenable to
change—but conceived of them as elements of a period which
was now definitely a *fait accompli*. On the other hand, this
enabled him to exhibit aspects of that period which were entirely unfamiliar to me at the time. And I soon realized that the
lifelessness of his prospective history was perhaps the price he
had to pay for the revealing hindsight it would afford. (Conversely, contemporary history can, and indeed must, show
things in a nascent state but is by definition prevented from
showing them in the light of knowledge available only to future
generations.)

Such revealing hindsight—revealing because it adduces new
evidence—should not be mistaken for the kind of hindsight
which falsifies historical reality by reading alien meanings into
it.[16] Droysen's all but Hegelian interpretation of Alexander goes
to the limit in this respect. After having indicated that Alexander
himself may have believed a Hellenized Asia to lie in the interest of his plans for world domination, Droysen introduces History in person, has her smile at Alexander's self-deception and
say: what was the goal to his ambition was to me the historical
means of achieving the Hellenization of Asia [17] (which in
Droysen's view ultimately served to facilitate the propagation of
Christianity). One feels tempted to follow the example of History and smile at these gratuitous speculations after the fact, yet
there is no doubt that they led Droysen to endow the Hellenistic
era with a dignity of its own.* The ways of the mind are inscrutable.

* Cf. pages 41–43.

So much for the historian's journey into the past. The journey continues: he must return to the upper world and put his booty to good use. Here follows a scheme of the mental operations in which he will have to engage to make the journey a success. They are about the reverse of those which helped him absorb the potential evidence.

The next logical step is for the historian to assimilate to himself the material collected, with the emphasis on his factual findings and finds. His stock-taking activities serve two purposes. First, they mark a transitional stage between research proper and interpretation—a stage which he can hardly afford to jump. If he failed to ponder and organize, somehow, his material he would not be able to assess its bearing on his initial hypotheses and freely to utilize it for analysis and in wider interpretative contexts. Second, these activities frequently amount to pursuits in their own right inasmuch as they are intended to disclose the shortcomings of histories at variance with the facts. Since especially large-scale histories cannot avoid beclouding or distorting part of historical reality, the task of exposing their errors is a running obligation. The results of the historian's efforts during this phase may exclusively benefit a major work he is preparing and therefore never come to light in the form of independent reports. To quote Burckhardt again, he advises a young colleague "simply to omit the mere rubbish of facts" in his prospective narrative (not without adding, though, that he should naturally study all that he omits).[18]

However, this advice sounds somewhat outmoded at a time when the syntheses of old are no longer fashionable. The rule today is, rather, a pronounced concern with that very "rubbish of facts" which Burckhardt wanted to clear away. Contemporary historiography abounds in fact-oriented accounts exhibiting the immediate yield of detailed research. They range from run-of-the-mill investigations which make you think of predatory raids into the past to inquiries which really involve self-forgetting immersion in the texts and remains. Of course, it is only these latter inquiries which live up to the scheme presented here. Altogether the genre of fact-oriented accounts largely coincides with what Herbert Butterfield calls "technical history." Butterfield expressly states that technical history presupposes an "act of self-emptying" on the historian's part [19] and at another place defines this type of history as a "limited and mundane realm of description and explanation, in which local and concrete things are achieved by a disciplined use of tangible evidence." [20]

The phrase "local and concrete things" points to one of the characteristics of the genre: its affinity for the small, the monographic form. There are good reasons for this. The state of passiveness in which any sensitive historian gathers the evidence palpably favors the influx of minutiae. And whenever he probes the sources to check the truth-to-fact of some inclusive narrative, some broader historical construction, he is likely to happen upon generalizations or macro-units which call for a fresh look at the diverse materials they allegedly cover.

It is further understood that the histories in this vein come into their own only if the stories they impart "can be taken over by the Catholic or Protestant or atheist." [21] The genre aspires to (unattainable) objective truth. The kind of objectivity it tries to achieve may be called "passive" because of its origin in a self which, though reactivated, is still at a low pitch and moreover refuses fully to assert itself for fear of blurring the communications received during its withdrawal from the scene.

Can anything be had for nothing? As products of a reduced self—reduced, that is, if there is enough of a self to admit of reduction—fact-oriented accounts are of necessity neutral and

colorless. Such interpretation as goes into them at all merely
serves to interrelate the data assembled in an unassuming way.
But even so these "technical" histories are more true to type
than are the many full-blown histories which inadvertently twist
the evidence to make it bear out whatever they express in terms
of present-day views, ideas, or subjective preferences. While in
them the historian's formative urges get the better of his curiosity about the real course of events, the accounts I have in
mind—accounts which confine themselves to taking stock of "local and concrete things"—unswervingly follow the realistic tendency. Bare and noncommittal as they may be, in doing so they
at least meet the "minimum requirement" of the historical approach.*

Their most outspoken counterparts in the cinematic medium
are documentary films designed to portray (physical) reality in
a straightforward manner. Here you have again a case where a
comparison between film and history proves rewarding. A few
documentaries I know picture appalling living conditions with a
matter-of-fact soberness which, as I have learned, results from
the deliberate suspension of their authors' creative powers.
Highly skilled craftsmen, the directors of these films proceed
from the conviction that pictorial beauty and suggestive editing
would interfere with their intention to let things be as they are.
They practice self-restraint as artists to produce the effect of
impersonal authenticity. Now the salient point is that their conduct is based on moral considerations. Joris Ivens relates that
during the shooting of *Borinage*, a 1934 documentary about the
miners in this Belgian coal district, he and his co-director Henri
Storck realized that their very subject matter required of them
photographic "simplicity." "We felt it would be insulting to people in such extreme hardship to use any style of photography

* See Chapter 2, especially pages 55–57.

that would prevent the direct honest communication of their pain to every spectator." [22] Human suffering, it appears, is conducive to detached reporting; the artist's conscience shows in artless photography. Since history is full of human suffering, similar attitudes and reflections may be at the bottom of many a fact-oriented historical account, deepening the significance of its pale objectivity.[23]

The journey continues. After having established and organized his facts, the historian moves on to their interpretation. He is about to complete his journey. But is the historian who returns from the past still the person he was when he left the present for it? In his critical comment on Collingwood's philosophy of history, Leo Strauss raises this very question and sagaciously answers it in the negative. (Collingwood himself was so convinced of the legitimacy of his insistence on the historian's present-mindedness that he would never have dreamed of asking such a thing.) Strauss arrives at the conclusion—a valid conclusion, as I see it—that, contrary to what Collingwood assumes, the historian does *not* retain his identity in the process: "He embarks on a journey whose end is hidden from him. He is not likely to return to the shores of his time as exactly the same man who departed from them." [24] Incidentally, he is not likely either to return to his point of departure.

The change of identity he undergoes must be traced to his stay in the past. To be precise, it is an aftermath of the discoveries which the historian is making in the state of self-effacement —that phase in which he opens himself up to the suggestions of the sources. Need I repeat that his findings may obstruct his original research designs and therefore determine him to alter the course of his investigation? At any rate, they are apt to tell him something he did not, and could not, know before. This

points to the direction of the change. It is inevitable that the
yield of the historian's active passivity should ferment in his
mind and thus eventually effect a broadening of its scope. Self-
effacement begets self-expansion. (I do not wish to imply that
the historian is a privileged person in this respect. Present-day
life being of the same ilk as the life of the past, everybody going
about the business of living may achieve such self-expansion,
provided he is capable of losing his self. And the historian himself, trained in productive absent-mindedness as he is, will certainly not only feed on sources which have ceased to flow.) In
consequence, Dilthey's belief that historical understanding calls
for the total mobilization of our being * turns out to be not
sufficiently specific. What is required of the historian is not
merely his "*whole* inner man" [25] as he happens to be but a self
which has expanded in the wake of its near-extinction.

The parallel, then, which I have drawn between Proust's Marcel and the historian cannot be fully upheld. Despite all that
they have in common they behave in a different manner. After
Marcel, shrunk to a stranger or photographer, has seen his
grandmother as she really looks, the palimpsest which his mind
represents during this involuntary excursion into camera-reality
dissolves again, and the loving Marcel underneath Marcel, the
impassive stranger, re-enters the scene. True, the historian
passes through the same phase of estrangement from his preferences and inclinations, but, unlike Marcel, he does not come out
of it unchanged. His self which after his return from the past
resumes control is enriched by the observations he has made
during its temporary recession. While the reinstated complete
Marcel falls back upon the ideas which he entertained of his
grandmother prior to her transformation into a photograph, the

* See pages 29–30, 43–44, 48, 62.

historian assimilates to himself the very reality which was concealed from him by his ideas of it.

This has a bearing on his position in the chronological order of things. The impact of the historian's journey on his mental build further invalidates the commonplace assumption that he is the son of his time. Actually he is the son of at least two times—his own and the time he is investigating. His mind is in a measure unlocalizable; it perambulates without a fixed abode.

Because of the complexity of his material the historian will have to avail himself of all imaginable modes of explanation. They may range from statistical surveys to imaginative guesses at purposes and meanings; and they are bound to vary with both his emphases and the characteristics of his particular subject matter. The history of ideas quite obviously requires a different treatment from, say, political or social history. Things human extending into multiple dimensions, one single type of explanation will rarely do; as a rule, several interpretative approaches must be interwoven to cover the case—any case—under scrutiny. Dilthey, instinct with a sense of wholeness, affirms the necessity for the historian to apply them jointly, arguing that they complement and reinforce each other.[26] So it makes sense to speak of a "web of interpretations." The historian's story is tantamount to such a web—at least to the extent that the events he relates lend themselves to being explained at all; whenever they prove to be unaccountable, his is largely a reporting job.

And what does the web of interpretations consist of? Conspicuous among its more articulate components is the science-oriented approach which takes its cue from the sciences proper, especially the behavioral sciences. Since its possibilities and limitations have been dealt with in Chapter 1, I shall confine myself to restating two major points made there: this approach is based on the fact that man is deeply embedded in nature; and its objective is to explain the past from the resultant regularities and uniformitiès in social life and human affairs in general.* Even though scientific explanations do not involve historical phenomena in their concreteness nor provide answers to specifically historical questions, they do isolate series of natural causes and effects which no historian intent on inclusive comprehension can afford to neglect. For him to frown on computers would be idle romanticism. (This is not said to gladden the hearts of the computer-minded. To mistake computers for a master key to interpretation means to deprive history of its peculiar flavor by reducing it to a science pure and simple.)

Certain aspects of his data—aspects not, or not fully, amenable to breakdowns in science fashion—may challenge the historian to resort to explanations in a morphological vein. Thus he feels time and again tempted to render intelligible the simultaneous occurrence of events in different areas of human endeavors by reference to the sway of a force or belief supposed to govern the period to which the syndrome belongs. Whether attempts along these lines will work depends entirely on the weight of the corroborative evidence. Some of them—for instance, Max Weber's theory of the conditioning power of Calvinist ethics, or Pirenne's idea of the beginnings of the European Middle Ages—are as fictitious as they are shining.[27] And they are hopelessly futile if, at a loss how to find a common denominator, they conjure up the "spirit" of a period. Croce's period spirits still seem to haunt minds in quest of lofty vistas. By the same token, morphological description offers itself as a tool for

---

* I shall again leave undiscussed the many regularities of conduct, motivation, etc., which, in any society, powerful agencies enjoin on people at large by means of force and/or persuasion. It goes without saying that events pertaining to this artificially induced nature are no less predictable than natural necessities.

the exploration of historical systems of ideas—e.g., Hellenistic syncretism, medieval Christianity, etc. Indeed, each such system invites inquiries into the structural relationships and the dynamic interplay between the various notions comprising it. Think of Basil Willey's *The Seventeenth Century Background* or, to mention a more recent example, Hans Blumenberg's remarkable studies of the change of thought systems at the beginning of the modern age.[28] There are, moreover, historical developments which favor a similar approach. The historian of art knows of sequences of successive, if not necessarily contiguous, artistic achievements which hang together according to a sort of internal logic because they substantiate, one after another, the implications and potentialities of the work or problem that opens the series.*

However, much as these methods of explanation (to which others may be added) help the historian to come to grips with the past, by themselves alone they do not suffice to make him understand it in the full sense of the word. Rather, true understanding encompasses them, informs them with direction and meaning. It is a mode of interpretation in its own right; and it owes its existence to a basic quality of historical phenomena which to ignore would be the death of history. Products of necessity as well as chance and freedom, these phenomena—immensely concrete and virtually inexhaustible phenomena—define, and fill, a universe which has many traits in common with the *Lebenswelt*. They stand out in it sphinx-like, as do their counterparts in the world we live in. And they would be impenetrable to us did we not in our dealings with them proceed after the very manner in which we proceed in everyday life when we assess, often seemingly on the spur of the moment, a person's character, argue about a political decision, ponder the possible

* For these sequences, see Chapter 6.

outcome of an individual or social crisis, etc. There is no other way for us to orient ourselves in the jungle through which we are passing. As he ventures into the thicket of things, the historian finds himself in the same precarious situation. So he too is obliged to draw on sundry value judgments, estimates, *ad hoc* hypotheses, adumbrations—running comments which constitute explanations of a special type. Altogether they make up what we call "understanding." In order to "understand" the phenomena that close in on him the historian will bring to bear on them a variety of such comments and glosses. These particular explanations are anything but digests or half-baked versions of scientific or morphological interpretations—which is to say that they cannot be dissolved or extended into statements about causal relationships, structural configurations, and the like. Nor do they easily admit of wider application. They are relatively self-contained; they result from, and respond to, unique encounters with opaque entities.

But in entrusting ourselves to them, do we not lapse into uncontrollable subjectivity? While they are undoubtedly subjective, they may nevertheless carry power of conviction. It all depends upon whether or not they conform to two conditions both of which enhance the significance of the processes of self-effacement and self-expansion. To be to the point, understanding must, first, be grounded in the historian's initial surrender to the facts. Second, its validity increases in direct ratio to the range of his human experience, the scope of his wisdom—faculties bound up with a reflective disposition and the knack of passive observation. Robert Graves's happy word: "History is an old man's game" [29]—he puts it into the mouth of the venerable Roman historian Asinius Pollio—subtly intimates that the development of historical understanding is contingent on the cultivation of these faculties. In addition to pressing home the need for them, Isaiah Berlin also takes a glance at the way in which historians give form and body to the explanations peculiar to understanding: "Historical explanation is to a large degree arrangement of the discovered facts in patterns which satisfy us because they accord with life as we know it and imagine it." [30] In other words, the insights which understanding yields tend to affect the shape of the narrative. The patterns of the historian's story reflect those of his accumulated life experience, nourished, as it were, by what the past confides to him.[31] In a way his story *is* his interpretation.

It may happen—although it does not happen often—that the understanding historian offers an interpretation which differs from the run of them. Burckhardt's notion of the awakening individual in the Renaissance is of this kind; and so is Marx's substructure-superstructure theory. The distinguishing feature of such explanations is that they seem to point beyond the material from which they are elicited. They introduce a new principle of explanation; they reveal—with one stroke, as it were—yet unsuspected contexts and relationships of a relatively wide scope; and they invariably involve matters of great import. These particular interpretations may be called "ideas." With them, the historian's journey definitely reaches its close. Historical ideas mark its ultimate destination.

That there is something very special about them can be inferred from the fact that perceptive historians marvel at their occurrence and try to describe the processes through which they may be arrived at. No sooner does an explanation in this vein present itself to the mind, says Isaiah Berlin (within contexts intended to emphasize the nonscientific aspects of history), than we immediately realize that "something deep-set and fundamental that has lain unquestioned and in darkness, is suddenly il-

luminated or prised out of its frame for closer inspection." [32]
Huizinga on his part coins the term "historical sensation" to
characterize the moment at which we touch on an idea or are
swayed by it. He speaks of "moments of special intellectual
clarity, moments of a sudden penetration of the spirit." He has
it, moreover, that our contact with an idea is "accompanied by
an utter conviction of genuineness and truth," even though we
hardly ever know whence it comes to us: it "can be evoked by a
line from a document or a chronicle, by a print, by a few notes
of an old song." [33] I might as well add that it can be evoked not
only by the sources to which it primarily applies but by "matters
remote from and apparently quite unconnected with the subject
of inquiry." [34] The historian may draw his inspiration from his
whole life experience.

What about the position of historical ideas in the hierarchy of
concepts? Festugière is convinced that he generalizes his empirical findings when he traces the vogue of religious mysticism in
the Hellenistic era to the exhaustion and self-abdication of
Greek reason (which he in turn attributes to the lack of experi-
mentation among the Greeks).[35] I am afraid he is deceiving
himself in thus identifying as a generalization what to all intents
and purposes is much more in the nature of an idea. To be sure,
historical ideas are generalizations to the extent that they are
derived from, and refer back to, a hard core of discovered data,
but at the same time they must be considered products of informed intuition which as such go beyond generalizations because they quiver with connotations and meanings not found in
the material occasioning them. Based upon absorption in the
facts, ideas have also other roots than the facts. They are genuine universals.[36] While it is always possible to proceed from an
idea down to its underlying material, the reverse way from the
material up to the idea is by no means a straight route. The idea

denies itself to additive research and an accumulation of detail. You will have to jump to capture it.

Nor should these singular interpretations be confused with the kind of ideas which form the backbone of traditional philosophy. Any philosophy implementing a total vision or postulating a total goal of mankind—and was this not the *raison d'être* of Western philosophy for most of the time?—climaxes in assumptions and norms which not merely pretend to unconditional validity but claim effectively to control all of reality. Unlike them, historical ideas have distinct boundaries; their inherent intention is to explain this or that section of the past. Burckhardt's awakening individual is the prototype of Renaissance man, not more, not less. In practice, traffic across the borders is pretty heavy. Historians longing for synthesis hanker after the consolation of philosophy, and philosophers of history devise over-all models for use in the lower regions. The philosophical idea of evolution has permeated major historical writings. Perhaps it is one of the more fortunate consequences of positivistic mentality that historians have become weary of such handouts from on high. Hexter, for instance, cautions his fellow historians against the dangers of too general concepts on the ground that they obscure rather than highlight conditions at a particular time and place.[37]

Huizinga says of Burckhardt that he "has long since joined the masters who are exalted above the antithesis of right and wrong."[38] Within the dimension in which this antithesis obtains no historical idea should be expected to be fully adequate. Each idea deserving of the name bears on a comparatively large portion of historical reality—which implies that the historian advancing it must keep at a certain distance from the events he is interpreting. But from this distant point of view he can neither perceive all the perhaps relevant facts nor avoid setting them in a perspective bound to conceal part of them. It has been observed that Burckhardt fails to take Renaissance economy and philosophy into account. In addition, if a historian verifying some idea inspects the material to which it applies from a lesser distance than the one at which the idea has been conceived, he will come across ever smaller units of that material; and they may convey suggestions which threaten to dissolve the idea of his concern. "It is a vain ambition," Huizinga objects to Burckhardt, "to want to describe *the* man of the Renaissance. The numerous types offered by that rich period are divided by other characteristics more basically than any individualism can unite them." [39] Devastating as this criticism is, I am not sure whether it is completely fair. For what does Huizinga do? He alters the distance to the subject; he plays off micro facts against a well-founded macro hypothesis.*

To the extent, then, that historical ideas are generalizations they cannot be "right" without being "wrong" also. The degree of their validity as generalizations depends upon the degree of their faithfulness to the available evidence. To repeat that in the world of history everything is a matter of degree is to restate one of the leitmotifs of this book. Gibbon's thesis about the decline of the Roman Empire has withered away, reminding one of those ruins whose mournful sight once moved him to intuit it; on the other hand, in the view of contemporary Renaissance scholars no important facts have yet been unearthed that would seriously upset Burckhardt's famous interpretation. [40]

And there is the dimension *above* that of right and wrong. In assigning Burckhardt a place in it, Huizinga wants to give us to understand that his idea is imperishable, no matter whether or not it proves to be correct. [41] Isaiah Berlin shows the same mag-

---

* The relations between micro and macro history will be discussed at length in Chapter 5.

nanimity with regard to the factual accuracy of the Marxist
doctrine: "Even if all its specific conclusions were proved false,
its importance in creating a wholly new attitude to social and
historical questions, and so opening new avenues of human
knowledge, would be unimpaired." [42] Since he and Huizinga
are certainly aware that an interpretation stands and falls with
its (relative) adequacy to the given facts, their indifference to
this vital issue presumably stems from their desire to throw into
relief the astounding survival capacity of historical ideas. Do not
even ideas which have been shown to be "wrong"—e.g., Max
Weber's ideal-typical construction of the implications of the
Protestant ethic—live on in the memory and retain something
of their initial splendor?

Historical ideas appear to be of lasting significance because
they connect the particular with the general in an articulate and
truly unique way. Any such connection being an uncertain venture, they resemble flashes illumining the night. This is why
their emergence in the historian's mind has been termed a "historical sensation" and said to "communicate a shock to the entire
system . . . the shock . . . of recognition." [43] They are nodal
points—points at which the concrete and the abstract really
meet and become one. Whenever this happens, the flow of indeterminate historical events is suddenly arrested and all that is
then exposed to view is seen in the light of an image or conception which takes it out of the transient flow to relate it to one or
another of the momentous problems and questions that are forever staring at us. Marx's substructure-superstructure theory and
Burckhardt's idea of the Renaissance are not only "right" generalizations: they make inroads into the realm of the general
truths (including those I have called philosophical ideas)—
truths which are of absolute validity, if empty, or aglow with
eternity like will-o'-the-wisps. Note that historical ideas do not

fuse with them but materialize at a lower level of abstraction. They mark the end of the historian's journey also in so far as they set a limit to his strivings for generality; beyond that limit he would lose touch with his materials. It is doubtful indeed whether the truths of the highest generality are capable at all of rousing the particulars they logically encompass. These extreme abstractions crystallize into statements so wide-meshed that the particulars—a series of historical events, or so—cannot but drop through the net. For the historian to haul them in the historical idea offers itself as the most general proposition—a threshold which he may transgress only at the risk of no longer being able to bring his findings home to the port of understanding.

Even though historical ideas issue from the whole self, they are not subjective in a sense that would interfere with their potential truth value. On the contrary, with them subjectivity is anything but a limiting factor. I have already indicated the reasons; they lie with the dynamic character of the historian's self. Schematically speaking, it comprises the messages he receives during its effacement and the experiences he undergoes as it is expanding. The objectifying effect of the fullness it thus achieves is strengthened by the movement in which it is engaged—a movement which renders it in a measure independent of its location in time. Historical ideas would seem to be the product of a dynamized self. But the term "product" is misleading. Actually, things happen the other way round. During the period of incubation a thousand possibilities of how best to explain his data pass before the historian's inner eye. So he must make his choice. And it is the fullness and relative mobility of his mind that enable him to select from among these possibilities the one which exceeds all the others in depth and comprehensiveness. The idea is not so much the product of his self as the result of a selective process, with his self acting as a divining rod; it is a discovery, not an outward projection. The discovery will be the more valid—i.e., the less "subjective"—the more it has benefited by all that the historian knows and imagines and is. This is what Bultmann means when he declares that "the most subjective interpretation of history is at the same time the most objective" [44]—or rather, what he would mean were he not bewitched by the sham profundity of the existentialist outlook. Subjectivity at its most intensive transcends itself. Historical ideas are objective precisely because of their indebtedness to un-mitigated subjectivity. The (approximate) objectivity to which they attain may be called "active" in contradistinction to the "passive" objectivity reached in the phase of self-reduction. If a screen separates us from the truth, these concrete-abstract ideas come closest to puncturing it.

In following the historian on his journey, I have deliberately omitted two difficulties confronting him en route. He moves about in a universe which, because of its nonhomogeneous structure, makes it necessary for him to negotiate many hurdles. And he travels through Time—a medium whose complexity fur-ther obstructs his advance. These difficulties call for close atten-tion. Did history not exist, one might almost say that it is an improbable undertaking.

5

The Structure of the Historical Universe

> "Nothing would further the progress of both the logic of science and the philosophy of history more than a rigorous analysis of the different ensemble types from the top to the bottom of the ladder."　　　RAYMOND ARON [1]

Histories differ in scope or magnitude, depending on the size of the spatiotemporal unit they cover. Those of the same scope are at the same level of generality. A monograph on the battle of Leuthen is of lower magnitude, or lesser generality, than an account of the Seven Years War, which in turn forms part of a narrative of still wider scope—say, a political history of 18th-century Europe. And so it goes on. The whole set calls to mind the Chinese gadget of the hollow ivory sphere which contains similar spheres of diminishing size, each freely circling in the womb of the next larger one. The diverse histories may also be arranged along a continuum one pole of which is occupied by syntheses of extreme generality—universal histories, that is—while the opposite pole would have to be assigned to investigations of atom-like events.

Differences in scope mark differences in distance. Any large-scale history—e.g., the history of a people—requires the narrator to step so far back from the given data that all the destinies of that people enter his field of vision.* Of course, in overviewing a big slice of the past, he cannot but lose sight of many circumstances responsible for his total impression of it. Conversely, Toynbee whose "intelligible fields of study"—the civilizations in their entirety—become visible only at an enormous distance from the evidence, speaks, not without condescension, of the "myopic" historians who, crawling deep below, ignore the grand vistas he himself is enjoying.[2]

Histories of the same magnitude have certain properties in common. Thus the historian of a century will select from among the sources other data than will the historian who concentrates on a decade or so. Nor should the two be expected to describe and specify the developments of their concern by way of comparisons of the same type or order. The comparable units vary with the level of generality at which the historian operates.

Altogether these different histories constitute the historical universe. For the sake of simplification I shall divide them into two major groups—micro and macro histories. It goes without saying that the boundaries between the two groups are fluid.

A paradigmatic instance of micro histories has already been mentioned: Panofsky's analysis of the uses which the high and later Middle Ages made of the models provided them by classical works of art and literature.† Such interpretative small-scale histories may be called "close-ups" because of their resemblance to the film shots of this name which isolate and magnify some visual detail—a face, a hand, a piece of furniture—to familiarize

---

* I might as well mention that the term "distance" carries also another meaning, here negligible. Whatever the scope of a history, it spreads over earlier and more recent events; and the historian's distance from them obviously increases with their chronological remoteness.
† See page 57.

us with its particular physiognomy. Falling into the micro dimension, close-up studies lie in the immediate neighborhood of
the bulk of fact-oriented accounts—that first yield of the historian's journey into the past—and moreover share with them the
devotion to minutiae and the affinity for the monographic form.
But unlike them, they explore their material to the full, instead
of confining themselves to neutral stock-taking. Close-ups are a
direct extension of those accounts. As a rule they result from
their authors' desire to supplement, refine, or indeed invalidate
notions and explanations which have been unquestioningly accepted by generations of macro historians. Jedin's close analysis
of the Councils of Constance and Basle serves a double purpose:
it qualifies the widely held belief that these assemblies were of
little consequence for the inner reform of the church; and it
highlights the lasting significance of their decrees which pro-
claimed the supremacy of general councils.[3] Hexter on his part
adduces detailed evidence in support of his thesis that the traditional opinion according to which the feudal aristocracy began
to degenerate in the Renaissance is nothing but an outworn
cliché.[4] As compared with close-ups, the high-magnitude views
they comment upon often strike one as rather sweeping and
inaccurate.

So God would be in detail? Two great historians—the Tolstoy
of *War and Peace* and Sir Lewis Namier—champion the doctrine epitomized by Aby Warburg's famous dictum. Both de-
clare the micro dimension to be the seat and fountainhead of
historical truth.

Tolstoy satirizes the many histories which attribute to the
Napoleons and Alexanders of our world the power to create or
destroy big empires. These histories, he argues, grossly exag-
gerate the range and impact of an individual's power. In addition, they would be solidly founded only if we still believed that

God subjects the peoples to the will of a personal ruler commissioned by Him to implement the plans of divine providence.[5] Yet theological explanations have had their day. And since modern historiography refuses to acknowledge them, we will again have to inquire into the nature of the mysterious force that brings about the movements of the peoples (or nations). In broaching this fundamental question, Tolstoy not only disposes of heroes, kings, generals, and ministers but rejects all propositions affecting him as an outgrowth of macro-thinking. He denies the influence of ideas on historical change and does not place any confidence in the validity, let alone relevance, of so-called sociological laws. In his view most historians indulge in abstract constructions which pass over the real facts they claim to embrace and represent.[6] His own answer testifies to his incomparable susceptibility to the ramifications and emanations of each single phenomenon—a sense of detail which, for instance, shows in his exacting description of the moth-catching lawyer in *Anna Karenina*. The force behind the movements of the peoples, says he, should not be sought above and outside them; rather, it consists in the innumerable activities of all the individual participants in the historical process.[7] To demonstrate this, he time and again confronts, in *War and Peace*, the undeniably real, if fragmentary, experiences of his characters—e.g., Pierre Bezukhov's during the battle of Borodino—with excerpts from histories and official accounts of the same period, this throwing into relief the unbridgeable gap between the empty generalizations and those first-hand impressions. With the artist's involvement in the concrete, Tolstoy imagines historical reality as an endless continuum of microscopic incidents, actions, and interactions which, through their sheer accumulation, produce the macroscopic upheavals, victories, and disasters featured in the run of textbooks. (By the way, he is not the only one to envision such an infinitesimal continuum. Fernand Léger, the French painter and film maker, dreamed of a monster film that would have to record the life of a man and a woman throughout twenty-four consecutive hours: their work, their silence, their intimacy. Nothing should be omitted; nor should the two protagonists ever be aware of the presence of the camera. Léger realized that the pictures he fancied were bound to be shocking sights because they would exhibit the normally hidden whirlpool of crude existence. "I think," he observed, "this would be so terrible a thing that people would run away horrified, calling for help as if caught in a world catastrophe." [8])

Quite logically, Tolstoy considers it the true historian's (unfulfillable) task to break down the macro entities into their smallest elements. His ideas about the interrelations between these tiny units reveal his dependence on 19th-century science. He falls into outright determinism. Human reason, he has it, obliges us to conceive of the events in the micro dimension as processes controlled by unalterable laws.[9] He further postulates that, if possible at all, a reconstruction of the chain of causes and effects in that dimension would yield the law of history as a whole. With Tolstoy, history is the realm of necessity—an extension of that of nature. (Interestingly, he refers to calculus in connection with the procedures to be used for the isolation of the micro units and their subsequent integration.[10] It is as if he anticipated the modern computers.)

Tolstoy's belief in an inexorable causal nexus gets him into deep waters. How reconcile the rule of necessity with the experience of human freedom? The solution he offers amounts to an awkward expedient: he sees no other way out but to degrade freedom to a phenomenon of our consciousness, something like a secondary quality. His main point is that in the world established by reason—the ideally real world—there is no place for

causally unexplainable actions. What we mistake for a free decision is, in the light of reason, the inevitable consequence of
given conditions. Freedom is an illusion. That the illusion nevertheless perpetuates itself must be laid to the impossibility for us
to account for the infinite number of elements that comprise
historical reality. The job of tracing the laws which govern their
interplay exceeds human efforts. This being so, we feel indeed
challenged to substitute freedom for what eludes our grasp.
Freedom is unknowable necessity.[11]

No doubt Tolstoy is a poor philosopher. He uncritically
adopts the philosophical commonplace ideas of his science-
oriented age and contrives to arrange them into a pattern permitting him to eat his cake and have it—rescue the free will and
yet uphold the deterministic dogma. It does not seem to occur
to Tolstoy that this "solution" prevents him from identifying
history as an intelligible and, perhaps, significant succession of
events. If freedom is merely a subjective phenomenon, necessity
continues to carry the day in the world about us: all that happens must happen and that is that.

But no sooner has Tolstoy, the would-be philosopher, had his
say than the real Tolstoy takes over. Giving short shrift to those
precarious speculations, the real Tolstoy—this unique personal
union of a mystic and an empiricist—endows indifferent necessity with a soul. That which must happen, he feels, also should
happen. At any rate, he is deeply convinced that in the case of
the Russian people everything will be for the good if only the
powers that be do not interfere with the live force moulding
Russia's future. Of course, to let things happen they will have to
know what is going on between all the actors in the play. Yet is
not, by Tolstoy's own premise, such knowledge forever unattainable? He overcomes this theoretically unmanageable difficulty by invoking the divinatory power of wisdom. Those he

calls wise intuitively acquire, or possess, the very knowledge
which is denied minds guided by reason alone. The wise keep
their ears to the ground; they have the gift of apprehending the
indistinct and often conflicting messages that constantly rise
from the dark recesses of everyday life; they themselves are part
of that force which generates the movements of the peoples.[12]

Tolstoy lends flesh and color to this vision: his Kutuzov is
wisdom incarnate. He does not plan and act; he waits and
listens. And it is his capacity for listening to, and interpreting,
the chorus of confused voices from root regions which enables
him to drive Napoleon into retreat. Kutuzov is an inspired
leader because he is loath to follow his inspiration. His sole
ambition is to bring to fruition the formless thoughts and desires
he finds inscribed in millions of Russian hearts. "He knows," as
Prince Andrey puts it, "that there is something stronger and
more important than his will—the inevitable march of events." [13]
(The inevitable march of events? Tolstoy's fixation to the
mechanistic notions of his time asserts itself everywhere. But
this does not impinge on the truth, embodied by his Kutuzov,
that really creative action is inseparable from intensive passive
observation.)

Toynbee relates that Namier once told him: "Toynbee, I study
the individual leaves, you the tree. The rest of the historians
study the clusters of branches, and we both think *they* are
wrong." [14] (He seems to have been polite enough not to tell
Toynbee what he thought of the study of the whole tree.)

Namier's field being political history, his metaphor of the
"clusters of branches" obviously bears on the ideological units
which are the stock-in-trade of the histories in his field. The
Whig interpretation of 18th-century England which he so effectively attacked not only accepted the dominant political ideas

and party programs of that century at face value but considered them nodal points of historical reality. The truth is, however, that these alleged units are projections of compounds of actions, reactions, and states of being which they camouflage rather than designate. They are sham entities. And since practically none of the real-life phenomena they veil falls into the ideological dimension to which they themselves belong, their inherent claim to be part of reality is thoroughly unjustified. Namier insists on the fictitious character of anything ideological. As he sees it, all histories which place the emphasis on political ideology, rational thought, and verbalized argument culminate in vague generalizations incapable of capturing the very reality they are meant to explain. Like Tolstoy, Namier rejects such macro histories with their panoramic views.

His negative attitude toward them is demonstrably influenced by Marx's substructure-superstructure theory. Namier too indulges in debunking the pretense to autonomy of ideas: he too stresses the role which material needs and social conditions play in their formation.[15] But for all this he is no Marxist. Not to mention his conservative temper, he is disinclined to turn from a political historian into a partisan, a *littérateur engagé*. More important, he feels strongly about exchanging one macro conception for another: Marx's imposing equation of (pre-)history with a succession of dialectically interrelated class struggles does not exert any appeal on him.[16] Rather, he wants to break away from the whole macro dimension—from all those broad and comprehensive thought patterns which ultimately constitute our conventional image of the world. The image they yield is deceptive because they exhaust themselves in establishing spurious links between phantom units of largely anonymous facts. Products of our consciousness, they are not so much self-contained insights as surface symptoms of inner-life processes. And what

he aims at is to get beneath the surface and explore the less
obtrusive, less visible real happenings in deep psychological lay-
ers. Namier's is a one-way route. This follows conclusively from
his indifference to synthesis and narration proper. John Brooke
says of him that he "never walked a step without looking in
every direction." [17] He cannot bring himself to neglect the individual leaves for the tree.

Namier himself acknowledges his indebtedness to Freud. He
requests historians to uncover the "psychological springs" of political ideas,[18] points to the share of "unconscious promptings"
in every action,[19] and categorically declares that a knowledge
of modern psychology—especially mass psychology—is indispensable for the advance of historiography.[20] Is he an orthodox
Freudian? "What matters most," he writes somewhere, "is the
underlying emotions, the music, to which ideas are a mere lib-
retto, often of very inferior quality . . ." [21] There is an artistic
strain in him (which distinctly shows in his prose). And his
aesthetic sensibilities may well have attuned him to the efforts
made in unison on all the fronts of contemporary art—efforts
which would hardly have developed in strength were it not for
the achievements of Freud and Marx. In any case, it is as if he
joined forces with those painters, poets, and musicians who
aspire to dissolve the traditional forms and modes of perceiving.
They proceed throughout from the big wholes and overarching
compositions of old to, in a way, fragmentary statements which,
perhaps, will never again jell into wholes. The (provisional)
result is an adjustment of our senses to what remains of the web
of used-up conventions once it is undone. (What remains is at
least incontestable.) So Namier resorts to psychoanalysis as a
means of disintegrating the standardized macro notions of political reality. If he is not a Marxist, he is not a strict follower of
Freud either.

The world of history, as it appears to him, offers a disquieting spectacle. While some of the political ideas peopling that world may be in accordance with the emotions, impulses, etc., which respond to the necessities of the hour, most of them are leftovers from days long since gone. But since they continue to kindle our imagination, they keep alive or even reactivate attitudes, fears, and expectations which have ceased to conform to the actual situation. These outdated habits of thought and behavior permanently disrupt the interplay of timely desires and hopes, thereby preventing us from meeting the present on terms of its own. Much as we try to repress them, they fill our unconscious and have a way of discharging themselves in uncalled-for demands and irresponsible outbursts. We are neurotics, at the mercy of traumatic experiences. With Namier, the principles and programs that determine political action are as a rule disturbances rather than reliable signposts. Indeed, he goes so far as to consider their absence a symptom of "greater national maturity." [22] There is a surrealistic aspect to the historico-political world he pictures: it is haunted by ghosts which, in the form of ideas and memories, invade our homes, offices, and brains.

His objective is to lay the ghosts—to trace, that is, the psychological motivations and mechanisms which, along with the material pressures of the moment, set things going in politics. Now these mainsprings of activities and events in the political area are not free-hovering agents but emanate from a very concrete nucleus; their carrier is the individual (or any group with an identifiable personality). It is individuals, Namier has it, who make up the aggregates which historians hypnotized by ideas and causes shuffle about at their pleasure, mistaking them for real units. They are not. The real units, his argument runs, yield only to micro analysis; to explain some phase of political history

one will have to study the lives of all the individuals involved in
it. The God he worships is not merely in detail but in biographical detail. (He might have wondered at Collingwood's total rejection of biography as part of the historical enterprise; yet if one
proceeds straight from a philosophical "idea of history," one is
bound to arrive at bizarre conclusions.) Namier's method is best
illustrated by his trail-blazing major work, that "fabulously microscopic examination of the composition of the successive
Houses of Commons under George III." [23] Note that, in applying
this method, he pays little attention to the prominent politicians
who wield influence and attract the professional biographers.
He is not a biographer in the usual sense. All his interest lies with
the curricula vitae of the little men, which afford more insight
into typical emotions and aspirations than do the careers of the
star performers. Entirely in keeping with this approach, Namier
champions historical investigations of a kind inaccessible to the
lonely scholar. He pleads for demographic history by way of cooperative effort—a program which has inspired the British *History of Parliament* presently in the making. His idea of micro
history, I should like to add, resembles Tolstoy's in that it foreshadows the advent of the computers. But is not every important innovation ushered in by dreams and gropings pregnant
with it?

In sum, Namier as well as Tolstoy hold that the ideologies
and big transactions on which our history books center arise
from an infinite number of small events exceeding them in reality. And both coincide in suggesting that, in the interest of
greater truth, macro historiography should be superseded by
collective micro studies.

However, this proposition stems from a wrong premise: Historical reality resides not only in detail, biographical or otherwise, but also extends into the macro dimension. Not all the

subjects of high-magnitude histories are constructions after the fact. There exist long-enduring events, such as wars, social or religious movements, slow adjustments of well-defined groups to changing environmental conditions, etc., which can be said to be tangible entities. Unfolding in lofty regions, some of them presumably escape the micro-historian's attention. Even though the names by which they are known may be imprecise abbreviations hazily covering a tangle of microscopic happenings, these events are more than sheer projections—provided they were experienced as units at the time of their occurrence. In 15th-century Europe the issue of church reform was a live concept, its high generality notwithstanding. Historical long-range events of this type are real to the extent that they stirred people to ponder their consequences, discuss alternatives, and advance possible solutions. Tolstoy's satire of traditional historiography is not entirely to the point. By the same token, the past has seen ideas come and go which, as they reached their apex, belonged no less to the realities of life than, say, an individual conflict,—no matter, for the rest, whether they were genuine or not. They have a peculiar substance, an irreducible content. And any historian treating them merely as derivatives of psychological processes misses part of what really happened and made people tick.

Small wonder that the Tolstoy-Namier position has given rise to various objections. Namier, to stay with him, has, among other things, been criticized for passing off his analytical method as a panacea. But while micro analysis is certainly fit to penetrate the ideological fog that veiled the practices of the corrupt politicians under George III, it does not apply to periods informed with authentic political ideas; the Puritan Revolution resists being psychologized away.[24] Butterfield, one of Namier's fiercest opponents, reproaches him with ignoring the reality of

such ideas. Namier and his followers, he remarks, corrode the
"avowed political purposes that give meaning as well as cohesion to the events of history"; [25] they fall prey to the "optical
illusion . . . that only the details matter"; [26] they are not
aware that, to write history, one must "possess also an eye for
generalities." [27] (It is probably not Butterfield, the mundane
"technical" historian, but Butterfield, the Christian believer, who
most deeply resents "Namierism," because it undermines all that
he believes in—the potential meaning of history, the intrinsic
value of ideas. As a Christian historian he takes significant continuity for granted and even assumes the existence of something
like "God's history," with a supernatural planner in charge of
human affairs.[28]) Nor has it eluded the critics that Namier, in
flagrant defiance of his professed concern with minutiae, sometimes substitutes the telescope for the microscope, setting large
portions of the past in a perspective of his choice. Was he not a
fervent Zionist? One might finally ask whether he really hits
rock-bottom in examining the psychological make-up of the individual. This allegedly smallest historical unit itself is an inexhaustible macrocosm. So reality again recedes when he is convinced he has come to grips with it.

The incidence of long-enduring events and ideas which more
or less lead a life of their own tends to suggest that macro
histories are in a measure independent of micro research.[29]
Even granted that these ideas, events, and wholesale arrangements grow out of the hustle and bustle of everyday preoccupations, they are apt to develop and change in ways which cannot
be sufficiently defined by a recourse to their elements. Discussing the relations between "these macroscopic phenomena" and
"the elementary, atomic data" from which they apparently issue,
Marrou insists that the former are as real as the latter and stresses
their relatively independent status: "They are realities of another

order, but, each in its own, all equally authentic." [30] For the rest, the fact that such macro realities are not fully traceable to the micro realities going into them—that interrelated events at low and higher levels exist, so to speak, side by side—is by no means an uncommon phenomenon. Most individuals behave differently in different dimensions of being. A good Christian may be a harsh landlord. Proust declares that it is "absurd to judge the poet by the man or by the opinions of his friends, as Sainte-Beuve does. As for the man, he is just a man, and can perfectly ignore what is thought by the poet who lives in him." [31]

The implication is that, contrary to what Namier and Tolstoy assume, political macro history may attain to a certain autonomy. (It is understood that this holds true also of histories in other areas.) If a political historian inquires, say, into the reasons for the overthrow of a regime or the causes of a war, he need not always probe the underworld of biographical detail but stands a fair chance of roughly explaining these events from motives, arguments, and reactions which belong to the same dimension in which he is operating. As long as big events loom large on the horizon they are perceived in their wholeness and therefore provoke reflections and measures of similar generality. On principle, from whatever distance a historian surveys the past, he will at each level of generality come across a causal nexus of a sort peculiar to that level—remember the concentric Chinese spheres, each moving around independently of the others. In his short histories of Rome and Greece, Rostovtzeff organizes the relevant major actions and actors into an intelligible texture without ever summoning micro facts.

Yet the texture is coarse and rather wide-meshed. Obviously the autonomy of large-scope histories is not to be depended upon. After having pleaded the case of macro autonomy over against Tolstoy's and Namier's excessive attacks on it, I now wish to show that its uncritical recognition involves heavy risks. To be sure, a political historian may plausibly fit together given high-magnitude events, ideas, and arguments, but if he sees his goal in the establishment of macroscopic contexts, he should not be expected satisfactorily to account for the past of his concern. The odds are rather that his narrative will misrepresent it. Macro histories overplaying their self-sufficiency are prone to go astray.

The reason is this: The higher the level of generality at which a historian operates, the more historical reality thins out. What he retains of the past when he looks at it from a great distance is wholesale situations, long-term developments, ideological trends, etc.—big chunks of events whose volume wanes or waxes in direct ratio to the distance. They are scattered over time; they leave many gaps to be filled. We do not learn enough about the past if we concentrate on the macro units. It is true, as Proust says, that the poet exists independently of the man in whom he lives, but it is equally true that the man does exist also; and the full story would tell us about the poet *and* the man. Moreover, with increasing distance the historian will find it increasingly difficult to lay hands on historical phenomena which are sufficiently specific and unquestionably real. Butterfield, this time in his capacity as a technical historian, observes that universal history "spreads over so wide an area that the knowledge can hardly avoid becoming too thin." [32] He is right: all that is discernible at the very high altitude where universal history comes into view are vaguely contoured giant units, vast generalizations of uncertain reliability.

Historians featuring the interplay of macro events naturally feel tempted to compensate, somehow, for the relative dearth of the material they care to seize upon. The dangers they thus incur have been spelled out by one no less than Bacon. He advises the historian not to deal with too long (or too shapeless) a period because "he cannot but meet with many blanks and spaces which he must be forced to fill up out of his own wit and conjecture." [33] There is no lack of obliging conjectures. To negotiate the "blanks and spaces" on his road, the historian eager to sustain macro autonomy may draw on his knowledge of the road's destination—hindsight being used as a cementing device rather than an eye-opener. Or he may introduce, "out of his own wit," ungiven motivations, philosophical ideas, etc., with a view to solidifying the fragile fabric he is weaving. The outcome are histories both incomplete and overdone. Gooch says of Guizot's historical work that it does not manifest "interest in the individual and the particular"; [34] and Sainte-Beuve criticizes it for being history "seen from a distance." Any such history, Sainte-Beuve elaborates, "undergoes a singular metamorphosis; it produces the illusion . . . that it is rational." Which leads him to conclude that "Guizot's history is far too logical to be true." [35] Need I expressly mention that the determined macro historian's admixtures and amendments should not be confused with responsible historical hypotheses? Since he often makes these additions unawares, the resultant histories abound with ambiguous concepts. Many seeming generalizations in them are in effect synthetic products, distilled from as well as instilled into the evidence.

Even though Tolstoy's and Namier's crushing verdict on traditional macro history overshoots the mark, it springs from a conception of what history in our age should be like, which I believe to be valid. History, they feel, comes into its own if it records, and makes us understand, the past as faithfully and completely as possible. Hale, discussing Bacon, says: "It [history] must be as full as possible, and as true to life as possible, not like those histories that 'do rather set forth the pomp of business

than the true and inward resorts [of them].' " [36] The basic importance of micro investigations lies in the fact that they are indispensable for any attempt to achieve such fullness. This does not
mean that the integration of micro findings of which Tolstoy
dreamed would enable us to get hold of the whole of history.
Not all of historical reality can be broken down into microscopic
elements. The whole of history also comprises events and developments which occur above the micro dimension. For this reason histories at higher levels of generality are as much of the
essence as studies of detail. But they suffer from incomplete-
ness; and if the historian does not want to fill the gaps in them
"out of his own wit and conjecture," he must explore the world
of small events as well. Macro history cannot become history in
the ideal sense unless it involves micro history. Now knowledge
of detail may be used in different ways. Frequently enough, it
serves as a sort of adornment. Macro historians, that is, avail
themselves of micro research, their own or not, to corroborate or
illustrate certain long-range views they have come to entertain
—views attached to the distance from which they look at events.
(To be sure, these views on their part may be derived from an
examination of the relevant source material, and are not some
generalizations more purposeful and goal-oriented than others?
And of course, the given facts, malleable as they are, rarely let
down a historian in search of evidence for his hunches. For the
rest historical reality is so rich in diversified data that you can
adduce from it evidence for almost everything you want to
prove.) The many details in Macaulay's histories seem invariably calculated, to confirm the meaning he attributes to the
periods and figures under consideration. All of them converge
toward his total of this or that situation—which gives the impression that his macro-scopic insight or intuitions do not so
much grow out of micro analysis but guide his selection of

concrete fact. Brilliant narrator that he is, he knows how effectively to handle corroborative detail. Toynbee, too, takes it for granted that the minutiae which the "myopic" historians contribute fulfill a worth-while function only if they support his large-scope constructions. To him we will return later in this chapter.

My proposition that in the interest of greater completeness macro history must involve micro history points to an involvement which is not merely a seeming one. It requires historians who, not satisfied with staying where they are, really journey to the past and get immersed in what they are finding there without much regard for their macro assumptions. These assumptions may or may not be confirmed by micro analysis for its own sake. Perhaps the historian engaged in it will happen on short-term causes defying the macro contexts he has established on the basis of macro evidence; or he will discover that apparently negligible exceptions from the general course of events carry implications apt to upset his appraisal of it. Think of Marc Bloch's *Feudal Society.**

This is why discerning historians aspiring to history in its fullness favor an interpenetration of macro and micro history. In spite of his belief in the authenticity of macroscopic realities, Marrou holds that the historian surveying a long stretch of the past had better begin "by getting to work himself, installed, first, at the level of the minute and precise investigation of detail." [37] Similarly Butterfield, for all his anti-Namier attitude, feels con-

* With the Tolstoy-Namier thesis that the infinitesimal continuum of atom-like events is more real than the sequences of large-scale events with which macro historians are dealing, the second major problem confronting the historian—the nature of time—comes into view. It will be tackled in the following chapter.

For the reference made to Bloch's *Feudal Society*, cf. this chapter, page 124.

strained to admit that macro history alone will not do and believes that the ideal kind of history would perhaps be "structure and narrative combined,"—a history which is both, "a story and a study." [38] *

This is in striking analogy with film: the big must be looked at from different distances to be understood; its analysis and interpretation involve a constant movement between the levels of generality. A statement by Pudovkin quoted in *Theory of Film* is to the point in this context:

> "In order to receive a clear and definite impression of a demonstration, the observer must perform certain actions. First he must climb upon the roof of a house to get a view from above of the procession as a whole and measure its dimension; next he must come down and look out through the first-floor window at the inscriptions carried by the demonstrators; finally, he must mingle with the crowd to gain an idea of the outward appearance of the participants." [39]

As I point out, the big can be adequately rendered only by a permanent movement from the whole to some detail, then back to the whole, etc.[40] The same holds true of the big in history. The macro historian will falsify his subject unless he inserts the close-ups gained by the micro studies—inserts them as integrant elements of his over-all pictures.

In consequence, the historian must be in a position freely to move between the macro and micro dimensions. This raises the issue of the structure of the historical universe—the first of the two major problems confronting any historian. Is it homogeneous, so that he may easily pass from one level to another? Substance and validity of macro history—its reality character—depend upon unhampered two-way traffic.

* The author's completed text for this chapter ends with this paragraph.

This traffic is controlled by two principles or laws which belong to material logic.* The first may be called the "law of perspective." I have shown in the preceding chapter that historical interpretation—"understanding"—ultimately involves the historian's expanded self, his life experience, his subjectivity. In other words, he must set things in a "perspective," conforming to his experiences, beliefs, and values, all of which are being rooted in self-effacement, passive observation.† Now there exists a definable relation between the role which matters of perspective are playing and the historian's distance from his material. Marrou observes "that to the degree that the level of the generality of the historical construction and the breadth of synthesis increase, the difficulties, perils, and uncertainty grow in the same proportion." [41] In other words, the impact of perspective treatment increases in direct ratio to the historian's distance from his material.

Why is this so? In the micro dimension a more or less dense fabric of given data canalizes the historian's imagination, his interpretative designs. As the distance from the data increases, they become scattered, thin out. The evidence thus loses its binding power, inviting less committed subjectivity to take over. (As already pointed out in earlier contexts, large-scale histories tend to assume an existential character.) The conflict of Pirenne's and Bark's theses about the origins of the Middle Ages decidedly involves this effect of perspective; [42] but one does not readily think of perspective in the case of close-ups, such as Panofsky's "principle of disjunction" or Jedin's Constance Coun-

* See Chapter 2, pages 47–48.
† Like the term "distance," the concept of "perspective" carries two meanings. It may define the manner in which histories ranging from a remote past to the present usually foreshorten or contract the former in favor of detailed accounts of the latter. Or it may serve to characterize a historian's peculiar slant on the past. Only the second meaning is of interest here.

cil analysis.[43] Here we again notice the importance of differences in degree in the intermediary area of history, already referred to.*

An observation made by Proust in his novel strikingly illustrates the fact that with the increasing scope of histories their composition is increasingly governed by the laws of perspective, as well as the consequences for the accessibility of the micro dimension from higher levels. On a carriage ride, earlier than the one referred to in chapter 3, Marcel sees sometimes two, sometimes three church steeples at a distance, dependent upon the angle from which he views the surroundings. Under the impression of their varying positions he imagines them to be three "maidens in a legend," slipping one behind another, so that only a single form appears.[44] Similarly, due not so much to oversight, neglect, and the like, as to the "law of perspective," macro historians must ignore part of the evidence at the outset. This function of perspective views which as such interfere with the accessibility of the material surveyed is the weightier the greater the distance. For example, general histories of the feudal society usually fail to do justice to its variety, which is covered up by their attempt to bring out the general features of this society; precisely its variety, however, is one of its essential characteristics.[45] Marc Bloch's *Feudal Society* suffers least from this necessary shortcoming, which obstructs the large-scale historian's intercourse with a portion of the sources and of micro histories. To be sure, the historian is theoretically free to explore the micro dimension as he pleases but in practice he will automatically prove insensitive to many of its contents, overlooking them or rationalizing them away as irrelevant. As Ferguson observes on the problems which would have to be faced by a new attempt at the synthesis, undertaken for his day by von Martin in *Sociology of the Renaissance* (1932), the author of such an attempt

* See Chapter 3, page 73, and again Chapter 8.

"will have to adjust his synthesis to take care of a great many inconvenient and unmanageable facts of which von Martin was happily unaware. But if something will be gained, something may also have been lost . . ." [46] Whether disparaged or simply not noticed, such contents are bound to drop out of the picture. What the macro historian does not see, he (partly) cannot see because it is overshadowed by what he does see.

Two supplementary remarks may be added to this discussion of the law of perspective. One is contributed by Aron's observation concerning the possibility of transforming one macro perspective into another. Stressing that subjective perspective is necessary for ensemble construction and that the historian must take cognizance of other perspectives to objectify his own as much as possible, he yet warns that there is between them "no numerical constant or equation." Their diversity is an "expression of life." [47] The other is a query: Are high-magnitude histories more affected by the "Zeitgeist" than histories at low levels of generality?

The second principle controlling the traffic between the micro and macro dimensions may be called the "law of levels." It bears on those micro events which are not overshadowed by the mechanisms of perspective but remain visible and are actually transported to the upper regions, going into the composition of large-scale histories.

What happens to them en route? In asking this, I deliberately confine myself to examining mainly traffic conditions on the way from "below" to "above." Also, I shall here disregard the deteriorating effect which the compositional exigencies of macro histories—especially general histories—produce on all micro findings incorporated in these histories.* The answer to the question raised then is that the micro events are threatened with

* This aspect will be discussed in Chapter 7.

losing some of their peculiarities and meanings when being transported to higher altitudes. They arrive up there in a damaged state.

Imagine, for example, three historical narratives, each of which includes a portrait of Luther—the first a history of the German people, the second dealing with the Reformation, and the third a full-fledged biography: I believe it to be highly probable that the three portraits involve different sets of meanings and therefore are in a measure incommensurable.

The "law of levels" is both illustrated and explained by the analogous phenomenon of the paradoxical relation between "close-ups" and long shots (shots of ensembles) in the cinematic narrative. In *Theory of Film*, this relation was explained with reference to the Griffith close-up of Mae Marsh's clasped hands in the trial episode of *Intolerance*, which "are not only integral components of the narrative but disclosures of new aspects of physical reality." As we are watching the big close-up of Mae Marsh's hands, "something strange is bound to happen: we will forget that they are just ordinary hands. Isolated from the rest of the body and greatly enlarged, the hands we know will change into unknown organisms quivering with a life of their own." [48] Similarly, the historian's close-up is apt to suggest possibilities and vistas not conveyed by the identical event in high-magnitude history. (The current fashion of presenting photographic detail of a work of art for separate enjoyment provides further evidence of this difference in quality and meaning; thus a bit of background scenery drawn from Gruenewald's Isenheim retable is vaguely reminiscent of a Japanese print.)

A theoretical elaboration may be added to this discussion of the law of levels. On principle, macro explanations claim to be valid for micro facts—for all particulars, that is—while micro insights on their part aspire to recognition in the macro dimension. Now since, to be valid, the former—the macro explanations and definitions—must at least partly be grounded in micro analysis, some of the implications of micro studies are likely to be in agreement with the macro historian's findings. But certainly not all of them, and perhaps not even the most significant ones. We have, then, two sets of generalizations or, rather, insights of a general nature—those which essentially belong to the macro dimension and those directly arrived at from "below" by way of micro analysis. It is the latter type of the general which Huizinga, in his criticism of Burckhardt, opposed to the idea of the Renaissance, which represents the first type of the general insight.* It is obvious that the generalities derived from micro investigations—and surrounding them like a fringe—are largely inconsistent with typical macro generalities. Can they be brought to fuse with the latter? Suffice it here to raise this problem involving the relations between the general and the particular.†

To conclude, the traffic between the micro and macro dimension is subject to severe restrictions. Because of the "law of perspective" part of the evidence drops out automatically. And because of the "law of levels" part of the virtually available evidence reaches its destination in an incomplete state. This means that the historical universe is of a nonhomogeneous structure. It comprises fields of varying density and is rippled by unaccountable eddies.

Radically speaking, the resultant traffic difficulties are unsurmountable. Toynbee's suggestion of a merger of the bird's-eye view and the fly's-eye view [49] is in principle unfulfillable. The

* See pages 99–100.
† This is resumed in Chapter 8.

two kinds of enquiry may co-exist, but they do not completely
fuse: as a rule, the bird swallows the fly.

How do sensitive historians react to this look of things? Here
are two examples.

Kristeller's Problem: Kristeller, the uncontested authority on
Renaissance thought, aims at a synthesis of his life-long research, a comprehensive intellectual history of the period so
familiar to him. But he shies away from this project because
of his awareness that he would have to sacrifice to it much of
what he knows and may still learn in the course of continued
research. It is as if he did not want to curtail or pass over any of
the precious insights which only full absorption in the sources
affords; as if he were afraid of the concealments and distortions
in the wake of the foreshortenings which the prospective
synthesis will most surely impose on him. His realistic passion
conflicts with his formative desire to make a "whole" of his
findings.

Diamond's Dream: Diamond asks himself whether a historian
engaged in a large-scale narrative might not be able to
avoid setting all events in the one perspective which corresponds to the distance bound up with the scope of his narrative.
Why should he not look at things from different distances as he
gets along? So does a wanderer who explores a landscape; he
will first take in the panorama as a whole and then walk toward
the far-distant mountain range, enjoying the ever-changing
sights about him. Many films proceed in this way. That Proust
knows how to combine immersion in minutiae and long-range
views will be seen in the following chapter. Diamond dreams of
an American history in which he plans, among other things, to
insert close-ups not as illustrations of his general assumptions
but, on the contrary, as self-contained entities apt to run counter

to his overall emphases. Also, some poem may be interpreted in depth on occasion.

This conception brings the historian's method into perfect analogy to "Griffith's admirable non-solution" of the dilemma of the cinematic and the theatrical in film as stated in *Theory of Film*:

> On the one hand he (Griffith) certainly aims at establishing dramatic continuity . . . ; on the other, he invariably inserts images which do not just serve to further the action or convey relevant moods but retain a degree of independence of the intrigue and thus succeed in summoning physical existence. This is precisely the significance of his first close-up. And so do his extreme long shots, his seething crowds, his street episodes and his many fragmentary scenes invite us to absorb them intensely. In watching these pictures or pictorial configurations, we may indeed forget the drama they punctuate in their own diffuse meanings.[50]

The analogy holds. And yet one should not throw out the child with the bath water: some attempts at an interpenetration of micro and macro history are more successful than others. In several cases the movement between different levels has resulted in an "idea," a new principle of explanation.* One will now better understand the peculiar truth value of ideas and their oblique relation to factual accuracy.

As a matter of course, the range of *intelligibility* of histories is a function of their width of scope. The higher their magnitude, the more of the past they may render intelligible. But the increase of intelligibility is bought at a price. What the historian gains in scope he loses in terms of (micro) information. "De-

* See pages 100 ff.

pending upon the level at which the historian places himself,"
says Lévi-Strauss, "he loses in information what he is gaining in
comprehension, and vice versa." [51] And he declares that for the
historian to escape this dilemma the only possibility is "to leave
history behind . . . either by going down below it . . . or
going up above it." [52]

The fact that the increase of intelligibility entails a dwindling
of information is a special case of the "principle of mental economy" * which seems to govern our social and intellectual universe. It is of a piece with Blumenberg's principle of the "economy of intentions" according to which the advance of scientific
knowledge is bound up with the abandonment of the metaphysical claim to total knowledge. Science, says he in his Galileo
analysis, accounts not for the whole of nature but for partial
processes. The *Lebenswelt* which Husserl opposes to this par-
ticularization is but a borderline concept; only if we could direct
our intentions equally to all parts of it would it come to life.[53]

The belief that the widening of the range of *intelligibility* involves an increase of *significance* is one of the basic tenets of
Western thought. Throughout the history of philosophy it has
been held that the highest principles, the highest abstractions,
not only define all the particulars they formally encompass but
also contain the essences of all that exists in the lower depths.
They are imagined as the "highest things" in terms of both generality and substance.

This shows, for instance, in that part of the gnostic scheme
which deals with the ascent of the soul from the "world" to the
upper spheres. According to it, the transition to a higher level is
tantamount to an advance in spiritual insight. "The negative law
that each order is unable to see the next higher one indirectly
entails the positive law that the transition of the soul to a higher

* Cf. Chapter 1, page 22, and Chapter 3, page 67.

order is at the same time an ascent in knowledge," says Jonas on the "subordinationism" of the system of Origen.[54] The repercussions of this scheme still make themselves felt in our days, and in diverse branches of knowledge. It is, for instance, at the bottom of Novikoff's all but Plotinian principle of "integrative levels of organization," which holds that the progress of evolution of the inanimate, animate and social worlds materializes at different levels each of which is governed by laws of its own; and that while one cannot understand high level phenomena without understanding those of the lower levels, our knowledge of a lower level does not enable us to predict what will occur at a higher level.[55]

I am referring here to this ingrained belief in the superior significance of the "highest things" only for the purpose of throwing into relief one of the underlying assumptions of the present study—the assumption that the traditional identification of the extreme abstractions—say, the idea of the "good" or that of "justice"—as the most inclusive and essential statements about the nature of things does not apply to history, or related approaches to reality.* When the historian ascends from the micro dimension to ever higher levels of generality, he will reach a point, marked by what I have called the "historical idea," beyond which, as he proceeds further to the dimension of "philosophical" ideas or extreme abstractions, the significance of his insights is bound to decrease instead of continuing to increase. Note the many drop-outs of micro facts in large-scale histories. The very high abstractions have no longer a bearing on the evidence they are meant to cover. They read ideas into things which the things do not include. But the historian, says Harnack, has "no right to place the factors and impelling ideas of a development

---

* For this, see again Chapter 8, especially pages 203 ff.

in a clearer light than they appear in the development itself." [56]
By doing precisely this, traditional philosophy has completely
obscured and, still worse, disparaged the kind of relations that
obtain between the particular and the general in the area of the
last things before the last.

Hence the relative legitimacy of the Tolstoi-Namier objections
to macro history. Close-up findings are significant in their own
right, no matter whether or not their implications coincide with,
or can be subsumed under, the broad views bound up with high
magnitude histories. It is not sufficiently exact just to envisage,
as Hexter does, a process in which "the particular and the individual define the content and the body of the general, while the
general helps to illuminate and make sense of the particular." [57]
How close-ups relate to the broad views of large-scale histories
in case they deviate from them will be considered in chapter 8
and may for the moment be left in the open.*

But this may be the place for an excursus on the significance
of close-ups for a solution to Toynbee's "quantity problem." [58]
Toynbee raises an important issue when, in *Reconsiderations*, he
claims that the historian must make an attempt to do justice to
the enormous quantity of accumulated historical knowledge.
The sheer quantity of it poses by itself the problem of what
might be its purpose. It demands, so to speak, to be put to some
meaningful use. But how can it be used?

The quantity of historical knowledge is taken care of in two
ways. One of them is the approach of the theologians and philosophers of history. But their approach does not bear on history
as a detachable reality open to scrutiny. Jewish-Christian theology springs from an existentialist relation to the past and the

* This is resumed in Chapter 8 pages 203–06 and pages 214–16.

history it means extends toward a future outside historical time. History as conceived by theology is salvation history at bottom —that is, it reaches beyond history in the modern sense of the word. The events that count are within the orbit of history *and* outside it. The same holds true of the great philosophies of history up to a point. Even though they remain within secular time, they explain, mostly under the influence of the theological assumption of a divine plan, the whole of the past in the light of a principle which at best conforms to part of the facts and usually is synonymous with a good cause whose ultimate triumph it is to support.

The other approach is more in keeping with the scientific spirit of the age. In trying to do something about the quantity of our accumulated historical knowledge, Toynbee organizes, as also Spengler does, the given material into large units— civilizations or, with Spengler, culture souls—whose development he analyzes for regularities.* But not only are the regularities thus established very general indeed, they also concern history only to the extent that it is part of nature. Aware of this, Toynbee, as we saw earlier, insists that these regularities are by no means necessary; that, on the contrary, Western civilization may take an entirely unpredictable course. His admission, however, is hardly consistent with his emphasis on regularities.

Let me now assume for the sake of the argument that the regularities traced are really relevant to the whole of history. Then they must all the more dovetail with histories at a lower level of generality. Toynbee actually claims that such an interpenetration of macro and micro history is indispensable. "The solution of the problem of quantity," he says, "lies in combining the panoramic with the myopic view." [59] Here the problem arises

* See pages 40–41.

whether this interpenetration of histories at different levels of generality is at all possible. According to the "law of levels" the contexts established at each level are valid for that level but do not apply to findings at other levels; which is to say that there is no way of deriving the regularities of macro history, as Toynbee does, from the facts and interpretations provided by micro history. It is therefore not surprising that Toynbee's own efforts to master the quantity of historical knowledge are not very encouraging. The regularities at which he arrives are rather irrelevant, not to mention that his insistence on the freedom of will and the unpredictability of history discredits them further.

To sum up: the effort to do justice to the enormous quantity of accumulated historical knowledge is bought at a price. It yields, on the whole, regularities of a rather indifferent and irrelevant character. These regularities "cover" only those historical developments which mark mankind's sinking back into nature. Finally, they represent observations which are at best valid only from the bird's-eye view. The micro events of monographs neither bear out nor directly negate what is seen from an inhabitable distance.

No doubt the sheer quantity of available historical knowledge seems to request of us that we should try to take care of it in one way or another. But does it pay to follow this request? So far any attempt at global history has resulted in irrelevant, all too general statements and arbitrary constructions—products of wishful thinking and existentialist needs. What is captured by these attempts is the sediments of the historical process, not its real joints and hidden depths. I am afraid lest the idea of universal history might be a mirage, a chimera teasing us. . . .

As I see it, the vast knowledge we possess should challenge us not to indulge in inadequate syntheses but to concentrate on close-ups and from them casually to range over the whole, assessing it in the form of aperçus. The whole may yield to such light-weight skirmishes more easily than to heavy frontal attack.

The nonhomogeneous structure of the historical universe carries two interrelated implications of interest. The first bears on the constantly growing body of the fact-oriented accounts—i.e., historical research proper—the kind of histories which roughly conform to Butterfield's "technical history." [60] The question is, are endeavors in this vein meaningful in their own right even if they are not touched off by interpretative concerns and high-level assumptions? Many a historian denies their independent value. They are scorned as dry-as-dust history,[61] considered a "waste of erudition" (Bloch).[62] Huizinga cautions against over-emphasis on "detailed historical research." [63] Other historians waver, carrying loads on both shoulders. So the late Meinecke. On the one hand, he endorses technical history on the ground that it not only establishes the facts but uncovers "hitherto unknown values of the past." [64] On the other, he subordinates technical history to the exposition of values. He calls technical research "mechanistic," holds that sheer fact-finding is pervaded with evaluations, and all in all degrades technical history to a means to an end.[65]

Perhaps the most incisive argument against the legitimacy of fact-finding for its own sake comes from Marc Bloch. He complains of the "split between preparation and execution," taking up the cudgels for guided research: each historian should "struggle with the documents" in the interest of his queries—a claim which goes hand in hand with the repudiation of research "in neutral gear." [66] But Bloch's argument rests on uncertain ground. It originates—I have mentioned this before *—in his unfounded suspicions, as a theoretician, of "passive observation"

* See page 85.

and in his preoccupation with scientific history. For the rest, it is
not the purpose of fact-oriented accounts to make it unnecessary
for the historian continually to test his models and regulative
ideas by micro research of his own.

Presumably the most convincing argument in defense of technical history has been provided by *Bury*. He declares that the
historian aiming at a "complete assemblage of the smallest facts"
in the faith that it "will tell in the end" labors for posterity,[67] is
"playing the long game." [68] Is he? Because of the "law of levels"
—the traffic difficulties between the micro and macro
dimensions—he is likely to lose the game: many micro data he
painstakingly assembles will never reach the upper regions of
synthesizing histories. Bury's reasoning does not stand the test
either.

So the question as to the meaningfulness of "technical history"
would seem to be unanswerable. There is only one single argument in its support which I believe to be conclusive. It is a theological argument, though. According to it, the "complete
assemblage of the smallest facts" is required for the reason that
nothing should go lost. It is as if the fact-oriented accounts
breathed pity with the dead. This vindicates the figure of the
collector.

The other implication of the nonhomogeneous structure of the
historical universe concerns the issue of the progress of historiography. The refinement of research methods, the increase of
research tools, the discovery of new evidence and the broadening of our horizon in its wake—all this speaks in favor of the belief, wide spread among historians, that historiography will
grow in comprehensiveness and, as many assume, objectivity.
This belief, certainly justified up to a point, is not even upset by

the awareness that macro histories are inherently subjective. The ensuing "limitations" of high-magnitude histories, it is held, may be gradually overcome by:

(1) the expansion of knowledge (Marrou, Pirenne, Kristeller; in a way, Hexter); [69]

(2) the recourse to comparative studies (Bloch, Pirenne); [70]

(3) the reliance on teamwork (Bloch, Marron, Kristeller).[71]

Both Bloch and Pirenne hope that in the end a "scientific elaboration of universal history" (Pirenne) [72] will arise. It is understood that they will be the dupes of their hopes. As for the idea of teamwork to arrive at a factual universal history, Lévi-Strauss criticizes it by pointing out that "so far as history aspires at meaningfulness, it condemns itself to making choices. . . . A truly total history would neutralize itself; its outcome would equal zero." [73] I might as well also mention E. H. Carr's pro-progress argument: historiography progresses as we turn from narrow to ever wider contexts of interrelationships, such as, in our days, the broad curves of socioeconomic developments. "The old interpretation is not rejected, but is both included and superseded in the new." [74] The flimsiness of this argument is obvious. If it falls to each successive generation to define the goals of progress in its own terms, then the nature of the historical process as a whole remains undefined. And Carr's idea that our interpretations of history become ever more comprehensive and hence attain to ever increasing objectivity hinges on this untenable concept of progress.

All this is more or less the product of wishful thinking. (In fact, that Bloch should conjure up the ghost of universal history is rather a shame.) As Valéry rightly insists, the subjectivity inherent in interpretative macro histories is unsurmountable; ". . .

since we cannot retain everything, and since we have to free ourselves from the infinitude of facts by judging . . ." [75] And may it not even transcend itself in the best of them? To try to overcome it is not only impossible but, under certain circumstances, outright devious. Since, accordingly, high-magnitude histories, including social histories with their pretense to objectivity, are subject to the "law of perspective," they cannot possibly take advantage of all the facts available. And if hitherto neglected or unknown facts are digged up and utilized in subsequent narratives, these in turn will then necessarily disregard other parts of the virtually inexhaustible material. In consequence, there is a limit to the accurate coverage of the facts— i.e., to the progress of historiography.

One might still ask whether historians should not be supposed to learn from the errors and misplaced emphases of their predecessors and thus, generation after generation, steadily improve on what went before. Improve, a new generation of historians may, but the avoidance of past errors hardly protects them from committing other ones, and depth of insight is not the privilege of the most recent age. It is difficult to imagine that Thucydides will ever be surpassed. The belief in the progress of historiography is largely in the nature of an illusion.

6
Ahasuerus, or the Riddle of Time

Modern historiography conceives of history as an immanent continuous process in linear or chronological time which on its part is thought of as a flow in an irreversible direction, a homogeneous medium indiscriminately comprising all events imaginable.[1] This conception, which owes much to the ascent and ascendancy of science, was preceded by notions giving a more restricted significance to linear time for an understanding of the past. The Greek historians did not fully establish a primacy of linear time over the cyclic time concept; in addition, there persists throughout the history of the Greek mind a dualism of a divine time and a time of men in the apperception of human events.[2] Even though the ancient Jews did not ignore history as a mundane process in time, yet they largely entertained an existential relation to it. They considered history a product of the interaction between them and God, identifying the events of the past as punishments or rewards meted out by Him to His chosen people.* The hoped-for redemption, envisioned by the apocalypses of later Judaism, marked not so much a new historical epoch as the divinely decreed end of human

* See pages 73–74.

history. Early Christian eschatology engulfed chronology also.[3] But since the parousia failed to come, the Church, while retaining the belief in ultimate resurrection, established herself in the world, with the result that she had to reconcile with each other two divergent times. St. Augustine calls them the time of nature and the time of grace or salvation and believes these two times to be insolubly intertwined in ways impenetrable to man.[4] Medieval chronicles, with their incoherent mixture of elements from both salvation history and mundane history, nicely reflect the attempt simultaneously to move within secular time and away from it. The anachronisms of medieval poems express a traditionalist attitude which seeks to blend the past with the present rather than to emphasize their diversity.[5] Incidentally, one does well to remember what Malinowski says of his Trobriands—that their reliance on magic does not prevent them from approaching many issues in a rational, all but scientific spirit.[6] By the same token, a sense of chronological time may have subsisted even throughout periods which in their art and literature mostly ignored its flow.

In studying our conception of chronological time, it would seem advisable to concentrate on a large-scale spatiotemporal unit—say, Western civilization—composed of successive events which are actually or potentially interrelated, so that their succession in time can be said to be of consequence. The reason is obvious: if events belong to two cultures or civilizations between which no interaction takes place, the fact of the succession or simultaneity of these events in chronological time is entirely irrelevant.

Here we may once more ponder the time concept underlying Spengler's panoramic world view, already touched upon in Chapter 1 in connection with Toynbee.* It will suffice to speak

* See page 39.

of him because he more radically isolates his diverse cultures from each other than Toynbee does. How are we to imagine the common temporal medium in which the Spenglerian cultures with their peculiar times emerge, develop, and perish? To the extent that Spengler admits of transitions between them (i.e., pseudomorphoses), they are embedded in the flow of chronological time which thus is reactivated; but whenever he insists on the complete autonomy of his cultures, the common temporal medium turns into a quasi timeless vacuum, an unthinkable negative counterpart of eternity. And chronological time itself as the common medium may reemerge only at the rare moments at which historical and natural processes coalesce —in prehistory which gives birth to all cultures and in case of changing relations between humanity and nature on a global scale. Weizsaecker calls the invention of nuclear energy such a turning point.

I shall inquire, then, into the validity of our conception of history as a process in chronological time within the context of one and the same civilization. Three important implications of this conception for the modern approach to history should be pointed out. First, in identifying history as a process in linear time, we tacitly assume that our knowledge of the moment at which an event emerges from the flow of time will help us to account for its occurrence. The date of the event is a value-laden fact. Accordingly, all events in the history of a people, a nation, or a civilization which take place at a given moment are supposed to occur then and there for reasons bound up, somehow, with that moment. Marrou expresses this assumption of the significance of the moment in chronological time when he says that through history man knows "what he is, where he comes from, why he finds himself placed in the situation that reveals itself as being his . . ." [7] In keeping with this premise, historians usually establish meaningful relationships, causal or otherwise, between successive groups of events, tracing the chronologically later ones to those preceding them.

Second, under the spell of the homogeneity and irreversible direction of chronological time, conventional historiography tends to focus on what is believed to be more or less continuous large-scale sequences of events and to follow the course of these units through the centuries. Many a general narrative relates, say, the history of a people or an institution in chronological order and, in doing so, inevitably attributes significance to the simultaneity of the multiple events that make up the sequence. Ranke's political histories, for instance, are full of excursions into the cultural field.* The underlying idea is that, in spite of all breaks and contingencies, each such inclusive unit has a life of its own—an individuality, as Meinecke puts it. Sometimes narratives in this vein seem to be intended to answer the question where do we come from (or where do we go, for that matter). The question would hardly be raised were it not for our confidence in the workings of calendric time.

Third, uncritical acceptance of the conception of flowing time kindles a desire to translate the formal property of an irreversible flow into content—to conceive, that is, of the historical process as a whole and to assign to that whole certain qualities; it may be imagined as an unfolding of potentialities, a development, or indeed a progress toward a better future. This desire proves irresistible. Not to mention Hegel, whose grandiose construction of the historical process still materializes in a no-man's land between temporality and eternity, even Marx, more down to earth though he is, cannot help yielding to the temptation to map out the course of history in its totality. What the philoso-

* Examples, from Ranke as well as from other historians, will be found in Chapter 7, where the problems of this view of simultaneity will be discussed more fully. See especially pages 173–75.

phers impose from above, numbers of historians try to achieve
from below. Haunted by the chimera of universal history (that
phantom-like counterpart of flowing time), Ranke speaks of a
"general historical life, which moves progressively from one nation or group of nations to another"; [8] Henri Pirenne [9] and
Marc Bloch [10] call universal history the goal of all historical
pursuits. Chronology thus acquires a material meaning of the
first magnitude.

At this point I should like to draw attention to several observations apt to invalidate our confidence in the continuity of the
historical process and, accordingly, the power of chronological
time. It is noteworthy that it is precisely anthropologists and art
historians—not any historians or philosophers of history—who
are aware of the problematic character of chronological time.
Henri Focillon, the art historian, insists on the inherent logic of
the unfolding of art forms, and he argues that simultaneous art
events often belong to different "ages." Art forms, he says, normally pass through an experimental state, a classic age, age of
refinement and baroque age, and "these ages or states present
the same formal characteristics at every epoch and in every environment." [11] Furthermore an art form asserts for these stages
its own time table, independently of historical necessities. "The
successive stages . . . are more or less lengthy, more or less intense, according to the style itself." [12] No wonder then that the
date is not usually "a focus, a point within which everything is
concentrated," but that the history of art alone, and not even
considering the relationship of events in different fields such as
politics, economics, and art, "displays, juxtaposed within the very
same moment, survivals and anticipations, and slow outmoded
forms that are the contemporaries of bold and rapid forms." [13]
Focillon also has the concept of the emergent "event" which

determines its environment rather than being produced by it. For example, "the most attentive study of the most homogeneous milieu, of the most closely woven concatenation of circumstances will not serve to give us the design of the towers of Laon," or, of course, the environment they created.[14] It emerges, rather, as "a highly efficient abruptness." [15] All these elements, together, account for Focillon's disbelief in the magic spell of simultaneity, the effectiveness of an alleged Zeitgeist.

Kubler, a student of Focillon's, has developed the latter's suggestions into a theory of great interest. In his little volume, *The Shapes of Time: Remarks on the History of Things*,[16] this brilliant art historian, who is an anthropologist to boot, attacks the preoccupation with periods and styles common among scholars in his field. Instead of emphasizing matters of chronology, he submits, the historian had better devote himself to the "discovery of the manifold shapes of time." [17] And what does Kubler understand by shaped times? Art works, or more frequently their elements, says he, can be arranged in the form of sequences, each composed of phenomena which hang together inasmuch as they represent successive "solutions" of problems originating with some need and touching off the whole series. One after another, these interlinked solutions bring out the various aspects of the initial problems and the possibilities inherent in them. So it would seem evident that the date of a specific art object is less important for its interpretation than its "age," meaning its position in the sequence to which it belongs. The fact that related consecutive solutions are often widely separated in terms of chronological time further suggests that each sequence evolves according to a time schedule all its own. Its time has a peculiar shape. This in turn implies that the time curves described by different sequences are likely to differ from each other. In consequence, chronologically simultaneous artistic achievements should be expected to occupy different places on their respective time curves, one appearing early in its series, a second being far remote from the opening gambit. They fall into the same period but differ in age.

Lévi-Strauss, too, repudiates the idea of a continuous historical process evolving in chronological time. But unlike Focillon-Kubler, he assigns different times not to logically interrelated series of event but to histories of different magnitudes, arguing that each of them organizes specific data into a sequence which sets a time of its own. Histories of different orders of magnitude like anecdotic history, biographic history, etc., are, he says, coded by separate "classes of dates based, schematically speaking, on hours, days, years, centuries, millennia, etc., as units." [18] It is not possible to proceed from the peculiar time of one class of history to that of another, but like mathematical incommensurables, "the dates belonging to any one of these classes are irrational in relation to all those belonging to the other classes." [19] While you may interrelate histories of the same class, there is a gulf between the time schedules of histories at different levels.[20]

Since Levi-Strauss's proposition mainly serves to implement the idea that the historical universe shows a nonhomogeneous structure, I shall in the following stay with Focillon-Kubler's theory, which has a more direct bearing on the problem at issue. If somewhat modified, its pithy argument against the overemphasis on chronological time in art history is also valid for history in general. The "historical process" inevitably involves a variety of areas. History of art marks only one of them; other areas comprise political affairs, social movements, philosophical doctrines, etc. Now successive events in one and the same area obviously stand a better chance of being meaningfully interrelated than those scattered over multiple areas: a genuine idea invariably gives rise to a host of ideas dependent on it, while,

for instance, the effects of social arrangements on cultural trends
are rather opaque. To simplify matters, it may be assumed that
the events in each single area follow each other according to a
sort of immanent logic.[21] They form an intelligible sequence.
Each such sequence unfolds in a time peculiar to it. Moreover,
the times of different sequences usually have different shapes, as
is strikingly illustrated by a little experiment which Sigmund
Diamond conducted at Harvard. He requested his students to
investigate different areas of American history and to periodize
the course of events on the basis of their respective findings.
One student specialized in political history, another in history of
literature, and so on. Finally they came together and compared
notes. The result was that the periods which they had separately
devised did not coincide.[22]

A profound general theory of a differentiated historical time
was stated by Herder, to whose argument W. von Leyden recently drew attention in an article on the concept of relative
time in history from which the passage concerning Herder
should be here incorporated in full.

> ". . . it is significant that Herder also held the view
> that everything carries within itself its own measure of
> time, or rather the measure of *its own time;* a measure
> that exists even if there is no other measure besides it.
> Presumably by this he meant that a thing *is* a clock, not
> that it *has* a clock. He stipulated that, if general ideas
> are to be banished from historical explanation, Newton's
> framework of absolute space and time must likewise be
> repudiated within this field. For, he argued, it will be
> found that two different things will never have the same
> measure of time and therefore innumerable times may exist
> in the universe 'at the same time.' To remove any doubt
> he explains that the idea of a measure common to all
> times, just as the idea of infinite space which 'was' the

sum-total of all places in the universe, is something introduced by the intellect: both absolute space and absolute
time are, properly speaking, a mere phantom. . . . To
the best of my knowledge, no one who has previously
considered Herder as a historiographer has discussed or
even pointed to this characteristic time doctrine." [23]

At a given historical moment, then, we are confronted with
numbers of events which, because of their location in different
areas, are simultaneous only in a formal sense. Indeed, the nature of each of these events cannot be properly defined unless
we take the position into account which it occupies in its particular sequence. The shaped times of the diverse areas overshadow the uniform flow of time.

Here the historical period comes into view, this spatiotemporal unit to which practically all histories of a certain
breadth of scope resort in an effort to pattern the course of
events. The period seems to be so indispensable a unit that it is
invented after the fact if it cannot be discovered in the material.
Nor is it swayed by the wavering opinions, partly nominalistic,
partly realistic, on the significance of periods.

Let us, then, take a look at the period. Any period, whether
"found" or established in retrospect, consists of incoherent
events or groups of events—a well-known phenomenon which
accounts, among other things, for the occurrence of events relatively unaffected by the Zeitgeist: thus the overstuffed interiors
of the second half of the nineteenth century belonged to the
same epoch as the thoughts born in them and yet were not their
contemporaries. The typical period, that phase of the historical
process, is a mixture of inconsistent elements. This is nothing to
wonder at. Is not the individual's mind incoherent also? * "Our

* Cf. the author's argument in Chapter 5, page 117. It is here resumed in
application to the problems of the structuring of time.

minds," says Valéry, ". . . are full of tendencies and thoughts
that are unaware of each other." [24] And Lichtenberg, about 150
years earlier: "I have frequently one opinion when I lie down
and another when I am standing, especially when I have eaten
little and feel weak." [25] Marc Bloch speaks of "the amazing in-
terior partitions" existing in our minds and by way of example
relates that the historian Gustave Lenôtre was "constantly
amazed to find so many excellent fathers of families among the
Terrorists." [26] The integrated personality no doubt belongs
among the favorite superstitions of modern psychology.

As might be expected, there is no lack either of statements
acknowledging the nonhomogeneous character of the historical
period. Marx speaks of the *"Ungleichzeitigkeit"* (nonsimultane-
ousness) of the ideological super-structure. Curtius insists that
literature differs from the arts in terms of movement, growth,
and continuity.[27] Schapiro believes that a unity of style throughout the culture of a period cannot, where it exists, be taken for
granted but requires explanation by some particular factor imposing it on the several areas.[28] Raymond Aron upholds the
independence of art with regard to its socioeconomic environment and defends the relative autonomy of the political area
against the champions of social history.[29] Mandelbaum, with a
special view to history of philosophy, favors the assumption of
independent, internally continuous special histories under the
name of "cultural pluralism." [30] Dilthey stresses not only the
unified context of the life of a period but also the existence of
opposing forces which turn against the one-sidedness of the
Zeitgeist, often continuing older ideas or anticipating the future.[31]

But it is two different things to notice a phenomenon and to
realize its potential meaning. None of these statements testifies
to an awareness of what the divergence of the elements that

comprise a period may imply for the significance of chronology. Even though Marx, for instance, is enough of a realist to perceive, and codify, "Ungleichzeitigkeit," he nevertheless clings to Hegel's idea of a dialectical historical process which involves the conventional identification of homogeneous linear time as the time of history.

In the light of Focillon-Kubler's views, however, the evidence rather suggests that this equation is open to doubt. Actually, history consists of events whose chronology tells us but little about their relationships and meanings. Since simultaneous events are more often than not intrinsically asynchronous, it makes no sense indeed to conceive of the historical process as a homogeneous flow. The image of that flow only veils the divergent times in which substantial sequences of historical events materialize. In referring to history, one should speak of the march of times rather than the "March of Time." Far from marching, calendric time is an empty vessel. Much as the concept of it is indispensable for science, it does not apply to human affairs. Its irrelevancy in this respect is confirmed by the mechanics of our memory. We may vividly recall certain events of our past without being able to date them. Perhaps the memory for qualities develops in inverse ratio to the chronological memory: the better equipped a person is to resuscitate the essential features of encounters that played a role in his life, the more easily will he misjudge their temporal distances from the present or play havoc with their chronological order. These errors must be laid to the difficulty for him to transfer his memories from their established places on his subjective time curve to their objective positions in chronological time—a time he never experienced. Nothing is more difficult than to experience it. This once more highlights its formal character, its emptiness. How should it carry content? As Walter Benjamin

judiciously observes, the idea of a progress of humanity is untenable mainly for the reason that it is insolubly bound up with
the idea of chronological time as the matrix of a meaningful
process.[32]

The upshot is that the period, so to speak, disintegrates before
our eyes. From a meaningful spatiotemporal unit it turns into a
kind of meeting place for chance encounters—something like
the waiting room of a railway station. But this is not all that
there is to it. Thus, Laslett is aware of the deceptiveness of general concepts projected back into the historical past, and he insists that history must seek to "reconstruct . . . in intricate
detail." [33] But understanding the whole society and large historical transformations affecting it is not therefore to be given up.
It is merely turned into a question of "all these tiny little movements and reactions," or "a question of minutiae, of residue as
you might say." [34]

In further pursuit of my argument I therefore wish to focus
on a case of great theoretical interest—Burckhardt's conception
of the period. The way he deals with it owes much to his ambiguous, largely negative attitude toward chronological narration.
(Note, by the way, that he, too, turned from his history teaching
to art teaching.) It is not that he would refrain from rendering, on occasion, a succession of all-embracing historical situations, but he does refuse to be put in the strait jacket of the
annalistic approach; [35] and a look at his major writings makes it
evident that he is reluctant to acknowledge the homogeneous
flow of time as a medium of consequence. In his *Weltgeschichtliche Betrachtungen* he withdraws from that flow into a timeless
realm in order to pass in review the varying relationships that
obtain, or may obtain, between freely developing culture and
the two institutionalized powers of the state and religion; and he

authenticates his observations by a plethora of examples culled from all quarters of world history with only superficial regard for their chronological order. *Die Zeit Constantins des Grossen* as well as *Die Kultur der Renaissance in Italien* testify to the same unconcern for the dynamics of the historical process. In both works Burckhardt brings time to a standstill and, having stemmed its flood, dwells on the cross section of immobilized phenomena which then present themselves for scrutiny. His account of them is a morphological description, not a chronological narrative. It covers a single historical period.

However, in thus repudiating chronology, Burckhardt again pays tribute to it, as is best illustrated by his *Renaissance*. In this unrivaled masterwork he explores, one by one, the variegated manifestations of Renaissance life, ranging from the rediscovery of antiquity to the free creation of states, from the new sense of personal values to social custom and mounting secularization. Does he want to demonstrate that, their simultaneity notwithstanding, the events he summons point in different directions? That not all that appears together actually also hangs together? He might, indeed, for his remark that "the highest in art does not depend directly upon the outward political life of the state" [36] clearly reveals his awareness of the incoherence of cultural epochs. Nevertheless, his declared objective is to interpret the Italian Renaissance as the age of the awakening individual—a conception, by the way, which is still considered a lasting contribution.[37] Now this conception, a genuine idea rather than a mere generalization, naturally implies that one and the same spirit of (secular) individualism asserts itself in virtually all the activities, aspirations, and modes of being that comprise the period. Consequently, the Renaissance must be thought of not as an incoherent conglomerate of events but as a whole with a meaning which pervades its every element. Burckhardt, that is,

steps out of chronological time only to entrust himself to its flow
in the end. Or so it looks. For once a period in its complexity is
recognized as an integrated whole, the shaped area times automatically recede into limbo, and, along with the total historical
process, chronology tends to re-assume significance.

The wary reader will already have noticed that this vindication of chronology flagrantly contradicts my original proposition
to the effect that chronological time is an empty vessel. I shall
presently show that the proposition suggested by Burckhardt's
interpretation of the Renaissance is as well-founded as the opposite anti-chronological one. Kubler in his otherwise legitimate
criticism of the art historians' overemphasis on periods decidedly overshoots the mark in almost precluding the possibility of
a confluence of area sequences: The "cross-section of the in-
stant," he contends, ". . . resembles a mosaic of pieces in
different developmental states. . . rather than a radical design
conferring its meaning upon all the pieces"; [38] and he insists
that the "cultural bundles" which make up a period "are juxtaposed largely by chance." [39] This holds presumably true, say, of
the Biedermeier period (which had to bear with the late Bee-
thoven) but does certainly not apply to the Renaissance and
many another era. The absence of periods with a "physiognomy" (Panofsky's expression) of their own would indeed be
rather surprising. The physiognomy distinguishing them may be
due to events, actions, moods of an authentic reality character.
And why not? Contemporaries commune with each other in various ways; so it is highly probable that their exchanges give rise
to cross-linkages between the accomplishments and transactions
of the moment.* Remember, too, the "principle of mental economy" according to which an individual's intensity at one point

* See pages 66–67.

makes for his inertia, his falling back into routine (or nature), at most others.* You cannot be original in all respects. Obviously this law—which must be largely held responsible for the stubborn existence of what might be called the "world"—favors the establishment of cross-linkages also. In consequence, even though simultaneous events as a rule occur in times of different shapes and moreover differ in "age," there is a fair chance that they will nevertheless show common features. Simultaneity may enforce a rapprochement; random coincidences may jell into a unified pattern. Do not, by the same token, the fragments of the self each of us believes to be sometimes converge and achieve unity or a semblance of it? To his observation on the amazing partitions in men's minds, Bloch adds another, which is no less significant: "Were Pascal, the mathematician, and Pascal, the Christian, strangers to each other? . . . it may be that (the) antithesis, correctly considered, is only the mask of a deeper solidarity." [40] At any rate the osmotic processes that constantly take place are always apt to produce a period or a situation which may indeed breathe a spirit affecting all areas and thus assume the character of a whole. Dilthey analyzed the unified structure of the age of enlightenment as an example of this kind of unity, which he calls "not a unity which can be expressed by one basic thought but rather an interconnection of the various single tendencies of life that gradually forms among them in the course of things." [41] There is an analogy between this precarious unity of a period and that of any entity we call a "gestalt." Bloch asks himself "if it is not futile to attempt to explain something which, in the present state of our knowledge of man, seems to be beyond our understanding—the ethos of a civilization and its power of attraction." [42]

But does the period as a whole then not become part and par-

* See Chapter 1, page 22, and Chapter 3, pages 66–67.

cel of the historical process, thereby establishing, by implication, homogeneous time as a medium pregnant with meanings? It should not be forgotten either that the old daydreams of mankind envision a far-distant future which cannot with any certainty be said to lie completely outside chronological time; and that the Greek conception of a progressive cultural development has managed to assert itself even in predominantly vertical-oriented times: Tertullian seems to have believed in a secular kind of progress; [43] St. Ambrose in his answer to the pagan Symmachus points to the "gradual invention of the arts and the advance of human history." [44] "While paganism in its old age began to plead for the authority of the old, most memorably about the worship of Victoria in the Roman Senate," says Edelstein about this doctrine of the early Christian writers, "the new creed had taken over that philosophy which paganism itself inaugurated in its youth." [45] Consider not least that we date the day of our birth; that we know of our position in the chain of generations; and that Death is shown with an hour-glass. *Les extrêmes se touchent:* our intrinsic being and the most empty mode of becoming are intertwined. So does Piaget trace mathematics back to biology. By the way, the increasing visibility of prehistory may further strengthen our confidence in the uncontestable role of calendric time.

Thus we are confronted with two mutually exclusive propositions neither of which can be dismissed. On the one hand, measurable time dissolves into thin air, superseded by the bundles of shaped times in which the manifold comprehensible series of events evolve. On the other, dating retains its significance inasmuch as these bundles tend to coalesce at certain moments which then are valid for all of them. It is this state of things which must have caused Burckhardt to disparage as well as endorse chronology. But he never cares to bring its inherent contradictions into the open. Benjamin on his part indulges in an undialectical approach; he drives home the nonentity of chronological time without manifesting the slightest concern over the other side of the picture. That there are two sides to it has rarely been recognized.

How deal with the dilemma in which we find ourselves? To come to grips with it I shall in the following no longer refer to the different area sequences and their peculiar time tables but focus on the relatively uniform periods or situations brought about by their confluence. Each such period is an antinomic entity embodying in a condensed form the two irreconcilable time conceptions. As a configuration of events which belong to series with different time schedules, the period does *not* arise from the homogeneous flow of time; rather, it sets a time of its own—which implies that the way it experiences temporality may not be identical with the experiences of chronologically earlier or later periods. You must, so to speak, jump from one period to another. That is, the transitions between successive periods are problematic. There may be breaks in the process; indeed, a period may, as an emergent "event" in Focillon's sense, arise from "nowhere." Dilthey quotes Burckhardt as saying about the spread of the belief in the beyond under the Roman Empire: "It is from hidden depths that such new trends usually receive their strength; they cannot be deduced from preceding conditions alone." [46] Similarly, Marx's conception of history is, in Alfred Schmidt's words, "a philosophy of world breaks, consciously abandoning the rule of continuous deduction from one principle." [47] Jonas believes that the movement of Gnosticism will be misunderstood so long as it is interpreted as a result of preceding ideas and beliefs rather than accepted as *sui generis* and arising from "something like an absolute origin, a radical new

beginning," [48] which as a new "prima causa" operates on the
material of existing ideas and motives.[49] Very similar views
were more recently set forth by Blumenberg in an article in
which the increasing interest of historians in the "threshold
times" between distinctive periods is explained from the fact
that they expose to the view of the historian "history itself,"
which in the classic periods remains "hidden under its manifestations." [50] In the view outlined by these statements, all histories featuring the "March of Time" are mirages—paintings on
a screen which hides the truth they pretend to render. Each period can be supposed to contribute a new picture; and the successive paintings thus produced cover, layer after layer, the ever-
expanding screen in a manner which is perfectly illustrated by
Clouzot's documentary film, *Le mystère Picasso*. It shows the
artist in the act of creation. We see: once Picasso has outlined
what he appears to have in mind, he immediately superposes
upon his initial sketch a second one which more often than not
relates only obliquely to the first; and in this way it goes on and
on, every new system of lines or color patches all but ignoring
its predecessor.[51]

Yet the same configuration of events which because of its
spontaneous emergence defies the historical process marks also a
moment of chronological time and has therefore its legitimate
place in it. So we are challenged to follow that process and think
in terms of linear transitions, temporal influences, and long-
range developments. The statements of this chapter which coincide in discrediting the a priori confidence in historical continuity
are not intended completely to deny the possibility of influences ranging over chronological time. But in order to speak of
them with a measure of certainty their existence must be authenticated in any specific case. I submit that this belongs to the
historian's most difficult tasks. Let alone that, because of the

scanty evidence, such influences are very elusive, part of them takes effect without leaving a trace. They work undercover: one word from you, long since forgotten, may have changed the mind of the man to whom it was once spoken. I have been deeply influenced by a casual remark a friend made to me two or three decades ago; his remark altered my approach to people and in a manner my whole outlook on life. When after a long separation we recently met again we reveled in memories and I could not help mentioning my indebtedness to him. He was immensely surprised; he did not remember having said anything of the sort to me. Substantial influences seem to be predestined to sink back into the dark.

It occurs to me that the only reliable informant on these matters, which are so difficult to ascertain, is a legendary figure—Ahasuerus, the Wandering Jew. He indeed would know first-hand about the developments and transitions, for he alone in all history has had the unsought opportunity to experience the process of becoming and decaying itself. (How unspeakably terrible he must look! To be sure, his face cannot have suffered from aging, but I imagine it to be many faces, each reflecting one of the periods which he traversed and all of them combining into ever new patterns, as he restlessly, and vainly, tries on his wanderings to reconstruct out of the times that shaped him the one time he is doomed to incarnate.)

In a sense, Ranke seems to have been aware of the paradoxal relation between the continuity of the historical process and the breaks in it, as appears when the passage already quoted in Chapter 1 is given in the full context, which runs:

> At every moment again something new may begin, something that can be traced only to the first and general source of all human action and inaction; no thing merely exists for the sake of the other outside of itself; there is none

that entirely resolves into the reality of the other. Yet
there is also at the same time a deep connection of things
of which no one is entirely free and which enters everywhere. By the side of freedom there is necessity. It resides
in that which is already formed and cannot any more be
undone, which forms the basis of every newly emerging
life and activity. That which became constitutes the connection with that which is becoming. But also this connection itself is not something which can be assumed
arbitrarily; it was in a certain way, thus and thus, not
otherwise . . . . A longer series of events—following
each other and side by side—, connected among each
other in this way, form a century, an epoch . . . .[52]

I have emphasized the double aspect of the period with a
purpose in mind; two modern attempts—are there more of
them?—to do justice to both the emptiness and the meaningfulness of chronological time assign to the concept of the period a
key position. Their discussion may help clarify the inextricable
dialectics between the flow of time and the temporal sequences
negating it.

To begin with Croce, his argument is outright fallacious.[53]
This inveterate idealist who does not want to be one boasts of
having dealt a deadly blow at Hegel's transcendental metaphysics. Hegel, says he, postulates an absolute spirit, or world
spirit, which is both immanent and transcendent; it realizes itself in the dialectical process of world history and at the same
time has its abode beyond history as the goal of this process.
Croce has it that this ontological transcendentalism will no
longer do. And he puts an end to it by dragging the absolute
spirit lock, stock and barrel into the immanency of the innerworldly universe. The spirit, he insists, is not an Absolute above
and outside of our changing world but materializes only within

history; to be precise, it provides us with concrete answers to the concrete questions raised in every given situation—questions which, of course, vary with the requirements of the moment. Croce, then, assumes the existence of comparatively autonomous situations or periods, each with a spirit peculiar to it. But if the manifestations of the spirit are inseparable from the specific needs of different periods, their meaningful connection in chronological time poses tremendous problems. Now Croce is so deeply concerned with the historical process that he nevertheless aspires to give chronological time its due. How does he solve the problems contingent on this task? He does not even see them. His heart's in the Highlands, his heart is not here. To say it bluntly, it still quivers with nostalgia for the idol he believes to have demolished. Oblivious of the fact that, according to his own premise, the spirit does not spread over the expanses of history but reveals itself exclusively in concrete situations, Croce in his otherwise admirable sketch, "Concerning the History of Historiography," [54] identifies its successive revelations from antiquity via the Middle Ages, the Renaissance, etc., to the present as phases of an intelligible dialectical process to which he moreover attributes a progressive quality. True, he tries to adjust the notion of a wholesale progress to his basic assumption of the complete immanency of the spirit by eliminating the idea of an absolute good and enhancing instead the spirit's effort to achieve a betterment of the conditions that obtain in any particular period. Yet this is a sheer playing with words in view of Croce's idealistic desire to equate the total historical process with a progressive movement, a movement toward "liberty." In sum, after having thrown out Hegel with great aplomb, Croce reintroduces him by the back door, unaware that what is possible to Hegel is denied to him. Indeed, while Hegel's transcendental spirit is fully qualified, alas!, to determine the direc-

tion of the whole of history, Croce's immanent spirit with its
concrete answers to concrete questions—arising from situations
beyond which we cannot ask—is not in a position to account for
the course of events. Croce evades rather than tackles the problems bound up with the antinomic character of chronological
time. Instead of asking how, if at all, the two contradictory time
conceptions can be related to each other—how, that is, chronological time can be reduced to nothingness and yet be
acknowledged—he undialectically, and absent-mindedly, presents them side by side. And the Hegelian he is wins out over
the Hegel-destroyer he would like to be.

And there is Proust's unique attempt to grapple with the per-
plexities of time. Strangely enough, its consequences for history
have not yet been realized. In dealing with it, I shall feature
only such traits of his novel as are relevant to my present
theme.[55]

Proust radically de-emphasizes chronology. With him, it appears, history is no process at all but a hodge-podge of kaleido-
scopic changes—something like clouds that gather and disperse
at random. In keeping with this Platonic view, he refuses to act
the historian and rejects the ideas of becoming and evolution.
There is no flow of time. What does exist is a discontinuous, non-
causal succession of situations, or worlds, or periods, which, in
Proust's own case, must be thought of as projections or counterparts of the selfs into which his being—but are we justified in
assuming an identical being underneath?—successively transforms itself. It is understood that these different worlds or situations reach fullness and fade away in times of different shapes.
With great ingenuity Proust demonstrates that each situation is
an entity in its own right that cannot be derived from preceding
ones and that indeed a jump would be needed to negotiate the

gulf between adjacent worlds. Throughout his novel he systematically veils the moments of their junction, so that we learn about a new world only after it is already in full swing. And to discredit completely our belief in the operating power of time, he removes the most imperishable, and most tenuous, connecting link between successive worlds—hope. Marcel, the protagonist of the novel and the embodiment of Proust's past selfs, anticipates future fulfillments in every situation; yet no sooner have his hopes come true than their magic dissolves, along with the self that nurtured them; and the succeeding self starts afresh on a path beset with other, if increasingly fewer, expectations. The gulf is unbridgeable; time, far from being the All-Father, does not father anything.

Why not then simply ignore it? This is precisely what Proust does. He invariably turns the spotlight on time atoms—memory images of incidents or impressions so short-lived that time has no time to mould them. Touched off by accidental bodily sensations, his involuntary memories assert themselves with complete indifference to chronology. The events they by and large evoke are much in the same nature as the seemingly insignificant minutiae of daily existence which Tolstoy calls more real and more significant than the big victories and heroes played up in the history books. Proust restores these microscopic units to their true position by presenting huge enlargements of them. Each such "close-up" consists of a texture of reflections, analogies, reminiscences, etc., which indiscriminately refer to all the worlds he, not only Marcel, has been passing and altogether serve to disclose the essential meanings of the incident from which they radiate and toward which they converge. The novel is replete with close-ups in this vein. They are penetrations in depth whose components—those meditations and recollections —follow unaccountable zigzag routes spreading over the whole scroll of the past. The patterns they form can no longer be defined in terms of time; in fact, their function is to lift things temporal into the near-timeless realm of essences.

So far it looks as if Proust, unconcerned for dialectics, confined himself to arguing the case of the discontinuous worlds and their shaped times. However, this is only part of the story. Even though Proust blurs chronology, he is at pains to keep it intact. Much as the close-ups with their time-confusing patterns tend to obstruct our awareness of a flow of events, they not only point to the situations occasioning them but are woven into a narrative which renders Marcel's successive selfs in their chronological order. On the whole, the novel abides by a strict itinerary. Or as Jauss puts it, behind the mosaic of anachronistic moments there lurks, concealed from view, the "precise clockwork of irreversible time." [56]

Not content with installing it, Proust tries to re-embed the chronologically successive worlds—worlds which are spontaneous creations arising from nowhere—in the flow of time. The reason is that he wants to make that flow an equal partner in the game. For he cannot resolve the antinomy with which he grapples unless he really confronts and dialectically reconciles with each other its two opposite aspects—the incoherent series of shaped times and chronological time as a homogeneous flow. His solution inevitably involves a detour: he establishes temporal continuity in retrospect. At the end of the novel, Marcel, who then becomes one with Proust, discovers that all his unconnected previous selfs were actually phases or stations of a way along which he had moved without ever knowing it. Only now, after the fact, he recognizes that this way through time had a destination; that it served the single purpose of preparing him for his vocation as an artist. And only now Proust, the artist, is in a position not only to identify the discontinuous worlds of his past as a continuity in time but also vicariously to redeem his past from the curse of time by incorporating its essences into a work of art whose timelessness renders them all the more invulnerable. He sets out to write the novel he has written.

The profundity of this solution should not lead one to overestimate the range of its validity. Proust succeeds in reinstating chronological time as a substantial medium only a posteriori; the story of his (or Marcel's) fragmentized life must have reached its terminus before it can reveal itself to him as a unified process. And the reconciliation he effects between the antithetic propositions at stake—his denial of the flow of time and his (belated) endorsement of it—hinges on his retreat into the dimension of art. But nothing of the sort applies to history. Neither has history an end nor is it amenable to aesthetic redemption.

The antinomy at the core of time is insoluble. Perhaps the truth is that it can be solved only at the end of Time. In a sense, Proust's personal solution foreshadows, or indeed signifies, this unthinkable end—the imaginary moment at which Ahasuerus, before disintegrating, may for the first time be able to look back on his wanderings through the periods.

7

General History and the Aesthetic Approach

Maurice Mandelbaum has recently drawn attention to a "rather strange fact"—that "those who have concerned themselves with the general problems of historiographical method have rarely discussed the question of how the methods of 'special histories,' such as histories of philosophy, or of art, or of technology, or of law, are related to what they regard as paradigmatic cases of historiographical practice." [1] The "paradigmatic cases" are narratives of a type which we most readily remember when we vaguely think of history as a branch of knowledge; what then immediately comes to mind is the history of some people or the history of an age. Altogether narratives in this vein constitute a species in its own right which, in keeping with Mandelbaum's definition, may be called "general history." (The term "general" was originally applied to political histories, which in their heyday occupied a privileged position.) Whether or not much cultivated today, general history is a major genre of modern historiography.

One of its chief characteristics lies precisely with the fact that it is general: it essentially differs from special histories in that it extends over a variety of areas. Whereas the special historian focuses on phenomena within one and the same area—relatively homogeneous phenomena at that—the general historian concerns himself with virtually all the events that make up the whole of a temporal sequence or a situation. It should be obvious that this difference is bound to carry methodological implications of consequence.

A general theoretical statement rarely reveals all the relevant aspects of the particulars it covers. So a look at their actual configurations will always prove rewarding, if not indispensable. On principle, for instance, it is certainly true that general historians may survey spatiotemporal units of any size, big ones or small ones; but is it not equally true that they by and large favor narratives which encompass wide expanses of the past? To all intents and purposes, general history falls into the macro dimension. Also, in practice the boundaries between the two genres are fluid. There is hardly a specialized inquiry that would not venture beyond its set confines. Such "transgressions" are all the more required if the events in a particular area cannot possibly be isolated from activities and changes outside that area. Stubbs's *Constitutional History* and Maitland's *History of English Law* enjoy the reputation of being the best (general) histories of medieval England; [2] that, say, a history of art should ever attain to a similar status seems highly implausible to me. For the rest, even if an area history takes on all the airs of a general narrative, it still retains a peculiar character. The apparent identity results from different intentions. The specializing historian makes inroads into neighboring domains, while the general historian tries to marshal masses of facts from diverse regions. Where the first seeks to supplement his specific insights, the second aspires to synthesis at the outset.

Indeed, the subject matter of general history must be imagined as representing a whole of a sort. Without a unifying frame of reference the genre would not be viable. Its very existence depends upon the possibility for the historian to relate his materials to a common denominator. Is the unity he looks for discovered or imposed? Assuredly, he will be inclined to believe that it is inherent in historical reality itself. And what does the unity consist of? There is no clear-cut answer to this either. Mandelbaum holds that the genre invariably centers on the life of society at large and that, accordingly, the general historian "is concerned with human thoughts and actions in their societal context and with their societal implications . . ." [3] Palpably inspired by the current infatuation with social history, this answer is incomplete and too narrow to fill the bill. The common substratum might as well be the identity of a people through the ages, or such an entity as an empire or a body of all-pervasive beliefs. Any substratum will do. And any of them can be supposed to give rise to the unifying arrangements and interpretations which are prerequisite to a narrative built from disparate elements. If the general historian does not succeed in interconnecting, somehow, these elements and impressing upon us continuity and cohesion, he had better relinquish his job. But to say this is to suggest that his whole undertaking rests on uncertain grounds. The unity he needs—does he trace or postulate it?—is not guaranteed; the facts he musters are refractory. And yet general history exists and subsists. How is this puzzling genre possible?

Whether he knows it or not, the general historian is in a predicament. He has to cope with a tremendous problem—the antinomy at the core of chronological time.* There is, on the one hand, no denying the partial significance of the passing of

* To be sure, he is also confronted with the difficulties arising from the nonhomogeneous structure of the historical universe (see Chapter 5). But to simplify matters I shall leave them undiscussed here; moreover, they concern historians of all denominations.

time for the whole of human affairs. Within certain limits and contexts, it makes sense to speak of developments over time and the common features of selected periods. This would seem to justify the general historian's pursuits up to a point. Favorable winds may allow of relatively smooth sailing as he proceeds to render and explain the general run of things. On the other hand, he is constantly prevented from proceeding this way because the events he tries to connect belong to different areas and therefore resist being treated as elements of a unified and meaningful temporal sequence. The reason why they do not easily lend themselves to participating in the joint enterprise must be laid to the fact that they are primarily members of sequences which evolve according to timetables peculiar to their respective areas. The opposite, no less powerful aspect of chronological time is that of an empty medium, a flow carrying with it phantom units and insignificant aggregates of happenings. As compared with the special historian, who in the ideal case moves along a time curve formed by a series of coherent phenomena, the general historian is at a disadvantage: he is caught in a cataract of times. (Since the antinomic character of Time has been mostly overlooked, the little attention paid to the methodological differences between the synthesizing and specializing approaches till now is not so strange after all.)

Once again, how is general history possible? The answer is simple enough. The genre can materialize only if the historian manages to dispose of the obstacles which spell doom to his project. Of course, it is not given him to bridge, let alone eliminate, the existing temporal chasms; nor is he in a position to transform the many random complexes of events he encounters into real live units. All that he is able to do about these permanent disturbances is to play them down as best he can. To achieve his ends, the general historian must take refuge in *manipulative expedients and devices,* permitting him to advance his narrative with a somnambulist's assurance. They are to make us (and him) forget that the highway of chronological time is in truth uneven and bumpy.

His efforts in this direction are facilitated by two circumstances. The first is the effect of the "law of perspective." Operating in the macro dimension, the general historian reviews the potentially available evidence from an appreciable distance. At the place he is occupying detail recedes and the air becomes rarefied. He is in a measure alone with himself—more alone than he would be in the micro dimension where hosts of facts are apt to crowd in on him. But the less he is exposed to their pressures, the more he will feel free (and entitled) to give rein to his formative powers. And this naturally relieves him of inhibitions in his recourse to expedients and adjustments.*

Second, since the story he tells unfolds at a comparatively high level of generality, the deceptive ease with which generalizations can be transferred from the milieu of their origin to any other environment stands him in good stead also. Once established, they claim independence and admit of all kinds of uses. Their apparent malleability is a boon to the synthesizing historian. Why indeed should he not capitalize on it to keep his narrative going? Of course, in doing so he is taking certain risks. Generalizations are fragile products which demand to be handled with care. Whenever they are removed from their native soil and made to sustain alien contexts, they may become dumb and no longer echo the meanings that led to their formation. In his *History of Europe,* Pirenne summarizes the state of affairs under the emperor Justinian as follows:

* See Chapter 5, pages 122–23, and again Chapter 8, "The General and the Particular," pages 203–06.

> Justinian, as we know, closed the school of Athens . . .
> But the dogmas and mysteries of religion provided an
> abundance of material for the passionate love of dialectic
> which had for so many centuries characterized Hellenic
> thought. No sooner did Christianity appear than the
> East began to teem with heresies; there were pitched
> battles in the great cities, Council attacked Council . . .[4]

Passionate love of dialectic? Teeming with heresies? The
opaqueness of this montage of generalizations cannot be more
complete. In the interest of story continuity they becloud the
very situation they are called upon to evoke.

No doubt the general historian's foremost concern is the un-
ruly *content* of his narrative. Perhaps the most conspicuous device to bring it into line consists in the adaptation to the historical medium of one or another of the several great philosophical
ideas which pretend to cover and explain the whole historical
process. (Need I repeat that philosophical and historical ideas
are two different things?) * Many a general history seems to be
informed with the ideas of progress, or evolution, or any mixture
of them. It is not as if the narrator would have to impose them
upon his material; the air is impregnated with these ideas, so
that they may appear to him as something given and self-
evident. Indeed, he may not recognize them as the speculative
abstractions they are when he falls back on them in his quest for
substantial unity. This is corroborated by the typical language
of historical writings; a discerning contemporary historian J. H.
Hexter has it that such words as "tended, grew out of, developed, evolved; trend, development, tendency, evolution,
growth" belong among their standing vocabulary.[5] (Under the

* See pages 101–03.

spell of the ideas at its bottom narrative historians sometimes represent the history of a people or the like as a succession of events which lead straight to the present. The result is a more or less closed success story which, because of its necessary reliance on teleological considerations, not only spawns falsifying hindsight but further tightens the bonds between the elements of the narrative, thereby smoothing away all the existing rifts, losses, abortive starts, inconsistencies.)

Along with the family of ideas which champion progress, perfectibility and/or some variant of the Darwinian scheme, philosophy also provides the model concept of cyclical change. And its biological version—the image of recurrent processes of organic growth and decay—likewise offers itself to historians as a convenient means of passing off large portions of the past as coherent and intelligible sequences. References to this image, which has been no less internalized than the notion of progress, even turn up in accounts otherwise impervious to biological analogies. "At the beginning of the Roman Empire," says Nilsson, "the world had become tired." [6] Clearly, philosophical ideas have a way of changing from valiant attempts at total interpretation into opiates and treacherous signposts.

I have mentioned these idea-oriented histories only to eliminate them at the outset. Wary of speculations which beg the question, conscientious historians try to get along without such ideological props or crutches. There are in fact numerous general narratives which give a wide berth to *a priori* assumptions about the direction and meaning of history; they neither equate it with a progressive movement nor presuppose that it runs in cycles. Pirenne, for instance, would not have dreamed of letting himself be guided, or misguided, by philosophical total views. It is these, so to speak, uncontaminated narratives which are of particular interest here because they best permit one to find out

about the less conspicuous devices needed for their build-up—
devices of which their authors *must* avail themselves in order to
be able to tell the story they wish to impart. To be sure, as the
responsible historians they are supposed to be, they certainly do
not want to manipulate its content; yet if they refrained from
making the appropriate adjustments, the whole edifice would
immediately collapse. So they will do what they have to do all
but against their will and often without being aware of it. The
genre forces the hand of its devotees. This explains why the adjustments to which they willy-nilly resort are much in the nature
of slight retouchings, soft pressures—you hardly notice the
magic.

Yet there they are. And quite understandably, many of them
serve to strengthen the impression of continuity over time. Now
the chronological sequence is threatened every moment with
dissolving into the divergent strands of events of which it is
composed, so that this impression can be upheld only against
overwhelmingly heavy odds. Small wonder that under such desperate circumstances even scrupulous historians see no other
way out than to adduce flighty arguments in support of the unified sequence. Two random examples may illustrate this.

> Paul Wendland in his *Die hellenistisch-roemische Kultur,*
> a true classic, accounts for the rise of superstitions under
> the Roman Empire as follows: "For the Imperial period
> it is symptomatic that an intensified religious life turns
> with vehement passion to the oriental cults. Extraneous
> factors encouraged this development." He summarily lists
> them and then continues: "The decline of culture and
> decay of the sciences conduce to every sort of supersti-
> tion." [7]

Obviously possessed with the urge to feature the sway of
longitudinal influences, Wendland draws on a totally imaginary

life experience—that superstitions largely result from the decay
of paideia (as Werner Jaeger would have said) and the decline
of science. Do they? True, Dodds in his *The Greeks and the Irrational* reasons in a similar way: he holds that the "failure of
nerve" (Gilbert Murray's term) in later antiquity was responsible for the acceptance of astrology and that we moderns are in
the same boat as the ancients—or rather, would be in it were it
not for the intervention of psychotherapy which, he hopes, will
immunize us against any new-fangled version of Chaldean beliefs.[8] But I venture to submit that there is also something to be
said in favor of the opposite interpretation according to which
psychotherapy, as commonly practiced today, would represent
not so much a sobering antidote as the modern counterpart of
Hellenistic astrology with its pseudo-scientific calculations and
directives. Over against Wendland one might as well contend
that scientific progress makes for an increase of superstitions.

> On occasion even Marc Bloch unduly stresses linear de-
> velopments. After having, in his *Feudal Society*, depicted
> the disastrous effects of the Arabic, Hungarian, and Scan-
> dinavian invasions, he declares that "a society cannot with
> impunity exist in a state of perpetual terror," and inserts
> the following transitional paragraph: "The havoc had
> nevertheless not been merely destructive. The very dis-
> order gave rise to certain modifications—some of them
> far-reaching—in the internal organization of Western Eu-
> rope."[9]

This paragraph in turn introduces a sketchy survey of what
happened in France and England once the worst was over.
Were all of the partly positive changes a direct consequence of
the incursions? Bloch suggests that they were by stating that the
havoc which the invaders wrought on Western Europe was not
merely destructive. But in this way he decidedly overburdens
the incursions with causal responsibilities.

Temporal continuity is inseparable from meaningful together-
ness. In addition to bolstering that continuity, the general historian will therefore automatically try to make any period of his
concern appear as a unity. This calls for adjustments of story
content, enabling him to blur the discrepancies between co-
existent events and turn the spotlight instead on their mutual
affinities. It is almost inevitable that, as a matter of expediency,
he should neglect intelligible area sequences over cross-
influences of his own invention.

From Ranke to the present, examples are found in highly re-
spected places. Whenever Ranke himself looks out of the win-
dow of political history to survey the neighboring regions of art,
philosophy, science, etc., he insists on explaining goings-on in
them from the total situation, at such and such a moment, of the
nations or peoples whose destinies he narrates. In other words,
he contrives to fit the cultural events of the period into a make-
shift scheme which is to give us the impression that they conform to the general state of affairs. But his very eagerness to
bring these events onto the common denominator of a whole
that moves in time prevents him from probing their essences,
their real historical positions. Ranke presents distorted pictures
of them, in defiance of his own claim that history should tell us
"wie es eigentlich gewesen." The profile of Erasmus in his
Deutsche Geschichte im Zeitalter der Reformation is as lifelike
and lifeless as a slick court painter's portraits.[10] And aside from
being irrelevant, his comments, in *Die Geschichte der Paepste,*
on Guido Reni, Palestrina, and other exponents of late Italian
16th-century culture are couched in terms so flowery and ama-
teurish that any college student today would be ashamed of
using them.[11] Note, though, that Burckhardt as a young man
knew parts of this famous work by heart.[12] (But none of us is
immune against magic splendor, however futile. I remember

having been in my youth completely under the spell of Thomas Mann's *Tonio Kroeger* with its elegiac, if ludicrous, nostalgia for the blond and blue-eyed doers. In fact, my whole generation was.)

The pattern set by Ranke is followed throughout. And often enough the narrator's compulsive efforts to interrelate things actually miles apart result in statements which are far-fetched, to say the least. The mirage of unity can be authenticated only by chimerical evidence. Somewhere in his *History of the Early Church* Hans Lietzmann dwells on the deterioration of the arts in later antiquity. Having mentioned that sculpture then lost its tradition, he opens the next paragraph with the sentence: "The economic distress of the second half of the third century also spoiled the spirit of literature." [13] This statement which correlates economic conditions and artistic manifestations for the sake of unification is nothing but a flimsy *ad hoc* improvisation without any basis in reality. The spirit of literature blossomed in Germany after World War I—at a time of acute economic distress, that is.

Or take again Wendland. In a section of his book, entitled "Individualismus," he lumps together a number of developments under this very heading:

> "This individualistic tendency, which in science leads to a division of professional branches, and everywhere to division of labor and a separation and mutual delimitation of spheres of interest, shows strongly also in literary production." [14]

A hypostasized generalization—the "individualistic tendency" —is here elevated to the central cause of a variety of phenomena, the fictitious thus begetting the real. Yet a look at the phenomena themselves suffices to make you realize that, for instance, scientific specialization cannot possibly have been an effect of that "cause." Wendland puts the cart not only before the horse but before the wrong horse. (By the way, his *Hellenistisch-roemische Kultur* is an inexhaustible repository for adjustments of this type. They climax in a veritable gem of a misstatement—the lapidar pronouncement: "With daemonic strength, Augustus also impressed unity on his time." [15] It would be difficult to establish the unity of a period in a more categorical and less conclusive manner.)

However, all these adjustments find their natural limit in the character of the material on which they bear. The past is threaded with unaccountable changes and incoherent compounds of events which stubbornly resist the kind of streamlining required by general history. Were it only for the historian's attempts to gear story content to the needs of the genre, the genre might falter for lack of sustenance. To maintain it as a going concern, he will have to supplement these attempts by *formal* expedients involving structure and composition. There is practically no general narrative that would not draw on them. What the narrator cannot accomplish in the dimension of content he expects to achieve in the aesthetic dimension.

And this brings the age-old controversy about the relations between history and art into focus. The extreme views taken of the matter by the ancient rhetoricians and antiquarians still retain exemplary significance. Robert Graves in his novel, *I, Claudius,* nicely epitomizes these views by introducing the Roman historians Livy and Pollio—the same Pollio whom he has say that "history is an old man's game"—as spokesmen of the two conflicting schools of thought. While Livy indicts Pollio of dullness, the latter insists that you cannot mix poetry and history:

> "Can't I? Indeed I can," said Livy. "Do you mean to say
> that I mustn't write a history with an epic theme because
> that's a prerogative of poetry . . . ?"

> "That is precisely what I do mean. History is a true record
> of what happened, how people lived and died, what they
> did and said; an epic theme merely distorts the record." [16]

Within the framework staked out by this dialogue, the debate
has been carried on throughout the modern age, with ambivalent attitudes by and large getting the better of analysis and argument. Symptomatic of the wavering are Bury's contradictory
comments on Thucydides: he praises Thucydides for repudiating Herodotus' epic designs and preferring "the demands of historical precision to the exigencies of literary art," but then again
defends his "speeches" as serving the "artistic purpose of pauses
in the action." [17] The prevailing indecision manifests itself in
the widespread opinion that history is a science as well as an
art.[18] Even in our days with their emphasis on scientific method
and social change historians find comfort in this formula which
veils rather than tackles the issues at stake.[19]

To come to grips with them one will have to discriminate between the two different functions which art may assume in historical writings. One of these functions is vital indeed. Con-
cretizing Meinecke's hints at it,[20] Marc Bloch elaborates on the
essential role of art in a statement which gets to the core of the
matter:

> "Human actions," says he, "are essentially very delicate
> phenomena, many aspects of which elude mathematical
> measurements. To translate them properly into words and,
> hence, to fathom them rightly . . . great delicacy of lan-
> guage and precise shadings of verbal tone are necessary."
> He concludes: "Between the expression of physical and
> human realities there is as much difference as between
> the task of a drill operator and that of a lutemaker: both

> work down to the last millimeter, but the driller uses pre-
> cision tools, while the lutemaker is guided primarily by
> his sensitivity to sound and touch . . . Will anyone deny
> that one may not feel with words as well as with fin-
> gers?" [21]

Art, then, fulfills an indispensable function if it is not so much a goal as a consequence of the historian's pursuits. The very nature of his explorations may enjoin on him a language which is impressive aesthetically; yet its peculiar beauty denotes only the depth of his understanding; it is a by-product, not a set objective. To the extent that the historian produces art he is not an artist but a perfect historian. This is what Namier means when he compares the great historian with a "great artist or doctor." [22] The emphasis is on the art of the great doctor; and the rationale of the comparison lies in the fact that both the doctor and the historian operate in the orbit of the *Lebenswelt,* dealing with human realities which, to be absorbed and acted upon, require of them the diagnostician's aesthetic sensibilities. Burckhardt is aware of this—he would be. "That is something these people as well as a few others no longer know," he writes to Gottfried Kinkel in 1847, "that real history writing requires that one live in that fine intellectual fluid which emanates to the searcher from all kinds of monuments, from art and poetry as much as from the historians proper . . ." [23]

The other function of art is nonessential to the medium. Art in this sense is an accretion, an adornment. As such it may still serve the legitimate extramural purpose of making the expert's accounts more palatable to the layman. History is also a public affair; and stylistic know-how need not interfere with scholarly accuracy. The Society of American Historians distributes awards for works which best combine "scholarship and literary excellence." [24] If the request for "literary excellence" means nothing more than that the historian should keep a watchful eye on his prose, the Society's policy will be objectionable only to professionals who believe indifference to the manner of representation to be a prerequisite of erudition.* Yet there is a limit to the historian's aesthetic strivings, a threshold beyond which they tend to encroach on his intrinsic preoccupations. (The late Garrett Mattingly's stories of the Armada and of Catherine of Aragon lie dangerously near to that border; I wonder whether they do not sometimes cross it.) No sooner does the historian aspire to the status of an artist (in addition to that of an historian)— arrogating to himself the artist's freedom to shape his material in accordance with his vision—than beauty as an unintended effect of his inquiries proper is superseded by beauty as a deliberate effort. And his triumph as an artist is apt to defeat the cause of history. In consequence, the saying that history is both a science and an art carries meaning only if it refers to art not as an external element but as an internal quality—art which, in a manner of speaking, remains anonymous because it primarily shows in the historian's capacity for self-effacement and self-expansion and in the import of his diagnostic probings.

Now the general historian cannot fully implement his narrative designs unless he pays special attention to the form of his story. This need not mean that he would reach out for, or indeed achieve, "literary excellence"; actually, he may be a poor writer. But it does mean that he must use specifically literary devices after the fashion of an artist bent on moulding his mate-

---

* Note that I am speaking here of writing as a craft in its own right, not of the kind of writing which is the great historian-diagnostician's prerogative. With him, the art of prose is contingent on his art as an interpreter. True, he must be able to "feel with words" in order adequately to convey his insights, but this does not necessarily imply that he is a consummate writer.

rial. In the case of general history, that is, the nonessential function of art becomes an essential one; aesthetic arrangements
turn from an external embellishment into an internal requirement. In conjunction with the pressures put on story content,
these arrangements are contrived to yield patterns which connect the unconnected, establish illusory contexts, and, all in all,
solidify the unity of temporal sequence. So the willing readers
are safely guided through Time. They are in about the same position as those caravans of vacationing tourists you meet everywhere in Europe—no by-roads for them, no opportunity to
deviate from the preordained routes planned by their respective
travel agencies. The general narrative so completely depends on
formal adjustments along these lines that even the most perceptive craftsman is powerless to evade them. Werner Kaegi has it
that Burckhardt's *Renaissance* includes formulations with which
"you don't exactly know if they are informed more by painstak-
ing consideration of the subject or by the formative need for a
formal delineation." [25]

Sham transitions are a much-favored surface expedient. They
create the illusion of a flow, substituting, in Croce's words,
"aesthetic coherence of representation for the logical coherence
here unobtainable." [26] The following example is drawn from
Nilsson:

> "While art in the Augustan age turned back to classicism
> and various trends appeared under the following emperors,
> a romantic return to the old (archaism) asserted itself in
> the second century with Hadrian . . ." [27]

Aside from toying with stereotyped generalizations of no
avail, Nilsson in this sentence throws a bridge joining the different art movements of successive periods. Yet it is a purely verbal
bridge, constructed with the aid of a single word, the not very
trustworthy conjunction "while." That gullible readers may nev-

ertheless fancy they are crossing a real bridge is quite another matter.

Pirenne's *History of Europe* is replete with similar dodges—perhaps for the reason that it speedily reviews a diversity of topics which must be brought together, somehow.

> Discussing the developments in Italy that led up to the Renaissance, Pirenne first elaborates on the North-Italian bourgeoisies—a paragraph closing with the praise of Florence. The subsequent topic is the Papal States. He introduces it by saying: "Neither in their wealth, nor in their political, social or intellectual activity would the Papal States bear comparison with Lombardy or Tuscany. They presented . . ." [28]

Built from an uncalled-for comparison, or confrontation, this threadbare transition testifies to the indomitable desire for stylistic adhesives.

> At another place, Pirenne deals with the rule of Alfonso V and the significance of Aragon for Spain: "It was Aragon that opened up for Spain, cut off from Europe by the Pyrenees, the only possible means of communication, the highway of the Mediterranean." Then he wants to interest us in Castile. But would not this change of subject be too much of a shock for us? To cushion it he inserts a transitional sentence which reads: "However, not Aragon but Castile was the true Spain. It was Castile . . ." [29] Follows information about things Castilian.

The sentence reminds me of the student of zoology whom his professor requests to tell him something about the elephant. Having been coached only for the fly, the student answers: The elephant is much, much bigger than the fly. As for the fly . . .

This polishing job would by itself alone hardly be of consequence, did it not fall into line with other, more substantial expedients. Altogether they aim at tightening the composition of

the general narrative, so that it assumes an air of wholeness reminiscent of works of art. In the absence of ideological props such
compositional arrangements will be all the more needed. The
task of simulating cohesion in the aesthetic dimension admits of
a variety of solutions. The narrator may organize successive
waves of events or states of being into something like an epic.
Or he proceeds, as a playwright would, with an eye to dramatic
suspense. Or he so shapes his story that it exudes a singular
mood—the case of Huizinga's *The Waning of the Middle Ages.*

What happens here has its counterpart in film. The cinematic
quality of film stories varies in direct ratio to their transparence
to camera-reality. Since this contingent and indeterminate reality is partly patterned—as is the historical universe with its long-
enduring events—stories, or fragments of them, can easily be
discovered in it. (Think of Flaherty's *Nanook,* and the like.)
They certainly are in character. And so are episodic films, the
episode by definition emerging from, and again disappearing in,
the flow of life. To be precise, their cinematic flavor is a function
of their porosity; they must be permeable to the chance manifestations of that life. Now many commercial films are not true
to the medium in this sense. Paying tribute to the prestige of the
established arts, they tell stories which are either adapted from
(successful) stage plays or novels, or modelled on them in terms
of structure and meaning. The "theatrical film," as this story
type may be called, sacrifices porosity to dense composition; and
it unfolds above the dimension of camera-reality instead of passing through it. In the play *Romeo and Juliet* the Friar's failure
to deliver Juliet's letter in time is significant inasmuch as it denotes the workings of Fate. But in the Castellani film *Romeo
and Juliet* the same event affects the spectator as an outside intervention unmotivated by what goes before, a story twist which
for no reason at all alters the course of action. The whole affair

belongs to an ideological continuum, not the material one to which film aspires. It is a sham entity which would have to be broken down into its psychophysical components to become an integral part of camera-life.[30]

The general narrative resembles the theatrical film. In both media compositional exigencies set the tune. None less than Rostovtzeff inadvertently surrenders to them by reducing, in his short history of Rome, the Spartacus revolt to a minor incident, a mere bagatelle.[31] No doubt he knew better. But he shrank from pulling down the structure he was about to erect.

All these devices and techniques follow a harmonizing tendency—which is to say that their underlying intentions flagrantly conflict with those of contemporary art. Joyce, Proust, and Virginia Woolf, the pioneers of the modern novel, no longer care to render biographical developments and chronological sequences after the manner of the older novel; on the contrary, they resolutely decompose (fictitious) continuity over time. Proust's work rests throughout upon the conviction not only that no man is a whole but that it is outright impossible to know a man because he himself changes while we try to clarify our original impressions of him.[32] As Erich Auerbach puts it, these modern writers "who prefer the exploitation of random everyday events, contained within a few hours and days, to the complete and chronological representation of a total exterior continuum . . . are guided by the consideration that it is a hopeless venture to try to be really complete within the total exterior continuum and yet to make what is essential stand out. Then too they hesitate to impose upon life, which is their subject, an order which it does not possess in itself." [33] In other words, they seek, and find, reality in atom-like happenings, each being thought of as a center of tremendous energies. The "order of life," ungiven them, may or may not exist. In fact, they rather doubt whether the small random units in which life, really tangible life, materializes are meaningfully interconnected, so that in the end the shadowy contours of a whole will delineate themselves at the horizon.

Modern art radically challenges the artistic ideals from which the general historian draws his inspiration—from which he must draw it to establish his genre. And because of the ensuing change of aesthetic sensibilities, his quest for aesthetic coherence has lost much of its appeal. Nor is the kind of "literary excellence" attainable to him in harmony with our way of seeing, our notions of style.[34] There is something passé about the beauty of Mattingly's magnificent histories.

The disruptive intentions of modern writers and artists are paralleled by the increasing misgivings of historians and thinkers about the synthesizing narrative, with its emphasis on the "total exterior continuum." It would be tempting to trace these similarities to a common source. But the *Zeitgeist* is a mirage; and cross-influences are often counterbalanced by sundry inconsistencies. Burckhardt combined an acute sense of discontinuity in human affairs with an outspoken predilection for harmonious wholeness in works of art.

Before turning to the misgivings and criticisms I have in mind, I should perhaps caution the reader against confusing them with the running attempts to check and question the faithfulness to reality of the general historian's accounts. Since its inception, modern historiography has made it its Penelope-like business to weave syntheses and unravel them again. This is beside the point here. What I do wish to stress is, rather, the negative attitude toward general history as such. Opposition to it comes from diverse quarters, asserting itself in direct and indirect ways.

Valéry's arguments against the genre would be still more convincing were it not for their provenance from his unflinching faith in the natural-science approach. Sagacious observer of the intellectual scene that he is, Valéry reproaches general history with leaving chaos unpenetrated and at the same time champions, in keeping with Focillon-Kubler's proposition, the study of what he calls "comprehensible series"—the very series featured in special histories: "I have derived something now and then from reading specialized histories—of architecture, geometry, navigation, political economy, tactics. In each of these fields, every event is clearly the child of another event," whereas in "all general history, every child seems to have a thousand fathers and vice versa." [35]

Valéry puts his fingers on the central problem: the general historian's fatal inclination to restore their fathers to all the foundlings in his care. He mistakes ancestry for explanation.[36] It is this obsessive *recherche de la paternité*, this overindulgence in origins, wholesale developments, and longitudinal influences which is the main target of contemporary attacks upon the genre. Hexter, for instance, as we know, seeks to explode the notion, dear to synthesizing historians, Marxist or not, that the feudal age was followed by the steady decline of the landed aristocracy and the concomitant rise of the bourgeoisie. He does so by arguing that the straight line of development suggested by this notion is nothing but an "imaginary construction," calculated to evoke the image of a consistent chain of becoming. In reality, he says, it neither explains the changes in question nor demonstrates their inevitability. His criticism is coupled with a recommendation: historiography might improve if "historian after historian re-examines the place and time with which he is mainly concerned, and seeks to contrive, for telling about what went on in that bounded place and time, a vocabulary of conceptions better suited to bring out its character than the fairly shopworn one now in use." [37]

Similarly, Peter Laslett disparages the habit, common among historians, of explaining the so-called Scientific Revolution of the 17th century from alleged large-scale socioeconomic developments, such as the coming of the middle class and of capitalist economies. A student of 17th-century society, Laslett denies the existence, in Stuart England, of a middle class in our sense of the word and by the same token chides the textbooks for relating the growth of the rational scientific outlook to the processes of economic rationalization. All of this is summed up in his objection to the imposition of imaginary unifying concepts and their use as levers for interpretation.[38]

Hans Blumenberg on his part takes exception to the widely sanctioned view according to which the idea of progress is a secularization of the eschatological interpretation of history. In this view the hope for infinite mundane progress would directly descend from the religious hope for ultimate redemption, transferring it from the supernatural to the innerworldly plane. Actually, there is no such lineage. Pointing to the origin of our conception of progress in the battle between the ancients and the moderns,[39] Blumenberg has it that the belief in its religious ancestry is an illusion pure and simple. That the illusion perpetuates itself must be laid to the surplus functions which that secular conception has come to assume: it has been burdened with the obligation to cater to the very human needs which once found their outlet in messianic prophecies. But while it is true that the Communist Manifesto stirs up about the same expectations as those aroused by these prophecies, it is no less true that its content, its substance proper, cannot be traced to them. Blumenberg's opposition to traditional *Geistesgeschichte* with its bias in favor of linear developments is based on a premise which I believe to be of crucial significance: he submits that we are entitled to speak of a spontaneous generation of thoughts and ideas.[40]

Passive resistance to general history adds to these frontal attacks. It has been observed that Namier persistently refuses to provide sustained narrative.[41] Burckhardt's ingrained suspicions of the genre show precisely in places where, for one reason or another, he sees fit to follow the turns and bends of a chronological sequence. The frequent use he makes of the word "nun"—approximately the English "now"—on these occasions is quite revealing. Take his account of the course of events that mark the era of the Greek tyrants: having related, for instance, that many a tyrant tried to ingratiate himself with the populace by remitting burdensome debts and confiscating the landed property of the nobles, he seems to be all set to report on the little success of the bribes; no sooner are the fickle masses won over to the tyrant's cause than it occurs to them that they might be even better off without a strong man at the top. But at this point a "nun" disrupts chronology: "Und *nun* (my italics)," Burckhardt continues, "—and now he [the tyrant] has to experience how much easier it is to seize power than to hold it." [42] The story is full of such "nuns." They literally puncture it, serving the narrator as loopholes. Through them he time and again escapes from the tyranny of the chronological order of things into more timeless regions where he is free to indulge in phenomenological descriptions, communicate his experiences, and give vent to his insights into the nature of man. To be sure, his account is still a story of sorts, but the influences connecting the "before" with the "after" turn slack like muscles. Burckhardt is not much concerned with them. He prefers to shift the emphasis from the

possible causes of past events to their consequences for posterity, their effects on the well-being of the contemporaries. Thus
he asks what the Greek polis contributed to the happiness and
unhappiness of its individual members.[43] His meditations about
"good furtune" and "misfortune" in history [44] raise moral questions in the form of a running comment on the colorful scenes
before the spectator's eye. Moral concern here insolubly fuses
with aesthetic interest. So does the art lover appraise beauty and
ugliness. It is noteworthy that, contrary to the general historian's
aesthetic arrangements, Burckhardt's escapes into the aesthetic
dimension are not meant to deepen the impression of chronological continuity but unmistakably intimate that history abounds
with contingencies which we must take in our stride.

However, this is not all that there is to it. Much as the arguments against general history appear to be justified, they have
not succeeded in suppressing the nostalgia for synthesis, for
large-scale narration. The genre is doomed to perish and yet
proves indestructible. It seems to fade away, succumbing to the
specialists' agoraphobia, their fear of all too wide themes and
spaces, and nevertheless continues to attract the minds. "If we
ask ourselves," says a contemporary historian, "what historians
have commanded the most lasting admiration, we shall find
. . . that they are . . . those who (like imaginative writers)
present men or societies or situations in many dimensions, at
many intersecting levels simultaneously . . ." [45]

The achievements of these past masters cast their spell even
over historians who are fully aware of the methodological tangle
in which any practitioner in the field is caught. I am thinking of
certain sporadic attempts to re-endow general history with theoretical respectability. As might be expected, they coincide in trying to reconcile the establishment of long-term developments
with the acknowledgment of all the facts and circumstances de-

fying them. One such attempt comes from a declared opponent of the genre. There is no better proof of its eternal attractiveness than Hexter's apparent lack of consequence. On the one hand, he blames the broad general narrative for indulging perforce in purely imaginary constructions and claims that it should be replaced by histories of more limited scope. On the other, he proposes a compromise apt to keep this very genre alive. The narrator, Hexter holds, might reduce its worst defects if, at each major change he comes across, he discontinues his story, with a view to relating that change to the conditions of the moment. So his inevitable concern with lasting influences will every now and then be checked by inquiries into the interaction between the divergent elements that make up (and disappear in) the procession of events along the "corridors of time." [46] Whether or not this compromise is workable remains to be seen.

The compilation of inclusive macro histories by way of cooperative effort may be said to represent another attempt in this vein. Their prototype is Lord Acton's *Cambridge Modern History*. In stringing together, and adjusting to each other, monographs by specialists, the editors of these composite works want to kill two birds with one stone—give the total chronological sequence and at the same time avoid the distortions, foreshortenings, etc., to which the narratives rendering it are prone. They want to construct macro history by aligning a series of micro histories. But this is a mechanical device. Histories at different levels of generality require different treatment; and it is extremely improbable that a collection of such monographs should achieve the kind of wholeness which is of the essence to general history.*

* Judging from its first volume, the forthcoming UNESCO *History of Mankind*, a product of international teamwork, is being organized in a slightly less mechanical manner. But even so it retains throughout the character of a compromise—not to mention that some of its features are rather controversial.

These compromises (to which still others might easily be
added) do not even pretend to solve the general historian's
problems. Is there a solution to them? The only real solution—
provided it is one—has been offered centuries ago. We owe its
rediscovery to Robert Merton who, with his flair for the genuine, has spotted it in *Tristram Shandy*.[47] Tristram's answer to
the question of how penetrate chaos is so memorable that I cannot resist the temptation of reproducing it to the full:

> Could a historiographer drive on his history, as a muleteer
> drives on his mule—straight forward;—for instance, from
> Rome all the way to *Loretto*, without ever once turning his
> head aside, either to the right hand or to the left,—he
> might venture to foretell you to an hour when he should
> get to his journey's end;—but the thing is, morally speak-
> ing, impossible: For, if he is a man of the least spirit, he
> will have fifty deviations from a straight line to make with
> this or that party as he goes along, which he can no ways
> avoid. He will have views and prospects to himself per-
> petually soliciting his eye, which he can no more help
> standing still to look at than he can fly; he will, moreover,
> have various
>> Accounts to reconcile;
>> Anecdotes to pick up;
>> Inscriptions to make out;
>> Stories to weave in;
>> Traditions to sift;
>> Personages to call upon;
>> Panegyrics to paste up at this door;
>> Pasquinades at that:—All which both the man and
> his mule are quite exempt from. To sum up all; there are
> archives at every stage to be look'd into, and rolls, records,
> documents, and endless genealogies, which justice ever
> and anon calls him back to stay the reading of:—In short,
> there is no end of it . . .[48]

Of course, this precisely is the rub in it. Just as Tristram himself never manages to expedite the narrative beyond his child-

hood days—there is so much to tell, so much to look into—it is, "morally speaking," impossible for any historian following him ever to reach Loretto. He is no muleteer after all.[49]

General history, then, is a hybrid, something between legend and the Ploetz, that imperishable annalistic manual which we as schoolboys used to memorize the dates of battles and kings. How explain the astounding longevity of this impossible genre? What to us appears as an "imaginary construction," has been the *raison d'être* of general history most of the time. Our preoccupation with the course of history is grounded in religious prophecy, theological computations, and metaphysical ideas about mankind's lot. Like all basic inquiries, the quest for the destinies of empires and peoples originates with the approach from "above"—a mode of apprehending and reasoning which only in the modern age has given way to the approach from "below." Not completely, though. The old questions, goals, and mirages linger on, joining forces with the needs and interests which arise from the historian's involvement in the affairs of his day. They too invite him to account for temporal sequence, the past as a whole. Indeed, under the impact of both these contemporary and traditional concerns he cannot help driving his mule straight to Loretto. General history might be more vulnerable to attacks did it not largely serve nonhistorical ends.

8
The Anteroom

One may define the area of historical reality, like that of photographic reality, as an anteroom area. Both realities are of a kind which does not lend itself to being dealt with in a definite way. The peculiar material in these areas eludes the grasp of systematic thought; nor can it be shaped in the form of a work of art. Like the statements we make about physical reality with the aid of the camera, those which result from our preoccupation with historical reality may certainly attain to a level above mere opinion; but they do not convey, or reach out for, ultimate truths, as do philosophy and art proper. They share their inherently provisional character with the material they record, explore, and penetrate. Now the whole realm to which photography as well as history in the modern sense belong has up to now been overshadowed by misconceptions founded on the traditional prejudice that there exists no field of knowledge in its own right between the hazy expanses in which we form opinions and the high-level areas harboring the products of man's most lofty aspirations. Thus photography has been misunderstood either as an art in the established sense or a sort of recording medium, yielding merely impressions of little avail; and exactly in the same way history has been misinterpreted as a matter of negligible opinions or a subject which can be adequately covered only by the philosopher or artist. In this treatise, I consider it my task to do for history what I have done for the photographic media in my *Theory of Film* [1]—to bring out and characterize the peculiar nature of an intermediary area which has not yet been fully recognized and valued as such.

This implies that, from the angle of philosophy or art, we, so to speak, stop in the anteroom when coming to terms with history on its own grounds. But what is the significance of our stay in the anteroom? Had we not better directly tackle the last things instead of idly focusing on the last before the last? Evidently, my task is not completed unless I speculate on the meaning of anteroom insight. I have pointed out in *Theory of Film* that the photographic media help us to overcome our abstractness by familiarizing us, for the first time as it were, with "this Earth which is our habitat" (Gabriel Marcel); [2] they help us to think *through* things, not above them. Otherwise expressed, the photographic media make it much easier for us to incorporate the transient phenomena of the outer world, thereby redeeming them from oblivion. Something of this kind will also have to be said of history.

PRELIMINARY DEMARCATION OF AREAS

For the purposes of the subsequent investigation I should first like to delimit, however provisionally, the area into which historiography falls. The differences between history and the scientific approach proper as well as art have already been made out in earlier contexts, in Chapters 1 and 7. And there is no need for expressly distinguishing historical knowledge from sheer opinion. What remains to be pondered is the relations between history and philosophy.

But how define philosophy in a general way? Such definitions are impossible independently of a definite frame of reference. The best is perhaps to characterize philosophical reasoning by those of its peculiarities which strongly impress themselves upon the historian. In a passage summarizing results of a historical survey of philosophy, Dilthey says: "We always saw operating in it the tendency to universality and toward reasons and causes, the direction of the mind at the whole of the given world. And always its metaphysical urge to penetrate into the core of this whole is found struggling with the positivist demand of general validity of its knowledge. These two aspects belong to its essence, and they distinguish it from the areas of culture most closely akin to it. In contrast to the sciences, it seeks to resolve the enigma of the world and of life itself; but in contrast to art and religion, it wants to give the solution in generally valid form." [3] It appears from this and from other examples,[4] that the historian is inclined to attribute to philosophy some such features as these:

First, philosophy aims at truths about man's ultimate concerns—the nature of being in general, of knowledge, of the good, of beauty, and not least of history. It deals with the very last things, assuming or doubting their existence. Hence, in part, its claim to highest significance.

Second, philosophical statements are of the highest generality, resting on the premise that they automatically cover all pertinent particulars. There is practically no philosophy of history that would not try to render intelligible the whole of history. Philosophy's claim to highest significance is also based on the conviction that its general statements about the world fully encompass that world.

Third, philosophical statements aspire to objective validity, or so at least does it appear to any historian aware of his dependence upon empirical evidence. Roughly speaking, one might

indeed say that philosophy, whether postulating or denying absolutes, wants to arrive at statements of unlimited authority—
statements which seek to emancipate themselves from the conditions of time and place. This lies in the nature of human reason. And it accounts for the preoccupation of contemporary
philosophy with the implications of historism.

Fourth, the historian may be struck by what often affects him
as the rather sweeping radicalism and rigidity of philosophical
truths. They do not seem to fit certain particulars of his interest;
and they tend to ignore, obscure, or minimize differences in degree to which he attaches importance. Jaeger, in *Paideia*, reproaches the "severe historians of philosophy" with dismissing
integral features "in Plato's picture of Socrates as mere poetic
decoration. It all seems to lie beneath the high level of abstract
thought on which philosophers ought to move and have their
being." [5]

Historiography differs from philosophy in all these respects.
Instead of proceeding from, or climaxing in, statements about the
meaning, or, for that matter, the meaninglessness, of history as
such, it is a distinctly empirical science which explores and in-
terprets given historical reality in exactly the same manner as
the photographic media render and penetrate the physical
world about us. History is much closer to the practically endless,
fortuitous, and indeterminate *Lebenswelt*—Husserl's term for
the basic dimension of daily life—than philosophy. Consequently, the historian would not dream of assigning to his findings and conclusions the kind of generality and validity peculiar
to philosophical statements. He is unconcerned for high abstractions and absolutes; at least he does not primarily care about
them.

The difference between the two approaches shows, for instance, in the history of ideas. While the philosopher, in dealing

with it, is bent on stressing the inherent potentialities of some
idea as the driving power behind its development—e.g., Jonas's
Gnosis—the historian (to the extent that he does not, like Kubler, connive at the behavioral sciences) prefers to drag the idea
whose unfolding in time he records through the underbrush of
history (which Jonas also tries to do); think of Daniel Halévy,[6]
or Bury's *The Idea of Progress*.[7] In fact, as we know, many historians nurture misgivings about and distrust the philosophical
approach. One might even speak of their resentment against
it—a sort of frustration traceable to the fact that they have
rarely the tools to meet the philosopher on his own ground. And
conversely, as viewed from the lofty regions of philosophy, the
historian devotes himself to the last things before the last, settling in an area which has the character of an anteroom. (Yet it
is this "anteroom" in which we breathe, move, and live.)

The boundaries between the areas of historiography and philosophy are fluid, as is illustrated by the existence of concepts
belonging to both areas. Originating with theological and metaphysical speculations, the concepts of universal history and
progress are a matter of concern to the historian also. Their ambiguous nature will be discussed in the course of the following
meditations, which bear on two issues of tremendous importance for both philosophy and history—the issue of historicity
and that of the general in its relation to the particular. These
meditations may shed light on the constitution of the anteroom.

HISTORICITY

The problem. Nineteenth-century historism is largely responsible for the firm establishment of the consciousness of man's historicity, the belief in the formative powers of time as well as
place. Dilthey was perhaps the first fully to realize the conse-

quences of this belief. According to it, there are no "eternal truths"; rather, all our thinking is a function of time. Consciousness of man as a historical being necessarily entails a conviction of the relativity of human knowledge. (Weizsaecker, as we know, has it that the natural laws are not immune against changes either, although this participation of nature in the historical process would be at a very slow pace.*)

Once historicity is recognized as part and parcel of the human condition, the problem arises as to how to reconcile the ensuing relativity of knowledge with the quest of reason for significant truths of general validity. It is the key problem of modern philosophy. All philosophical attempts to solve it try to find a way out of the dilemma confronting contemporary thought; they seek, that is, to legitimate the efforts of reason to get hold of absolutes, sometimes even suggesting their attainability, and at the same time to uphold the idea of historicity. These attempts can be divided into two groups.

Two "solutions." There are, first, numbers of alleged solutions which may be called "transcendental"; altogether they are an aftermath, or indeed the backwash, of secularized theological concepts and traditional metaphysics, with the idea of evolution being thrown into the bargain. They proclaim, at the outset, the possibility of timeless truths, positing a realm of absolute values, norms, and the like. So Ranke and Droysen, in a sense Scheler,[8] Rickert,[9] Troeltsch,[10] Meinecke,[11] etc. All of them attempt to escape the clutches of historical relativism which they are nevertheless obliged to affirm, and, in keeping with the demands of reason, to regain access to the lost paradise—that realm outside time which they nostalgically envision. How do they do it? To say it plainly, by way of some subterfuge or other. What hap-

* See Chapter 1, page 21.

pens is invariably the same: you still believe you are swimming
in the stream of time and all of a sudden you find yourself
ashore, face to face with eternity. It is great fun to watch these
thinkers move ahead toward their castles in the air. Somewhere
en route they inevitably perform what to all intents and purposes resembles the famous Indian rope trick.

The solutions of the other group, which I should like to term
"immanentist," proceed the other way round. They repudiate
the conception of timelessness and any assumption of an ontological character. With them, historicity is a basic tenet which,
once adopted, precludes the recourse to eternal truths. So the
only possibility of salvaging the absolute is for the philosophers
of this denomination to place themselves in the immanence of
the historical process and bring historicity to its ultimate logical
conclusion. These more recent attempts begin to take shape
with Dilthey's desperate labors. He rejects the independent existence of timeless norms, purposes, or values,[12] and instead
champions "full recognition of the immanence in the historical
consciousness even of those values and norms which claim to be
absolute." [13] And he endeavors to show that generally valid
truths may grow out of history itself.

> "This," he says, "at first appears as an insoluble riddle.
> We must construct the whole from the parts, while only
> in the whole is to be found the element which imparts
> meaning and thus determines the position of a given part.
> But we already saw that this is what in fact moves history
> itself. . . . History itself creates values, whose validity
> derives from an explication of the conditions contained in
> life, as for example the sanctity of contract, or the recogni-
> tion of the dignity and worth in every individual, looked
> at as man. These truths are generally valid because, if
> applied in the historical world at any point, they will make
> a regulation possible.[14]

In another place he concludes that "not the relativity of
every view of the world is the last word of the mind that passed
through all of them, but its sovereignty against each of them,
and the positive knowledge of how in the plural attitudes of the
mind we have the one reality of the world given to us." [15] Comment on Dilthey's position: he is still immersed in the very
philosophical tradition he fights. This is also shown by his obsession with big schemes and arrangements. Croce and Collingwood, too, want to elicit the objective from the flow of time.
Building from, and exploiting, Dilthey, the Heidegger of *Sein
und Zeit* goes farthest in this direction; he postulates a historicity of being itself, thus radically uprooting the subject-object
relation, and the venerable notions of substance and essence in
its wake. (But radicalism is not necessarily a virtue; and of the
subject-object relation Hans Jonas judiciously says that it "is not
a lapse but the privilege, burden and duty of man." [16]) The immanentist trend which is at the bottom of existentialism has
spawned a partly syncretistic literature—e.g., Karl Mannheim's
1924 essay, *"Historismus,"* [17] with its borrowings from Dilthey,
Weber, etc., and its irrelevant classificatory finesse. Mannheim
rejects the recourse to the static absolute, endorsing the histori-
cist assumption that there is no absolute truth. Truths and
values can be grasped only in perspective. But we need not despair for that reason because we are justified in assuming that
each "truth" is the last word within its own concrete situation
and that the different perspectives form a hierarchy in the total
historical process.—It is evident that all solutions in this vein
must "absolutize" history in order to retrieve the absolute from
it. This is precisely what Gadamer does in his Heidegger-
influenced *Wahrheit und Methode*,[18] which amounts to a
smooth fusion of major immanentist motifs. Symptomatically, he
resumes Dilthey's emphasis on *Wirkungszusammenhaenge* and

Wirkungsgeschichte.[19] Indeed, with him, the nonexistentialist main current of immanentism comes to completion: he hallows historical continuity and sanctifies actual tradition without looking for truth criteria outside. But in this way history becomes a stuffy closed system which, in accordance with Hegel's dictum, "*What is real, is rational*," [20] shuts out the lost causes, the unrealized possibilities. History as a success story—Burckhardt would never have accepted the underlying assumptions of modern hermeneutics.

Historical relativity. All these solutions are fallacious. Their failure to deal effectively with the implications of historism must be traced to their reliance on an oversimplified notion of historical relativity. Both the transcendental epigones and the immanentists start from the premise that history is a continuity unfolding in homogeneous time. If this be the case, then indeed historical relativity becomes inescapable; and all efforts nevertheless to justify the quest of reason for absolutes, ontological or not, necessarily involve expedients, doubtful intellectual maneuvers.

However, as I have tried to show in Chapter 6, the traditional conception of historical time requires qualification. Because of the antinomy at its core, time not only conforms to the conventional image of a flow but must also be imagined as being not such a flow. We live in a cataract of times. And there are "pockets" and voids amidst these temporal currents, vaguely reminiscent of interference phenomena. This leads me to speak, in a provisional way, of the "limited" relativity of certain ideas emerging from such pockets. Historical relativity thus turns from a matter of course into a puzzling problem. What I have, in effect, said in Chapter 4 about historical ideas, e.g., Marx's or Burckhardt's,* certainly also holds for general philosophical

* See pages 99–103.

truths: they must be thought of as lying both inside and outside flowing time. Is their inherent claim to temporal exterritoriality justified? Or does their share in historical relativity invalidate any such claim?

Proposition. In posing these questions, I start out on a proposition which differs from the transcendental as well as the immanentist solutions. The former focus on a realm of absolute values and norms which they set apart and distinguish from all that is only temporal. Yet this distinction—which moreover implies that the absolute is of higher significance than the time-bound and relative—loses its meaning once the paradoxal nature of time is recognized. With the immanentists, on the other hand, the temporal so completely sucks up the absolute that it seems possible to eternalize the time-conditioned truths themselves. But if time is no longer conceived of as a continuous flow, this solution is untenable also.

From the angle of my proposition, philosophical truths have a double aspect. Neither can the timeless be stripped of the vestiges of temporality, nor does the temporal wholly engulf the timeless. Rather, we are forced to assume that the two aspects of truths exist side by side, relating to each other in ways which I believe to be theoretically undefinable.* Something like an analogy may be found in the "complementarity principle" of the quantum physicists. My assumption is that speculations on the total nature of the universe are called for, or indeed indispensable, as gambles in Kafka's sense.[21] They meaningfully enter the scene on (unpredictable) occasions and then presumably fulfill a vital function.

The co-existence of both aspects, so difficult to imagine, tends

---

* Here the category of *tact* comes in. Cf. later in this chapter the subsections "Co-existence," pages 205–06, and "The nameless," pages 214–16.

to imply that the seeming alternative of transcendentalism, with its penchant for the ontological, or immanentism, with its total acceptance of historicity and its affinity for existentialism, is no genuine alternative either. Even though they point in opposite directions, the two approaches will have to be thought together, the "side-by-side" replacing the "either-or." [22] Hence the problematic character of Loewith's attempt to get away from the consequences of historicity by sympathetically referring to ancient cosmology and all that it stands for; this is an escape into plain ontological transcendentalism rather than a timely answer to our present intellectual situation.[23] Similarly open to criticism is the reverse attempt—Adorno's unfettered dialectics which eliminates ontology altogether.[24] His rejection of any ontological stipulation in favor of an infinite dialectics which penetrates all concrete things and entities seems inseparable from a certain arbitrariness, an absence of content and direction in these series of material evaluations. The concept of Utopia is then necessarily used by him in a purely formal way, as a borderline concept which at the end invariably emerges like a *deus ex machina*. But Utopian thought makes sense only if it assumes the form of a vision or intuition with a definite content of a sort. Therefore the radical immanence of the dialectical process will not do; some ontological fixations are needed to imbue it with significance and direction.

And how are we to connect successive general truths with each other? If the emphasis is put on time as a homogeneous flow, such ideas as evolution and progress which establish contexts between chronologically successive phases are bound to gain momentum. Accordingly, Dilthey tries to ascertain the objectivity of the Geisteswissenschaften by assuming that relevant knowledge expands and advances in the historical process. If, conversely, chronological time is considered an empty vessel, the establishment of meaningful relations between successive truths becomes rather difficult. The same Dilthey who adopts the idea of progress [25] drops it as soon as he begins to doubt the magic of flowing time; then he prefers to speculate on "types of Weltanschauungen." [26] His wavering in this respect strikes me as profound. The two extremes between which he meanders are marked by Hegel's "world spirit" and Heidegger's "*Sein-koennen*" which swallows up all objectivity, and with it, one should think, all relationships between successive truths. As for the idea of progress (which feeds on a questionable analogy with the learning process) it reaches its full scope only if it is applied to history as a whole. But can it be applied in such a wholesale manner at all? Blumenberg, as we know, sees this application of it as the result of a forced adaptation of its limited original form (in which it had been restricted to theoretical processes and the area of aesthetics), to serve the heterogeneous, theological notion of eschatology. What happened was that the idea of progress "had to widen its originally limited . . . scope and overextend it . . . to answer a question which theology, having given virulence to it, had left behind, as it were, towering in the open, masterless and unsatiated." [27] Any definition of the inherent antithetic character of this concept (which follows from the double aspect of general truths) is doomed to failure. Here is a rather lopsided definition which I submit for what it is worth: the idea of progress presents itself differently from different periods whose succession may or may not amount to a progress.

Ideas and philosophical truths come closest to puncturing the screen that separates us from what we fathom to be Truth. The *coincidentia oppositorum*, which Cusa in *De visione Dei* called "the wall of paradise behind which dwells God," [28] does not materialize this side of the screen.

THE GENERAL AND THE PARTICULAR

The intellectual universe. The second issue of importance for
the constitution of the anteroom arises from the high generality
of all philosophical truths about man's ultimate concerns. It is
considered a matter of course that these truths (e.g., Kant's
categorical imperative) apply to all particulars they are supposed to cover. Do they?* Here is where my argument concerning the nonhomogeneous structure of the historical universe
comes in.† If meaningfully extended, this argument has a definite bearing on the issues at stake. In fact, the historical universe
is only a borderline case of the general intellectual universe. I
submit that what holds of the former is valid of the latter also.
Our intellectual universe is not homogeneous either; there are
no less traffic difficulties in it than in the historical orbit proper.
To get from "above" to "below"—from the philosophical abstractions, that is, down to the concrete insights formally falling
under them—one has to introduce numbers of new definitions as
he moves along. The constructions and expedients needed to apply the categorical imperative to an individual case are an example. Another is the evasiveness of stereotyped national images. They conform to reality in general but dissolve as soon as
one gets down to concrete cases. An analysis of their strange
evasiveness might prove rewarding. Also the relation of the general and the particular in the treatment and subject of Tilly's
Vendée which was analyzed in Chapter 1 ‡ should be compared
for this problem as it appears in the present context.

In sum, philosophical truths cover only insufficiently the expe-

* The theological idea of the living God is the *only* extremely high abstrac-
tion which admits of full concretion in every individual case.
† See Chapter 5, pages 122–27.
‡ See pages 29–31.

riences and occurrences they generalize. You may distill these truths from a variety of empirical observations (or arrive at them by fits and starts), but the return trip to the concretions requires many supplementary assumptions. The general does not fully encompass the particulars. (For this whole theory, see my *Soziologie als Wissenschaft;* [29] also Dilthey.[30])

Universal history. I should now elaborate on the intrinsic dialectic of this borderline concept which, like progress, belongs to both philosophy and history. Anglo-Saxon empiricism and positivism is important as a revolt against the "phantom" character of general metaphysics. These schools of thought side with the particular against the general—but at what costs! In this context, Kant is significant. In the treatise, *Idea of a Universal History from a Cosmopolitan Point of View,* he commends the cultivation of empirical history and stresses that to be "thoroughly versed" in it is a requirement for the philosophic mind, but explicitly maintains that this idea "is no doubt to a certain extent of an *a priori* character." [31] Kant predicts that exactly because of "the praiseworthy circumstantiality with which our history is now written" (in the end—for reasons which express the principle of mental economy, namely, "to cope with the burden of history as transmitted to them" *—) our "remote posterity . . . will surely estimate the history of the oldest times, of which the documentary records may have been long lost, only from the point of view of what interests them . . ." [32]

Proceeding from the antinomy of the general and the particular, I believe that universal history has become illegitimate if it does not recognize this basic antinomy of history. It is no longer legitimate to think "from above to below"—starting out, that is,

* For the principle of mental economy, see especially Chapter 1, page 22, and Chapter 5, page 130.

from some philosophic conception of universal history. With that approach, we would be in danger of becoming spellbound by ideas about the general. We must rather proceed "from below to above" to pursue these without harm. But particularly needed here is critical comment on the illusion that world history can be produced from "below" by compiling and unifying the results of historical research. This was anticipated by the criticisms of Lévi-Strauss and Valéry which were quoted in Chapter 5.* A fitting example for applying them would be the *Unesco World History,* of which Wittram correctly judges that it sets "a very wide frame, while no informing conception is to be discerned; none at any rate that is very convincing." [33]

Here a point should be made of a fact already mentioned †— that the idea of a universal history tends to call forth an existential approach to it, and that the existential genre stands the best chance of materializing when the whole of history comes into view. . . . The larger the scope of a narrative, the more urgently heuristic assumptions and unifying ideas suggest themselves. At the high altitudes reality recedes and man is alone with himself. . . . Or does then reality answer him? . . .

Co-existence. The kind of relation that actually obtains between the general and the particular carries an implication of great interest. To the extent that philosophical truths base their claim to highest significance on their inclusiveness, their applicability to the particular insights and facts by logical subsumption, this claim is illusory. It would be valid only if the particular could, so to speak, blindly be inferred from the general into whose orbit it falls. But this is not the case. There is no general definition of, say, beauty that would lead one straight to an appropri-

* See page 137.
† See page 75.

ate definition of the peculiar beauty of a specific work of art; that general definition exceeds the latter in range, while lagging behind it in fullness of meaning. To be sure, philosophical truths have a significance of their own, but they need not be significant in the sense of rules which decisively determine, let alone exhaust, the meaning of the subordinate particulars. Hence the futility of attempts to trace a syndrome of particular thoughts to some general concepts and passing these off as the "philosophy" behind that syndrome. The thoughts and notions of, say, a historian may not at all converge toward a philosophy. And if they converge, this philosophy need not be the fountainhead of his particular insights. The general truth and a pertinent concrete conception may exist side by side, without their relation being reducible to the fact that logically the abstraction implies the concretion. "Tact" is required to define this relation in each particular case.

In fact, the establishment of the general and the settling of the particular are two separate operations. Marquand in his novel, *Point of No Return*,[34] nicely satirizes their matter-of-course subsumption by sociologists and, I should like to add, philosophers. The protagonist of this novel is extremely puzzled when he finds out that the people who, in a sociological study of his hometown, are bracketed as members of the upper lower middle-class, the middle middle-class, etc., are the very same people whom he knew so well in his childhood days. His surprise at their unexpected identity highlights the relative irrelevancy of their logical alignment.—The saying that the exception confirms the rule is quite to the point—provided we understand by exception that which follows the rule.

BURCKHARDT

Before developing the consequences of these meditations for the
relations between the areas of philosophy and history, I wish
to present a model case of what may be called anteroom thinking and conduct. Burckhardt's opus reflects, somehow, the arguments offered here. Not as if he were aware of the theoretical
foundations upon which his procedures rest or indeed cared to
bring them into the open. But he responds to the phenomenon
of time and the uneven structure of the intellectual universe
with the accuracy of a seismograph, a sensitivity unsurpassed by
any modern historian.

Some of Burckhardt's attitudes and opinions might call for
criticism. His aversion to mass movements and revolutions as
well as his visions of the future caused him to take a rather one-
sided stand against the idea of progress, which does not fit into
the over-all picture.[35] Time and again he shows himself overwhelmed by the grandeur of the historical process. This accounts for his absurd large-scale teleological speculations, including his insistence that history tends to offer compensations
for ill-fortune and suffering. His terms of *Glück* and *Unglück,* as
was pointed out, fuse moral concern with aesthetic interest. On
occasion, he could seem an outspoken anti-Semite.[36] And he
praises war.[37] Here also belongs Burckhardt's worship of ge-
nius, connected with his loathing of any history featuring mass
movements as the sources of historical change. But all this
hardly reduces the significance of his practical recognition of the
antinomies that condition thought in the area of history.

Historicity in general. Here should be mentioned Burckhardt's
avowed amateur attitude toward history. Burckhardt ap-

proaches his material in a casual way. He is deliberately unsys-
tematic, repudiating anything that looks like a construction imposed from without. He somewhere declares that concepts and
periods must be kept fluid. He often ponders possibilities that
might have come true without deciding in favor of any of them.
Of the past he picks up what attracts and interests him, as he
strolls through the world of history; and he never accounts for
the reasons of his choices.

Even though he is of course a professional, Burckhardt behaves toward history like an amateur who follows his inclinations. But he does so because the professional in him is deeply
convinced that history is no science. The "archdilettante," as
Burckhardt calls himself in a letter,[38] would seem to be the only
type who can deal adequately with it. One knows of amateurs
who turn into professionals; here a professional insists on re-
maining an amateur for the sake of his particular subject matter.

Nor does he ever feel the slightest inhibition to pass value
judgments on individuals and events. And as an amateur,
Burckhardt is not only historical-minded but also profoundly
humane. He never forgets the individual and his suffering in the
course of events. He never hints of the blessings in the wake of
despotic rulers without mentioning that the crimes they committed in order to seize and solidify power can under no circumstances be justified. His humaneness is palpably grounded in
theology. But while being a Christian he is also moulded by his
classical heritage: hence his constant wavering between compassion for the defeated and admiration of world-historical
deeds.

Time. Burckhardt's ambiguity with regard to chronology and his
conception of the period have been discussed already. His sensi-
tiveness for the dialectics between chronological time and the

time shapes that thread history, his inclination to deal with meaningful patterns of events instead of exploring their chronology, and his sense of the incoherence of any period were referred to in those contexts.* It remains to point to his wavering between antiquarian and present interest. Although Burckhardt's declared intention is to relate only what "interests" him, he does not believe our conceptions of the past to be one-sidedly conditioned by our present needs. Burckhardt's achievement as a historian illustrates that the fact that everyone views the world from his present condition does not imply that his outlook is fully determined by the present world situation. Not all his concern for the past can be derived from contemporary apprehensions or despair at the catastrophies he foresees but he is driven to certain sections of the past also because he as a present person embraces the past for its own sake. "Anyway one should be capable," he says, "to turn temporarily completely away from interests to knowledge, because it is knowledge; especially what is historical one must be able to contemplate even though it may have no direct relation to our faring well or ill; and if it has such a relation, one yet should be able to look upon it objectively." [39] In a measure, his present concerns are identical with a compassionate urge to uncover lost causes in history. He not only views the past in the light of the present but turns to the present from a primary involvement in the past.

The general and the particular. Burckhardt no doubt endorses "absolutes"—e.g., his image of man and his belief in man's unchangeability; his (apparently somewhat philistine) worship of normalcy manifest in his writings on art with their bias in favor of Raphael as against Michelangelo's superhuman grandeur; [40] and not least his express effort to uphold the consciousness of

* See Chapter 6, pages 150–52 and 155, and Chapter 7, page 186.

(cultural) continuity, referred to below. But these standing motifs go together with a characterization of concrete events and figures as phenomena in their own right. His descriptions and profiles do not just illustrate his general views; rather, they often relate obliquely to them. In his introduction to a course of lectures on the time of the Thirty Years War which he gave in Basel in 1848, Burckhardt, as Kaegi relates, denied that the whole of that time could be rendered by one single term of great generality. (Kaegi supposes that Counter Reformation was the term Burckhardt had in mind at this occasion.) "Here it would be wrong to want to prove with utter precision and perhaps to comprise everything by one word," he said, ". . . The character and essence of the European mind wants to be touched at a thousand ends at a time." [41] The general and the particular here exist side by side in a way which would call for close analysis.

While explicitly repudiating universal history, Burckhardt nevertheless feels attracted by it. He deprecates "world-historical perspectives" [42] and speaks of the need of "being absolved from mere narration, which should be replaced by manuals." [43] Instead of a systematic approach, which he detests, he favors single observations of interest, cross sections, etc., as revealing "that which repeats itself, the constant and typical," which is "something which strikes a chord in us and which we understand." [44] Yet it seems that Burckhardt exempts general *cultural* histories, which in a particular way relate to the present, from his verdict on universal history. He in fact describes as his guiding idea "the movement of culture, the succession of levels of human formation both as it appears connected with the different peoples and nations and within the individual people or nation." To which he adds, as if by afterthought, that "Actually, one should especially emphasize those facts from

which threads reach into our own time and form of humanity." [45]

Burckhardt's dealings with philosophy and theology testify to
the same ambiguity or "fear of the fixed" (in which he resembles
Erasmus). Of philosophy of history, he remarks: "It is a centaur,
a contradiction in terms; for history is co-ordinating and hence
non-philosophy, philosophy subordinating and hence non-
history." [46] And of Hegel in particular he says that "This brisk
anticipation of a world plan leads to errors because it starts out
from incorrect premises—as we are not privy to and do not
know the purposes of eternal wisdom." [47] Yet, in spite of these
misgivings, he cannot help philosophizing à la Hegel on occasion [48] and recognizes a relationship to Hegel, as in a passage
noted by Wind: "All the same, we are deeply indebted to the
centaur, and it is a pleasure to come across him now and then
on the fringe of the forest of historical study." [49]

A like ambiguity as toward the philosophy of history obtains
with respect to theology. Even though he rejects theology,
Burckhardt sometimes indulges in outright absurd teleological
speculations, going so far as to invoke providence.

ANTEROOM THINKING

The objective. Only now am I in a position to approach my final
objective—a redefinition, and rehabilitation, of certain modes of
thinking peculiar to historians. Not to them alone. Their ways of
arguing and reflecting prevail throughout the area into which
history falls—an area which borders on the world of daily life—
the *Lebenswelt*—and extends to the confines of philosophy
proper. In it, which has all the traits of an intermediary area, we
usually concentrate not so much on the last things as on the last
before the last.

I speak of rehabilitation within this context because the categories which assume so vital a function in the area of history have long since been overshadowed by the impact of the philosophical tradition. From the philosopher's point of view, as I have tried to show in the opening sections of this chapter, this in-between area must be characterized as an anteroom. The statements made in it have not the kind of truth-value virtually inherent in philosophical statements. They lag behind them in terms of comprehensiveness; nor do they even aspire to the latter's binding power and range of validity. On the other hand, most historians feel uneasy about philosophy's claim to superior significance. The philosopher's approach, they feel, obscures the autonomous meaning and the legitimacy of their own endeavors.

In conjunction with my criticism of the concept of historicity, my argument concerning the nonhomogeneous structure of the intellectual universe can profitably be used for an adequate appraisal of typical anteroom modes of thought. To summarize the implications of this argument, philosophical truths do not fully cover the particulars logically subsumable under them. Their high generality notwithstanding, they are limited in scope. So the peculiar significance and dignity to which they attain at their own level does not necessarily impinge on the significance and dignity of many a less general view or judgment.

Matters of degree. Since, like the two aspects of time, the general and the particular are co-existent, hanging together in a manner difficult to make out, it becomes possible to upgrade the importance of differences in degree; as, for example, the degree of engagement which I stressed as decisive for differentiating "existential" and true histories in Chapter 3.* The philosopher is

* See pages 73–74.

likely to neglect these differences in differentiations which concern general principles rather than the phenomena seemingly encompassed by them. Once Croce and Collingwood have stated the undeniable truth that fact-finding involves interpretation and that, in consequence, pure facts are inaccessible to the historian, they believe to have said all there is to it.* So, with them, the factual evaporates. But they are only right on principle—which does not mean everything. What actually counts in this respect is the degree to which a historian is able to efface his self in his contacts with the given data. In defending Dutch historiography against the German approach of the time, Huizinga remarks that the German historian will often blame the Dutch for never following a problem up to its logical end. "Especially he will keenly feel the lack of clear-cut conclusions suitable for schematization." Huizinga, who naturally sides with Dutch laxity, explains this seeming shortcoming from the urge "of apprehending things not so much by schematic abstract concepts, but rather by an envisioning of them." [50] And commenting on Michelet's *"L'histoire c'est une resurrection"* and Taine's *"L'histoire c'est à peu près voir les hommes d'autrefois"* he says that what matters is the *à peu près*, the "more or less." It is a resurrection, he says, that "takes places in the sphere of the dream, a seeing of intangible figures, a hearing of half-understood words." [51] Taken with Huizinga's rehabilitation of the antiquarian interest in the same context,[52] this is one of the best definitions I have come across so far of the historians breakthrough into the realm of ideas. It shows Huizinga's awareness that his ideas transcend subjectivity even though they grow out of it, and thus disposes, at one stroke, of the quarrel about the share of subjectivity in the historian's knowledge. Indeed, a stopping mid-way may be ultimate wisdom in the anteroom.

* See Chapter 3, pages 63–64.

Hence throughout this book my concern with shades and approximations. In a similar sense, I have argued in my article, "The Challenge of Qualitative Content Analysis," [53] that the pseudo-scientific methodological strictness in which our social scientists indulge often proves less adequate to their particular subject-matter than the "impressionist" approach decried by them. Accuracy in the approximate is apt to exceed statistical elaborations in precision.

The nameless. Because of their generality and concomitant abstractness, philosophical truths tend to assume a radical character. They favor either-or decisions, develop a penchant for exclusiveness, and have a way of freezing into dogmas. Different philosophical doctrines resist attempts at mediation, just as a party championing some idea splits into two or more groups—which then oppose each other—once the different aspects of the common idea begin to assert themselves at the expense of the affinity which kept them together.[54] There seems nothing of consequence to be left in the interstices between these truths. Or rather, under the spell of the traditional belief in the all-encompassing significance of the high abstractions all that is left there is from the outset disparaged as eclectic syncretism, a compromise of a sort. (Was not Erasmus called a compromiser because of his wavering between Church dogma and Reformation?) This threatens to overshadow, or to cast unfounded suspicions on, potential truths whose only resemblance to bad compromises consists in their location in the gaps that separate from each other, say, Marx and the early socialists, planned economy and the economy of the "invisible hand," or whatever sharp-edged propositions may capture our imagination. The source of the hasty disparagement of such truths is the deep-rooted confidence in the unlimited range of the general. But this confidence is unjustified; the insight into the nonhomogeneous structure of the intellectual universe disposes of it. With acceptance of this insight the ground is prepared for a theoretical acknowledgment of the nameless possibilities that may be assumed to exist, and to wait for recognition, in the interstices of the extant doctrines of high generality.

How take cognizance of these hidden possibilities? Certainly not by trying to deduce them from those doctrines; any such attempt might indeed result in a compromise. Yet if the truths in the interstices cannot be won by way of deduction from an established conception or principle, they may well arise out of absorption in configurations of particulars. "If, however, this consciousness which . . . grew self-sufficient at some time comes to doubt itself," says Blumenberg in his *"Melanchthons Einspruch gegen Kopernikus,"* "then there appear, from out of the darkness in which history keeps those who failed, the contourless figures of those who contradicted; and even the small-minded, inflexible character who did not want to look through Galileo's telescope to see the forbidden sight of the moons of Jupiter may find late vindication by an eminent scholar's saying of him that to applaud him is by no means impossible for a reasonable being." [55] I have pointed out on earlier occasions that the general views emerging from a historical micro study need not be identical with those underlying a corresponding large-scale history.* In other words, if A moves from "above" to "below" and B in the reverse direction, the two will not necessarily meet somewhere in between or land at each other's starting point. An example is to be found in Marx, who, in his *Pariser Commune,* does not confine himself to a general definition of the petty bourgeoisie on which he then bases his whole analysis, but tries to characterize the petit bourgeois of the period inde-

* See Chapter 5, pages 126–27.

pendently of, and beyond, the general theoretical concept. Procedures of this kind you often find in remote places of his writings.[56] Hence, too, Kafka's "strange mixture of hopelessness and
a constructive will which did not in his case cancel each other
out but by their wrestling with each other were driven to rise
to infinitely complicated expressions" (Brod).[57] The difficulty of
deducing the truths in the interstices from the high-level
statements, principles, or doctrines under whose rule they
fall does not imply that they were sheer mirages. Sometimes that which is buried under an imposing either-or may
shine forth from a casual aperçu, written at the margin of a
close-up.

Sancho Panza. The "side-by-side" principle I have proposed
here would then apply to the relations between the timeless and
the temporal as well as to those of the general and the particular. What does this imply for historians and other inveterate
anteroom dwellers? It requires them to acknowledge the possible significance of philosophical truths with their claim to objective validity (which precludes Heidegger and his existentialist
aftercrop) and at the same time to be aware of their limitations
in terms of absoluteness and controlling power (which precludes any definite ontological position). Ambiguity is of the
essence in this intermediary area. A constant effort is needed on
the part of those inhabiting it to meet the conflicting necessities
with which they are faced at every turn of the road. They find
themselves in a precarious situation which even invites them to
gamble with absolutes, all kinds of quixotic ideas about universal truth. These peculiar preoccupations call forth specific attitudes, one of which appears to be particularly fitting because it
breathes a true anteroom spirit. It takes on shape in a letter
which Burckhardt wrote to Nietzsche about the latter's *Ver-*

mischte Meinungen und Sprueche. As condensed by Loewith, Burckhardt's letter includes the following passage: "As an 'indolent pilgrim,' he never penetrated, as is known, into the very temple of thought but all his life was content to entertain himself in the courts and halls of the Peribolos, being content to think in images; with a 'mixture of fear and pleasure' he therefore watched, where he dared not follow, how surely Nietzsche treaded on 'dizzying cliffs', trying to see in his imagination the things he might perceive deep down below and in the far distance." [58] On another occasion he calls philosophy of history "a sort of pastime." [59] Indeed the simple man in us would be lost in boredom and dreariness were it not for the queer and unverifiable speculations which he cannot help pondering on and on. There is something of an Epicurean about Burckhardt—of a Sancho Panza who calls to mind the image which Kafka draws of this memorable plain figure: "Without making any boast of it Sancho Panza succeeded in the course of years, by devouring a great number of romances of chivalry and adventure in the evening and night hours, in so diverting from him his demon, whom he later called Don Quixote, that his demon thereupon set out in perfect freedom on the maddest exploits, which, however, for the lack of a preordained object, which should have been Sancho Panza himself, harmed nobody. A free man, Sancho Panza philosophically followed Don Quixote on his crusades, perhaps out of a sense of responsibility, and had of them a great and edifying entertainment to the end . . ." [60] The definition which Kafka here gives of Sancho Panza as a *free man* has a Utopian character. It points to a Utopia of the in-between —a terra incognita in the hollows between the lands we know.

In Lieu of Epilogue

(From Notes of the Author)

Focus on the "genuine" hidden in the interstices between dog-matized beliefs of the world, thus establishing tradition of lost causes; giving names to the hitherto unnamed.

> . . . But as soon as a man with originality comes along, and consequently does not say: one must take the world as it is, but saying: whatever the world may be, I remain true to a simplicity which I do not intend to change according to the good pleasure of the world; the moment that word is heard, there is as it were a transformation in the whole of existence, as in the fairy story—when the word is said the magic castle, which has been under a spell for a hundred years, opens again and everything comes to life: in the same way existence becomes all eyes. The Angels grow busy, look about with curiosity to see what is going to happen, for that is what interests them. On the other side: dark and sinister demons who have sat idle for a long while gnawing their fingers—jump up, stretch their limbs: for, they say, "this is something for us." . . .[61]
>
> (Concerning: Genuineness)
> Kafka quoting Kierkegaard (Brod, Kafka, 180f., 1963)

Notes

CHAPTER 1

1. Cf., for instance, Droysen, *Historik*, Muenchen, 1960, pp. 17–18.
2. See Dilthey, *Gesammelte Schriften*, Stuttgart-Goettingen, 1957–62, vol. VII, pp. 70, 79, 82–3, 85, 90, 118, 131, and *passim*.
3. Rickert, *Die Probleme der Geschichtsphilosophie*, Heidelberg, 1924, p. 74, and *passim*.
4. Cf. for instance, the journal *History and Theory*, (The Hague); Gardiner, ed., *Theories of History*, Glencoe, Ill., 1959; Gottschalk, ed., *Generalization in the Writing of History*, Chicago, 1963, Hook, ed., *Philosophy and History*, New York, 1963.
5. Valéry, *History and Politics*, New York, 1962, vol. 10, pp. 11, 122.
6. Mommsen, "Historische Methode," in Besson, ed., *Geschichte* (Fischer Buecherei), Frankfurt a.M., 1961, pp. 79–80.
7. Bloch, *Apologie pour l'histoire ou métier d'historien*, Paris, 1964, p. xiv.
8. See Bagby, *Culture and History*, Berkeley and Los Angeles, 1959, pp. 48–50. Cf. also Bock, *The Acceptance of Histories: Toward a Perspective For Social Science*, Berkeley and Los Angeles, 1956, *passim*. For an exposition of the argument see Mink, "The Autonomy of Historical Understanding," *History and Theory* (Middletown, Conn., 1966) vol. V, no. 1, pp. 28–44.
9. For an early reference in this vein, see Kant's *Idee zu einer allgemeinen Geschichte in weltbuergerlicher Absicht;* English

translation in Gardiner (ed.), *Theories of History*, Glencoe, Ill., 1959, pp. 21–34.

10. Murray, *Five Stages of Greek Religion* (Anchor Book), New York, pp. xi, xii.
11. See Brooke, "Namier and Namierism," *History and Theory* (The Hague, 1964), Vol. III, no. 3: 338–9.
12. Dodds, *The Greeks and the Irrational*, Boston, 1957, p. 252.
13. See Schmidt, *Der Begriff der Natur in der Lehre von Marx*, Frankfurt a.M., 1962, pp. 39, 48, 50.
14. v. Weizsaecker, *Geschichte der Natur*, Goettingen, 1958, pp. 37–43.
15. Cf. Schmidt, op. cit., p. 48.
16. v. Weizsaecker, op. cit., p. 69.
17. See Kracauer, "Die Gruppe als Ideentraeger," in *Das Ornament der Masse*, Frankfurt a.M., 1963, p. 141.
18. For this paragraph, see Kracauer, ibid., *passim*.
19. Dodds, op. cit., p. 243, exemplifies the long survival of religious rites, quoting Matthew Arnold's happy phrase of the "extreme slowness of things."
20. Plato, *Republic*, 496 d. (Quoted by Murray, op. cit., pp. 79–80.)
21. Tocqueville, *Souvenirs de Alexis de Tocqueville*, Paris, 1893, p. 36.
22. Klapper, *The Effects of Mass Communication*, Glencoe, Ill., 1960, discusses at length the findings of contemporary social-science research regarding regularities in the formation and transmission of opinions.
23. See McPhee, *Formal Theories of Mass Behavior*, Glencoe, Ill., 1963.
24. Mentioned by Butterfield, *Man on His Past . . .* , Boston, 1960, pp. 138–9.
25. After having stated that power is evil and that those wielding it are least interested in culture, Burckhardt, *"Weltgeschichtliche Betrachtungen,"* in *Jacob Burckhardt Gesamtausgabe*, Stuttgart, Berlin & Leipzig, vol. VII, 1929, p. 73, continues: "But he who wants power and wants culture—perhaps they both are blind tools of a third, still unknown." By the way, Butterfield, *Christianity and History* (Scribner's paperback), New York, p. 109, compares this unknown "intelligence" to a "composer . . . who composes the music as we go along . . ."
26. Quoted by Gadamer, *Wahrheit und Methode*, Tuebingen, 1960,

p. 192, from Ranke, *Weltgeschichte*, IX, p. xiii f.—Butterfield, *Man on His Past* . . . , Boston, 1960, p. 106, refers to the same Ranke statement.

27. v. Weizsaecker, op. cit., pp. 115–116.

28. See Kracauer, *Theory of Film* . . . , New York, 1960, pp. 66–67.

29. In keeping with this argument, Jonas, *Gnosis und spaetantiker Geist*, vol. I, Goettingen, 1964, pp. 58–64, insists that certain historical phenomena prove inaccessible to psychological and sociological explanations. Thus he says about the emergence of the Gnostic *"Seinshaltung"* in late antiquity: "What concerns us here is the 'remainder' a priori left in the calculus of empirical factors, however plausible the 'motivations' that can be derived from them: that integral principle of meaning which, conditioned and conditioning at once, already determines the conversion of those factors in the new spiritual context: that, in short, which cannot be 'explained' at all, but can only be 'understood' as one whole disclosure of human being at this moment in history". (loc. cit., p. 62; English translation for this quotation by Jonas).

30. See Tilly, "The Analysis of a Counter-Revolution," *History and Theory* (The Hague, 1963), vol. III, no. 1: 30–58. (Tilly's study has meanwhile been expanded into a book: *The Vendée*, Cambridge, Mass., 1964).

31. Burckhardt, op. cit., p. 26. Cf. also Croce, *History: Its Theory and Practice*, New York, 1960, I, p. 102; II, p. 291.

32. Hexter, *Reappraisals in History*, Evanston, Ill., 1961, p. 21. Gallie, "The Historical Understanding," *History and Theory* (The Hague, 1963), vol. III, no. 2: 169, too declares "that history is a species or special application of the genre story." But not unlike Dilthey—to be precise, the Kantian in Dilthey—he seems to conceive of the difference between history and science mainly as a difference in modes of approach.

33. Hexter, op. cit., p. 39.

34. Cf. Blumenberg, " 'Saekularisation', Kritik einer Kategorie historischer Illegitimitaet," in Kuhn and Wiedmann, eds., *Die Philosophie und die Frage nach dem Fortschritt*, Muenchen, 1964, pp. 204–65, *passim*. See also Jauss, "Ursprung und Bedeutung der Fortschrittsidee in der 'Querelle des Anciens et des Modernes,' " ibid., pp. 51–72, *passim*.

35. Cf. Schmidt, op. cit., p. 39.

36. Cf., for instance, Hexter, op. cit., pp. 15–16. For a similar criticism of Comte, see Bury, *The Idea of Progress* . . . , New York, 1955, pp. 302–3.

37. Dilthey, *Gesammelte Schriften,* vol. I, p. 107.

38. Cf. Lowe, *On Economic Knowledge,* New York, 1965, pp. 192–3. Carr, *What Is History?,* New York, 1962, p. 90.

39. For a qualification of this statement with respect to Marx, see Schmidt, "Zum Verhaeltnis von Geschichte und Natur im dialektischen Materialismus," in *Existentialismus und Marxismus,* Frankfurt a.M., 1965, p. 123.

40. Quoted from Spengler, "The World-as-History," in Gardiner, ed., *Theories of History,* op. cit., p. 194.

41. Frankfort, "The Dying God," *Journal of the Warburg and Courtauld Institutes* (London, 1958), vol. XXI, nos. 3–4: 151.

42. For this particular point, see Frankfort, *The Birth of Civilization in the Near East* (Anchor Book), New York, pp. 17–18.

43. See, for instance, Toynbee, *Reconsiderations,* London, 1961, p. 238.

44. Jonas, op. cit., pp. 73–74, praises Spengler for having discovered "Arabic" culture and introduced the concept of "pseudo-morphosis" to account for its destinies in a world dominated by Greek culture.

45. Mink, "The Autonomy of Historical Understanding," *History and Theory* (Middletown, Conn., 1966), vol. V, no. 1: 35, points out that "the history of natural science is not wanting either in examples of false theories which led to happy discoveries."

46. Cf., for instance, Dilthey, *Gesammelte Schriften,* vol. VII, pp. 70–71, where he defines the *Geisteswissenschaften* as follows: "They are all founded in experience, in the expressions for experiences, and in the understanding of these expressions,"—Or ibid., p. 131: "The total of what appears to us in experience and understanding is life, as a nexus encompassing the human species."

47. Huizinga, "The Task of Cultural History," in *Men and Ideas: Essays by Johan Huizinga,* New York, 1959, p. 54, in an admirable passage calls the historian's contact with the past "an entry into an atmosphere, . . . one of the many forms of reaching beyond oneself, of experiencing truth, which are given to man."—Berlin, "History and Theory: The Concept of Scientific History," *History and Theory* (The Hague, 1960), vol.

I, no. 1: 23, claims that the historian should offer us "something full enough and concrete enough to meet our conception of public life . . . seen from as many points of view and at as many levels as possible, including as many components, factors, aspects, as the widest and deepest knowledge, the greatest analytical power, insight, imagination, can present."

48. Quoted from Reinhold Niebuhr, "The Diversity and Unity of History," in Meyerhoff, ed., *The Philosophy of History in Our Time*, Garden City, N.Y., 1959, p. 315.

49. See quote from Berlin, cited in n.46.

CHAPTER 2

1. Kristeller, "Some Problems of Historical Knowledge," *The Journal of Philosophy* (New York, Feb. 16, 1961), vol. LVIII, no. 4: 87.

2. Quoted by Blumenberg, "Das Fernrohr und die Ohnmacht der Wahrheit," p. 45, from Husserl, *Die Krisis der europaeischen Wissenschaften. . .* , Den Haag, 1962, p. 448. The original text reads: ". . . die Wissenschaft schwebt so wie in einem leeren Raum ueber der Lebenswelt."

3. See Loewith, *Jacob Burckhardt . . .* , Luzern, 1936, p. 274.

4. Cf. Alfred Schmidt, *Der Begriff der Natur in der Lehre von Marx*, Frankfurt a.M., 1962, p. 27.

5. Cf. Mandelbaum, *The Problem of Historical Knowledge . . .* , New York, 1936, *passim*. He assumes "that events in the real world"—meaning historical reality—"possess a determinate structure of their own, which is apprehended, but not transformed, by the mind" (p. 239). The unmitigated realism underlying this statement is one of Mandelbaum's chief arguments against historical relativism.

6. Cf. C. J. Hempel, "Explanation in Science and in History," see William Dray, ed., *Philosophical Analysis and History*, New York, London, 1966, pp. 95–126, *passim;* Ernest Nagel, "Determinism in History," *ibid.* pp. 347–82, *passim*.

7. Quoted from Butterfield, *Man on His Past . . .* , Boston, 1960, p. 60.

8. Vossler, "Rankes historisches Problem," in Vossler, *Geist und Geschichte*, Muenchen, 1964, pp. 189–90. My translation.

9. Butterfield, op. cit., p. 104.

10. Quoted from Stern, ed., *The Varieties of History*, New York, 1956, p. 57. Translated by the editor.

11. Gooch, *History and Historians in the Nineteenth Century*, Boston, 1959, p. 74. Gooch, ibid., pp. 74–75, calls Ranke's book "a convenient summary of the main external facts," offering little interpretation; and he relates that "half a century later he [Ranke] was only persuaded with difficulty to include it in his collected works." Vossler, op. cit., especially pp. 190–91, elaborates on the implications of Ranke's desire to show "wie es eigentlich gewesen;" he emphasizes that Ranke neither approved of a "pure" history which exhausts itself in the "photographic" recording of the facts nor rejected an "immanent" philosophy of history—one that grows out of intimate familiarity with the given data instead of being imposed upon them from without.

12. Heine, *Lutezia, Sämtliche Werke*, vol. 9, Leipzig, 1910, p. 9.

13. To the extent that the following pages deal with the photographic media, they are based on material drawn mainly from the first two chapters of my book, *Theory of Film* . . . , New York, 1960.

14. Quoted from Gay-Lussac's speech in the French House of Peers, July 30, 1839, by Eder, *History of Photography*, New York, 1945, p. 242.

15. Quoted by Eder, ibid., p. 341.

16. Quoted by Sadoul, *L'Invention du cinéma, 1832–1897*, Paris, 1946, p. 246.

17. Quoted from Gay-Lussac's speech of July 30, 1839, by Eder, op. cit., p. 242.

18. See Freund, *La Photographie en France au dix-neuvième siècle* . . . , Paris, 1936, pp. 117–19.

19. For an analysis of Proust's approach to photography, see Kracauer, *Theory of Film* . . . , New York, 1960, pp. 14–15.

20. Droysen, *Historik* . . . , Muenchen, 1960, p. 285, says: ". . . The narrative presentation does not want to give a picture, a photography of that which once was . . . but our apperception of important events from that standpoint, from that point of view.

21. Namier, *Avenues of History*, London, 1952, p. 8.

22. Bloch, *Apologie pour l'histoire*, Paris, 1964, p. 72.

23. Quoted by Freund, op. cit., p. 103.

24. See Marrou, *De la connaissance historique*, Paris, 1962, p. 53.

25. See Newhall, *The History of Photography* . . . , New York, 1949, p. 71.

26. Ibid., pp. 75–6; Freund, op. cit., p. 113.

27. The experimental photographer Andreas Feininger, "Photographic Control Processes", *The Complete Photographer* (New York, 1942), vol. 8, issue 43: 2802, bluntly states that the goal of photography is "not the achievement of highest possible 'likeness' of the depicted subject, but the creation of an abstract work of art, featuring composition instead of documentation."

28. For an analysis of the French *avant-garde* of the 'twenties and early 'thirties, see Kracauer, op. cit., pp. 177–92.

29. Cf. Geyl, "Huizinga as Accuser of His Age, "*History and Theory* (The Hague, 1963), vol. II, no. 3: 231–62, *passim;* esp. pp. 241–45, 257.

30. Ibid., p. 262.

31. Kracauer, op. cit., pp. 12–13.

32. Quoted by Newhall, op. cit., p. 144, from John A. Tennant's 1921 review of a New York Stieglitz exhibition.

33. Quoted, ibid., p. 150, from an article by the photographer Paul Strand in *Seven Arts*, 1917, vol. 2, pp. 524–25.

34. Quoted from Stern, ed., *The Varieties of History*, New York, 1956, p. 57.

35. Cf. Panofsky, *Renaissance and Renascences in Western Art*, Stockholm, 1960, pp. 84, 87 ff.

36. Quoted from Caillois, "Le Cinéma, le meurtre et la tragédie," *Revue internationale de filmologie*, vol. II, no. 5 (Paris, n.d.), p. 87.

37. *Conversations-Lexikon der Gegenwart*, Brockhaus, Leipzig, 1840, Bd. 4. Article: "Raumer, Friedrich von". (Author's initials unidentifiable.) I am greatly indebted to Prof. Reinhart Koselleck for having brought to my attention this early reference to the relationships between historiography and photography.

38. See Sève, "Cinéma et méthode," *Revue internationale de filmologie* (Paris, July–Aug. 1947), vol. I, no. 1: 45; see also pp. 30–31.

CHAPTER 3

1. Burckhardt, *Die Kultur der Renaissance in Italien*, Wien (Phaidon Verlag), p. 1.

2. Cf. Berlin, "History and Theory . . . ," *History and Theory* (The Hague, 1960), vol. I, no. 1: 27.

3. See Croce, *History: Its Theory and Practice*, New York, 1960, p. 19.
4. Ibid. p. 12.
5. Collingwood, *The Idea of History*, New York, 1956. (A Galaxy Book) See, for instance, p. 305.
6. Ibid. p. 282 ff.
7. Cf. ibid. pp. 328–34.
8. Croce, op. cit. p. 25.
9. Cf., for example, Marrou, "Comment comprendre le métier d'historien," in Samaran, ed., *L'Histoire et ses méthodes*, Paris, 1961, p. 1505; Carl L. Becker, "What Are Historical Facts?" in Meyerhoff, ed., *The Philosophy of History in Our Time*, Garden City, N.Y., 1959, p. 133; etc.
10. Carr, *What is History?*, New York, 1962, p. 54. Incidentally, Carr goes to the limit, or rather beyond it, in following his own advice; he sees fit to derive certain changes in outlook which the Meinecke of 1907 underwent in the 'twenties and 'thirties from the simultaneous short-term changes of his political environment (ibid. pp. 48–49). With Carr, the historian is not only the son of his time but the chameleon-like offspring of fractions of it.
11. Butterfield, *Man on His Past . . .*, Boston, 1960, p. 25.
12. Collingwood, op. cit. p. 229.
13. Gooch, *History and Historians in the Nineteenth Century*, Boston, 1959, p. 21.
14. Marrou, op. cit. p. 1506.
15. Cf. Carr, op. cit. p. 44, and Gooch, op. cit. p. 461.
16. Quoted by Gooch, ibid. p. 461.
17. Marc Bloch, *Feudal Society*, Chicago, 1964, vol. 2, p. 307.
18. Finley, *Thucydides*, University of Michigan Press, 1963, p. 74.
19. Quoted from Hexter, *Reappraisals in History*, Evanston, Ill., 1961, p. 2. For the reference to Maitland and Stubbs, I am indebted to Prof. Sigmund Diamond.
20. In his "Foreword" to Hexter's *Reappraisals . . .*, Prof. Laslett (Trinity College, Cambridge) raises a question which points in this direction. He asks "whether the whole enterprise of accounting for the dramatic events of the middle of the seventeenth century in England is not to some extent misconceived. Is it right to assume, as always seems to be assumed, that a long-term, overall explanation is necessariliy called for? And he adds

that "it may not be justifiable . . . to suppose that great events have great causes." (p. xiii)

21. Personal information by Prof. France V. Scholes, who kindly permitted me to make use of it.

22. Collingwood, op. cit. pp. 269–70.—Blumenberg, "Das Fernrohr und die Ohnmacht der Wahrheit," p. 21, emphasizes Galileo's aggressiveness as a scientist. He, the "founder of natural science"(p. 73), says Blumenberg, "is not the man who would simply look at things and patiently give himself up to his object; what he preceives always foreshadows the contexts of a theory, bears on the complex of theses comprising it." (My translation.)

23. Collingwood, op. cit. pp. 243, 266–68.

24. Ibid. p. 281.

25. MacDonald, *Murder Gone Mad,* New York, 1965, p. 39. (An Avon Book)

26. Collingwood, op. cit. pp. 304–5.

27. Cf. Lord Acton's remarks on this subject, as quoted by Butterfield, *Man on His Past* . . . , Boston, 1960, p. 220. See also Marrou, "Comment comprendre le métier d'historien," in Samaran, ed., *L'Histoire et ses méthodes,* Paris, 1961, p. 1521.

28. Ratner, "History as Inquiry," in Hook, ed., *Philosophy and History,* New York, 1963, p. 329.

29. Valéry, *History and Politics,* New York, 1962, p. 8. (Cf. also Valéry, *Oeuvres,* II, Pléiade, 1960, p. 917: *"L'histoire alimente l'histoire."*)

30. Nietzsche, Friedrich, "Vom Nutzen und Nachteil der Historie fuer das Leben," *Unzeitgemaesse Betrachtungen, Zweites Stueck,* Leipzig, 1930, p. 137.

31. Ibid. p. 156.

32. Ibid. p. 177.

33. Cf. Aron, *Dimensions de la conscience historique,* Paris, 1961, p. 13.

34. Burckhardt, "Historische Fragmente aus dem Nachlass," in *Jacob Burckhardt Gesamtausgabe,* Bd. VII, Stuttgart, Berlin und Leipzig, 1929, p. 225.

35. For instance, Droysen, *Historik,* Muenchen, 1960, p. 306, identifies the "didactic presentation" as a legitimate form of historical narrative and declares it to be its objective "to apprehend the essence and sum total of the past from the stand-

point reached here and now, and . . . to explain and to deepen that which is, and is earned, in the present by its past becoming."

36. Meinecke, "Historicism and Its Problems," in Stern, ed., *The Varieties of History* . . . , New York, 1956 (A Meridian Book), pp. 267–88. For the quote, see ibid. p. 411, note 14.

37. Marc Bloch, *The Historian's Craft,* New York, 1959, pp. 65–66. The original reads: "Naturellement il le faut, ce choix raisonné des questions, extrêmement souple . . . . L'itinéraire que l'explorateur établit, au départ, il sait bien d'avance qu'il ne le suivra pas de point en point." Bloch, *Apologie pour l'histoire ou métier d'historien,* 5th ed., Paris, 1964, p. 26.

38. Max Weber's "ideal-types" give rise to exactly the same doubts.

39. Turning against the followers of the Croce-Collingwood school of thought, Hexter, op. cit. p. 8 n., defines this difference with unsurpassable clarity: "I do not for a moment intend to imply that current dilemmas have not suggested *problems* for historical investigation. It is obvious that such dilemmas are among the numerous and entirely legitimate points of origin of historical study. The actual issue, however, has nothing to do with the point of origin of historical studies, but with the mode of treatment of historical problems."

40. See Burckhardt, "Weltgeschichtliche Betrachtungen," in Jacob *Burckhardt Gesamtausgabe,* Band VII, Stuttgart, Berlin und Leipzig, 1929, p. 13.

41. Cf., for instance, Geyl, *Debates with Historians,* New York, 1958 (A Meridian paperback), pp. 196 and 221; Bury, *The Ancient Greek Historians,* New York, 1958 (A Dover paperback), pp. 246–7; Marrou, "Comment comprendre le métier d'historien," in Samaran, ed., *L'Histoire et ses méthodes,* Paris, 1961, pp. 1505, 1506; Raymond Aron, *Dimensions de la conscience historique,* Paris, 1961, pp. 24 and 11, 13, 172.

42. Burckhardt, op. cit. p. 206, values highly "unsere unerfuellte Sehnsucht nach dem Untergegangenen."

43. Huizinga, *Im Bann der Geschichte* . . . , Basel, 1943, p. 92.

44. See John Brooke about Namier, as quoted by Mehta, "The Flight of Crook-Taloned Birds," *The New Yorker,* Dec. 15, 1962, p. 93.

45. Harnack, *History of Dogma,* New York, 1961 (Dover books), vol. I, p. 39.

46. Lovejoy, "Present Standpoints and Past History," in Meyerhoff,

ed., *The Philosophy of History in Our Time,* Garden City, N.Y., 1959, p. 174.
47. Ibid. p. 180.—Geyl, op. cit. p. 196, expresses himself in a similar vein.
48. For an analogy to this phenomenon in the domain of film, see Kracauer, *Theory of Film* . . . , New York, 1960, pp. 151–52 (under the title: "Music recaptured").
49. Rostovtzeff, *The Social and Economic History of the Roman Empire,* Oxford, 1926, p. 541.
50. Proust, *Remembrance of Things Past,* New York, 1932 and 1934, vol. I, pp. 543–45.
51. Graves, *The Greek Myths,* Baltimore, Maryland, 1955, vol. I, p. 112.

CHAPTER 4

1. See Stern, "Introduction," in Stern, ed., *The Varieties of History* (a Meridian Book), New York, 1956, p. 31.
2. Geyl, *Debates With Historians* (a Meridian Book), New York, 1958, pp. 39–40.—As might be expected, opinions on Macaulay are divided. For instance, Hale, "Introduction," in Hale, ed., *The Evolution of British Historiography* (a Meridian Book), Cleveland and New York, 1964, p. 45, praises him precisely for his inquisitiveness as a traveler.
3. Cf. Gadamer, *Wahrheit und Methode,* Tuebingen, 1960, p. 198.
4. Vossler, "Rankes historisches Problem," in Vossler, *Geist und Geschichte* . . . Muenchen, 1964, pp. 194–95, strongly emphasizes the religious foundations of Ranke's approach.
5. See Dilthey, *Gesammelte Schriften,* Stuttgart-Goettingen, vol. V, 1957 & 1961, pp. 281, 281–82, n.—To mention a recent comment on this Ranke statement, Gerhard Ritter, "Scientific History . . . ," *History and Theory* (The Hague, 1961), vol. I, no. 3: 265, endorses it in glowing terms, obviously with a view to disparaging the indulgence in constructions and the over-aggressiveness of certain contemporary historians. (Ritter's paper was originally published in Germany in 1958.)
6. Proust, *Remembrance of Things Past,* New York, 1932 and 1934, vol. I, pp. 814–15. (Translated by C. K. Scott Moncrieff.) —Cf. also Kracauer, *Theory of Film* . . . , New York, 1960, pp. 14–15.

7. Cf. Schuetz, "The Stranger," *The American Journal of Sociology* (May 1944), vol. XLIX, no. 6: 499–507.
8. Quoted from Toynbee, ed. and transl., *Greek Historical Thought* (a Mentor Book), New York, 1952, p. 43.—It goes without saying that Polybius is another case in point. See, for instance, Bury, *The Ancient Greek Historians* (a Dover Book), New York, 1958, pp. 191–219.
9. When interviewed by Mehta, John Brooke and Toynbee expressed themselves in this sense. See Mehta, "The Flight of Crook-Taloned Birds," *The New Yorker*, Dec. 15, 1962, pp. 74, 82.—Within this context Burckhardt's reference to the frequent incidence of emigrants in the Italy of the Renaissance and his emphasis on their great achievements seem of special interest to me. See Burckhardt, *Die Kultur der Renaissance in Italien*, Phaidon Verlag, Wien, p. 78, und Kaegi, *Jacob Burckhardt: Eine Biographie*, vol. III, Basel, 1956, p. 715.
10. Schopenhauer, *Saemtliche Werke*, Wiesbaden, 1949, vol. 2 ("Die Welt als Wille und Vorstellung", drittes Buch, Kap. 34), pp. 464–65, says: "Vor ein Bild hat jeder sich hinzustellen wie vor einen Fuersten, abwartend, ob und was es zu ihm sprechen werde; und, wie jenen, auch dieses nicht selbst anzureden: denn da wuerde er nur sich selber vernehmen."
11. Cf. Bailyn, "The Problems of the Working Historian: A Comment," in Hook, ed., *Philosophy and History*, New York, 1963, p. 98.
12. Marc Bloch, *The Historian's Craft*, New York, 1959, p. 65–66.
13. Mills, *The Sociological Imagination*, New York, 1959, p. 196.
14. Quoted by Willey, *The Seventeenth Century Background* (a Doubleday Anchor Book), Garden City, New York, 1953, p. 43.
15. Burckhardt, *Griechische Kulturgeschichte* (Kroeners Taschenausgabe, Baende 58, 59, 60), Leipzig, Band 58, pp. 7-8. The passage reads as follows: ". . . gerade mit heftiger Anstrengung ist hier das Resultat am wenigsten zu erzwingen: ein leises Aufhorchen bei gleichmaessigem Fleiss fuehrt weiter."—See also Loewith, *Jacob Burckhardt . . .* , Luzern, 1936, pp. 186-87.
16. Harnack, *History of Dogma* (Dover Books), New York, 1961, Book I, vol. 1, pp. 37–8, judiciously observes: ". . . the historian falls into vagueness as soon as he seeks and professes to find behind the demonstrable ideas and aims which have moved a period, others of which, as a matter of fact, that period

itself knew nothing at all." (Translated from the third German edition by Neil Buchanan.)

17. Droysen, *Historik* . . . , Muenchen, 1960, p. 245.

18. In a letter of March 30, 1870, Burckhardt writes to Bernhard Kugler: "Ich rathe ferner zum einfachen Weglassen des blossen Tatsachenschuttes—nicht aus dem Studium, wohl aber aus der Darstellung." Quoted from Max Burckhardt, sel. and ed., *Jacob Burckhardt: Briefe,* Bremen, 1965, p. 275.

19. Butterfield, "Moral Judgments in History," in Meyerhoff, ed., *The Philosophy of History in Our Time* (a Doubleday Anchor Book), Garden City, New York, 1959, p. 229.—The excerpt is drawn from Butterfield, *History and Human Relations,* London, 1931.

20. Butterfield, *Man On His Past* (a Beacon Book), Boston, 1960, p. 139.

21. Ibid., p. 139.

22. Quoted by Kracauer, *Theory of Film* . . . , New York, 1960, p. 202, from Ivens, "Borinage—A Documentary Experience," *Film Culture* (New York, 1956), vol. II, no. 1: 9.

23. Butterfield, "Moral Judgments . . ." (see note 19), p. 244, alludes to this possibility when he says that the (technical) historian may assist the cause of morality by describing, in concrete detail and in an objective manner, a wholesale massacre, the consequences of religious persecution, or the goings-on in a concentration camp. For the rest, Butterfield's idea of technical history itself originates in an intricate mixture of theological and scientific notions.

24. Strauss, "On Collingwood's Philosophy of History," *The Review of Metaphysics* (Montreal, June 1952), vol. V, no. 4: 583.

25. Quoted from Hale, "Introduction" (see note 2), p. 42, where he cites a letter of Carlyle to John Stuart Mill in which Carlyle writes: History "is an address (literally out of Heaven, for did not God order it all?) to our *whole* inner man; to every faculty of Head and Heart, from the deepest to the slightest . . . "

26. Dilthey, *Gesammelte Schriften,* Stuttgart—Goettingen, vol. VII, 1958 & 1961, p. 164, writes: "Relish in the art of narration, probing explanation, application of systematic knowledge to it, analysis into particular causal nexuses and the principle of development, these elements combine, re-enforcing each other." —Cf. also Berlin, "History and Theory . . . ," *History and*

Theory (The Hague, 1960), vol. I, no. 1: 24, where he expresses himself in a similar vein.

27. See, for instance, Kolko, "Max Weber on America: Theory and Evidence," *History and Theory* (The Hague, 1961), vol. I, no. 3: 243–60, *passim*, esp. pp. 259–60.

28. Cf., for example, Blumenberg, *Die Kopernikanische Wende,* Frankfurt a.M., 1965, and his *Paradigmen zu einer Metaphorologie,* Bonn, 1960.—I should also mention that Jonas, *Gnosis und spaetantiker Geist,* vols. I and II, Goettingen, 1964 and 1954, offers outstanding examples of historico-morphological analysis.

29. Graves, *I, Claudius* (a Vintage Book), New York, 1961, p. 116.

30. Berlin, "History and Theory . . ." (see note 26), p. 24.—For similar references to the importance of wide human experience, see Marrou, *De la connaissance historique,* Paris, 1962, pp. 79–80 (where he mistakenly ascribes Graves' "boutade": "History is an old man's game" to the emperor Claudius); Hexter, *Reappraisals in History,* Northwestern University Press, 1961, pp. 43, 199.

31. See the quote in Loewith, *Jacob Burckhardt,* Luzern, 1936, p. 188: "No reference work in the world can replace with its quotes that chemical compound into which a proposition found by ourselves enters with our divining and our attentiveness, so that a real intellectual property is formed." Loewith quotes from *Gesamtausgabe,* Basel, 1929–33, vol. 8, p. 8.

32. Berlin, op. cit., p. 24.

33. Huizinga, "The Task of Cultural History," in Huizinga, *Men and Ideas* (a Meridian Book), New York, 1959, pp. 53–4.

34. Aydelotte, "Notes on the Problem of Historical Generalization," in Gottschalk, ed., *Generalization in the Writing of History,* Chicago, 1963, p. 167.

35. See Festugière, *La Révélation d'Hermès Trismégiste.* Vol. I: *L'Astrologie et les sciences occultes,* Paris, 1944, pp. 7, 356.

36. For comment on the range of validity of historical generalizations, see, for instance, Dilthey, *Gesammelte Schriften,* vol. VII (see note 26), p. 188, where he deals with the formation of concepts in the *Geisteswissenschaften.* "Here, the formation of concepts," he says," is . . . not a simple generalization which obtains from a series of particular cases that which is common to them. The concept expresses a *type*."—Cf. also Benjamin, "Ursprung des deutschen Trauerspiels," in Benjamin, *Schriften,*

Frankfurt a.M., 1955, vol. I, pp. 141–365. In the "Erkennt-niskritische Vorrede" to this treatise (pp. 141–74) Benjamin emphatically insists on the difference between "generalization" and "idea." See esp. pp. 155–64.

37. See Hexter, *Reappraisals in History* (see note 30), pp. 202, 204.

38. Huizinga, "Renaissance and Realism," in Huizinga, *Men and Ideas* . . . (a Meridian Book), New York, 1959, p. 288.

39. Huizinga, "The Problem of the Renaissance," in Huizinga, op. cit. p. 287.

40. Personal communication by Prof. P. O. Kristeller.

41. Huizinga, "Renaissance and Realism" (see note 37), pp. 288–89. Speaking of the masters whom Burckhardt has joined, Huizinga says that "one no longer asks what the opinions of such men were but what their spirit is."

42. Berlin, *Karl Marx: His Life and Environment* (a Galaxy Book), New York, 1959, pp. 43–44.

43. Berlin, "History and Theory . . . (see note 26), p. 24.

44. Bultmann, *History and Eschatology* . . . (a Harper Torch-book), New York, 1962, p. 122.

CHAPTER 5

1. Aron, *Dimensions de la conscience historique*, Paris, 1961, p. 19.

2. Even though Toynbee admits the necessity of micro history, for which see the excursus on the "quantity problem," pp. 125–28 his emotional prejudice against it is very strong indeed. Mehta, "The Flight of Crook-Taloned Birds," *The New Yorker*, Dec. 8, 1962, p. 92, reports that, in a conversation with him, Toynbee "comforted himself with the thought that the days of the microscope historians are probably numbered."

3. Jedin, *Bischöfliches Konzil oder Kirchenparlament?* Basel, 1963.

4. Hexter, "The Education of the Aristocracy in the Renaissance," in Hexter, *Reappraisals in History*, Evanston, Ill., 1961, pp. 45–70.

5. Tolstoy, *War and Peace*, Baltimore, 1951, vol. II, pp. 1400–1401.

6. Ibid., p. 1425.—Cf. Berlin, *The Hedgehog and the Fox*, New York, 1953, pp. 19, 26, 29.

7. Tolstoy, op. cit., p. 1425.

8. Kracauer, *Theory of Film*, New York, 1960, pp. 63–64.—For the

quote, see Léger, "A propos du cinéma," in L'Herbier, ed., *Intelligence du cinématographe*, Paris, 1946, p. 340.

9. Tolstoy, op. cit., p. 977.
10. Berlin, op. cit., p. 31.
11. Tolstoy, op. cit., p. 1440.
12. Cf. Berlin, op. cit., pp. 68–72.
13. Tolstoy, op. cit., p. 886.
14. Mehta, "The Flight of Crook-Taloned Birds," *The New Yorker*, Dec. 15, 1962, pp. 82–83.
15. John Brooke, as quoted by Mehta, ibid., pp. 74, 87, points out Marx's influence on Namier.
16. Talmon, "The Ordeal of Sir Lewis Namier," *Commentary* (New York, March 1962), vol. 33, no. 3, pp. 242, 243.
17. Mehta, op. cit., p. 93.
18. Ibid., p. 78.
19. Namier, "Human Nature in Politics," in Stern, ed., *The Varieties of History, New York,* 1956 (A Meridian Book), p. 382.
20. Ibid., pp. 382, 384.
21. Ibid., p. 384.
22. Ibid., p. 386.
23. Talmon, op. cit., p. 242.
24. Mehta, op. cit., p. 106.
25. Butterfield, *George III and the Historians*, New York, 1959, p. 210.
26. Ibid., p. 213.
27. Ibid., p. 213.
28. Mehta, op. cit., p. 119.—Cf. Butterfield, *Christianity and History*, New York, 1949, passim.
29. For a discussion of this issue, see the papers "Methodological Individualisms: Definition and Reduction" by Max Brodbeck and "Societal Laws" by Maurice Mandelbaum in Dray, ed., *Philosophical Analysis and History*, New York, 1966. In keeping with my own assumption, both authors emphasize that certain historical and sociological macro concepts enjoy a modicum of independence, that they resist being dissolved into micro elements. But, with both of them, formal argument and logical sophistication get the better of material analysis proper.
30. Marrou, "Comment comprendre le métier d'historien," in Samaran, ed., *L'Histoire et ses méthodes*, Paris, 1961, p. 1499.
31. Proust, *Contre Sainte-Beuve*, Paris, 1954, pp. 176–77.

32. Butterfield, *Man on His Past,* Boston, 1960 (A Beacon Paperback). p. 44.
33. Quoted from Bacon's *Advancement of Learning* by Hale, "Introduction," in Hale, ed., *The Evolution of British Historiography from Bacon to Namier,* Cleveland and New York, 1964 (A Meridian Book), p. 17.
34. Gooch, *History and Historians in the Nineteenth Century,* Boston, 1959 (a Beacon Paperback), p. 182.
35. Quoted from Sainte-Beuve, *Causeries,* vol. I, by Gooch, ibid.
36. Hale, op. cit., p. 17.
37. Marrou, op. cit., p. 1532.
38. Butterfield, *George III and the Historians,* p. 205.
39. Quoted in Kracauer, *Theory of Film,* p. 51, from Freund, *La Photographie en France au dix-neuvième siècle,* Paris, 1936, p. 92.
40. Ibid.
41. Marrou, op. cit., p. 1529.
42. Cf. Bark, *Origins of the Medieval World,* Garden City, N.Y., 1960 (a Doubleday Anchor Book), passim; especially the criticism of the Pirenne thesis in the chapter "The Problem of Medieval Beginnings."
43. For Panofsky, cf. above, Chapter 2, p. 43 and n. 32; for Jedin, *Bischöfliches Konzil oder Kirchenparlament?,* especially his analysis of the *Haec Sancta* decree on pp. 10–13.
44. Proust, *Remembrance of Things Past,* New York, 1934, vol. I, pp. 138–39.
45. Example provided by Professor Diamond.
46. Ferguson, "Introduction," in Alfred von Martin, *Sociology of the Renaissance,* New York and Evanston, 1963 (a Harper Torchbook), p. xiii.
47. Aron, op. cit., p. 14.
48. Cf. Kracauer, op. cit., pp. 47–48.
49. Cf. Toynbee, *Reconsiderations,* New York, 1964; esp. pp. 124, 134–35.
50. Kracauer, op. cit., p. 231.
51. Lévi-Strauss, *La Pensée sauvage,* Paris, 1962, p. 346.
52. Ibid., p. 347.
53. For all of the foregoing, see Blumenberg, "Lebenswelt und Technisierung unter Aspekten der Phänomenologie," *Sguardi su la filosofia contemporanea,* vol. LI (1963), esp. pp. 20 ff.;

and Blumenberg, "Das Fernrohr und die Ohnmacht der Wahrheit," in Galilei, *Sidereus Nuncius,* Frankfurt am Main, 1965, esp. pp. 44–45 and 72–73.

54. Jonas, *Gnosis und spaetantiker Geist,* Part II, 1, Göttingen, 1954, p. 189.

55. See Novikoff, "The Concept of Integrative Levels and Biology," in *Science,* vol. 101 (1945), pp. 209–15.

56. Harnack, *History of Dogma,* New York, 1961 (a Dover Book), vol. I, p. 132.

57. Hexter, op. cit., p. 210.

58. Cf. Toynbee, op. cit., "The Problem of Quantity in the Study of Human Affairs," *passim.*

59. Ibid., p. 134.

60. See Chapter 4, p. 77.

61. For instance, cf. Bullock, "The Historian's Purpose: History and Metahistory," in Meyerhoff, ed., *The Philosophy of History in our Time,* Garden City, N.Y., 1959 (a Doubleday Anchor Book), p. 293: "the desolate wastes of an arid historical erudition."

62. Bloch, *The Historian's Craft,* New York, 1959, p. 86.

63. Huizinga, *Im Bann der Geschichte,* Basel, 1943, p. 12.

64. Meinecke, "Historicism and Its Problems," in Stern, ed., *The Varieties of History,* New York, 1956 (a Meridian Book), p. 275.

65. Ibid., pp. 275 and 273. Meinecke's position, which would subordinate technical to interpretative history, is paralleled by that of Guthrie, in a statement on the same subject: "There are the natural scholars whose bent it is to establish the text of an author or date a series of pots; and there are others who feel more concerned to put the results of such scientific work in a larger setting, to assess their place in the classical tradition and their relevance to the present day . . . . may I be forgiven for saying that we are just now in especial need of the interpretative type?" Guthrie, "People and Traditions," in Guthrie—Van Groningen, *Tradition and Personal Achievement in Classical Antiquity,* London, 1960, pp. 9–10.

66. Bloch, op. cit., p. 86.

67. Bury, "History as a Science," in Stern, ed., op. cit., p. 219.

68. Bury, *The Ancient Greek Historians,* New York, 1958 (a Dover Book), p. 246.

69. See Marrou, *De la connaissance historique,* 4th ed., Paris 1962,

p. 235: " . . . it is natural that historical research, like every intellectual discipline knowing continuous development, should have progressed with time . . . "—Pirenne, "What Are Historians Trying to Do?" in Meyerhoff, ed., *The Philosophy of History in our Time*, Garden City, N.Y., 1959 (a Doubleday Anchor Book), p. 98: "The more these accounts multiply, the more the infinite reality is freed from its veils."—Kristeller, "Some Problems of Historical Knowledge," *The Journal of Philosophy*, vol. LVIII, no. 4 (February 16, 1961), p. 97: "It is the steady task of historical enquiry to advance the frontier of established knowledge and to reduce the area of unverified opinion."—Hexter, op. cit., p. 190: " . . . with respect to the more distinctly time-bound conceptions, a shaking-down process takes place. They get sifted out after a while; but a considerable residue, not contaminated by them, remains."

70. Cf. Pirenne, op. cit., p. 99: "The comparative method permits history to appear in its true perspective." For Bloch's view, see n. 71.

71. Bloch believes that comparative history calls for teamwork. On determining an occurrence of feudal phases in the history of societies other than the European, he says in *Feudal Society*, Chicago, 1964, vol. II, p. 446: "It is by no means impossible that societies different from our own should have passed through a phase closely resembling that which has just been defined. If so, it is legitimate to call them feudal during that phase. But the work of comparison thus involved is clearly beyond the powers of one man."—Marrou, "Comment comprendre le métier d'historien," in: Samaran, *L'Histoire et ses méthodes*, Paris, 1961, pp. 1515–16, says: " . . . even a historical work of a very personal character, conceived and carried out over the sources by one researcher, is nevertheless the culminating point of an immense collective effort . . . The historian appears to us as the architect who . . . must call in a whole series of separate crafts."—An aspect stressed by Kristeller, op. cit., p. 88, is that the "various historical disciplines, just as the various sciences, developed from specific social, historical, and intellectual circumstances, and are sustained by personal, national, religious, institutional, or professional interests. Some of them overlap, and, on the other hand, there are no man's lands not yet occupied by any of them. It is only through a gradual expansion of knowledge, and through an increasing degree of inter-

departmental collaboration, that we can hope to come closer to a unified historical knowledge."

72. Pirenne, op. cit., p. 99.
73. Lévi-Strauss, op. cit., p. 340.
74. Carr, *What is History?*, New York, 1962, p. 165.
75. Valéry, "Historical Fact," in *History and Politics: Collected Works*, vol. X, New York, 1962, p. 121.

CHAPTER 6

1. Cf. for instance, Kristeller, "The Moral Thought of Renaissance Humanism," in *Chapters in Western Civilization*, vol. I, 3rd ed., New York, 1961, p. 290, where he argues from the premise, among others, that we must "accept continuity as basic to history." Compare, however, this chapter, n. 21, for another aspect of Kristeller's view.

2. Cf. especially Vidal-Naquet, "Temps des dieux et temps des hommes. Essai sur quelques aspects de l'expérience temporelle chez les Grecs," in *Revue de l'Histoire des Religions*, vol. CLVII, no. 1 (Jan.–March 1960), pp. 55–80, *passim.*

3. See Blumenberg, " 'Säkularisation.' Kritik einer Kategorie historischer Illegitimität," in Kuhn and Wiedmann, eds., *Die Philosophie und die Frage nach dem Fortschritt*, München, 1964, p. 243, where the differences between the idea of progress and eschatology are pointed out.

4. See Marrou, "Das Janusantlitz der historischen Zeit bei Augustin," in Andresen, ed., *Zum Augustin-Gespräch der Gegenwart*, Darmstadt, 1962, especially pp. 376–77.

5. Bloch, *Feudal Society*, Chicago, 1964, vol. I, p. 91.

6. Malinowski, *Magic, Science and Religion*, Garden City, N. Y., 1954 (a Doubleday Anchor Book), especially pp. 26, 28–30, 33–35.

7. Marrou, Comment comprendre le métier d'historien," in Samaran, ed., *L'Histoire et ses méthodes*. Paris, 1961, p. 1476.

8. Ranke, *Universal History: The Oldest Historical Group of Nations and the Greeks*, London, 1884, pp. xi–xiv and 2, quoted by Butterfield, *Man on His Past*, Boston, 1960 (a Beacon paperback), p. 124.

9. See Henri Pirenne, "What Are Historians Trying to Do?" in Meyerhoff, ed., *The Philosophy of History in Our Time*, Garden City, N.Y., 1959 (a Doubleday Anchor Book), pp. 88–89.

10. Marc Bloch, *The Historian's Craft*, New York, 1959, p. 47.

[French title: *Apologie pour l'histoire ou métier d'historien,* Paris, 1949–50.]

11. Focillon, *The Life of Forms in Art,* New York, 1948, p. 10.
12. Ibid., p. 10.
13. Ibid., p. 55.
14. Ibid., p. 60.
15. Ibid., p. 63.
16. Kubler, *The Shape of Time,* New Haven and London, 1962, Cf. *passim.*
17. Kubler, op. cit., p. 12.
18. Lévi-Strauss, *La Pensée sauvage,* Paris, 1962, p. 345.
19. Ibid., p. 344.
20. Cf. the examples given ibid., p. 343, and especially pp. 344–45, where the magnitude level of modern and contemporary history is compared with that of prehistory: "Coded in the system of prehistory, even the most famous episodes of modern and contemporary history cease to be relevant, except perhaps . . . . certain massive aspects of demographic development as looked at on a global scale, the invention of the steam engine, and the discovery of electricity and nuclear energy."

  Marc Bloch, op. cit., pp. 183–4, also touches upon a need to conceive of histories of different magnitudes in the context of his discussion of the independent establishing of the shape of sequences independently for each area. As he wittily puts it: "A religious history of the reign of Philip Augustus? An economic history of the reign of Louis XV? Why not: 'Journal of what happened in my laboratory during the second presidency of Grévy,' by Louis Pasteur? Or, inversely: 'Diplomatic history of Europe from Newton to Einstein.'"
21. Kristeller, op. cit., p. 291, explaining the presence of medieval and modern traits in the Renaissance as well as of traits peculiar to itself affirms this at least inasmuch as "in a complex, but articulated civilization each area of culture may have its own line of development."
22. Personal communication by Prof. Diamond.
23. W.von Leyden, "History and the Concept of Relative Time," *History and Theory* (The Hague, 1963), vol. II, no. 3, pp. 279–80; citing Herder's *Metakritik* (1799), Pt. I, sec. 2, 84, in *Sämmtliche Werke,* Pt. 16 (Cotta, 1830).
24. Valéry, *History and Politics, Collected Works,* vol. X, New York, 1962, p. 93.

25. Lichtenberg, *Aphorismen, Briefe, Schriften,* Stuttgart, 1953, p. 21.
26. Bloch, op. cit., p. 151.
27. Curtius, *European Literature and the Latin Middle Ages,* New York, 1953, p. 14.
28. Meyer Schapiro, "Style," in Kroeber, ed., *Anthropology Today,* Chicago, 1953, p. 295.
29. Aron, *Dimensions de la conscience historique,* Paris, 1961, pp. 115–16 and 270.
30. Mandelbaum, "The History of Ideas, Intellectual History, and the History of Philosophy," *History and Theory,* Beiheft 5 (The Hague, 1965), pp. 50–52.
31. Dilthey, *Der Aufbau der geschichtlichen Welt in den Geisteswissenschaften,* in *Gesammelte Schriften,* vol. VII, Stuttgart and Göttingen, 1961, pp. 178 and 183.
32. Benjamin, *Geschichtsphilosophische Thesen,* in *Schriften.* Frankfurt am Main, 1955, vol. I, p. 502.
33. Laslett, "Commentary," in Crombie, ed., *Scientific Change* (*Symposium on History of Science, University of Oxford 9–15 July 1961*), London, 1963, p. 863.
34. Ibid.
35. Cf. Kaegi, *Jacob Burckhardt,* vol. II, Basel, 1950, p. 185.
36. Quoted by Kaegi, op. cit., vol. III, Basel, 1956, p. 95.
37. See, for instance, Kristeller, "Changing Views of the Intellectual History of the Renaissance since Jacob Burckhardt," in Helton, ed., *The Renaissance: A Reconsideration of the Theories and Interpretations of the Age,* Madison, 1961, pp. 29–30.
38. Kubler, op. cit., p. 28.
39. Ibid., p. 122.
40. Bloch, op. cit., p. 152.
41. Dilthey, loc. cit., p. 185.
42. Bloch, *Feudal Society,* vol. II, pp. 306–7.
43. Cf. Lovejoy, *Essays in the History of Ideas,* New York, 1960 (a Capricorn Book), p. 320.
44. See Rand, *Founders of the Middle Ages,* New York, 1957 (a Dover Book), p. 17.
45. Edelstein, "The Greco-Roman Concept of Scientific Progress," *Ithaca, 26 VIII–2 IX 1962,* Paris, p. 57.
46. Dilthey, *Einleitung in die Geisteswissenschaften, Gesammelte Schriften,* vol. I, Stuttgart and Göttingen, 1959, 1962, p. 256.

47. Schmidt, *Der Begriff der Natur in der Lehre von Marx*. Frankfurt am Main, 1962, p. 27.

48. Jonas, *Gnosis und spätantiker Geist*, Part I, Göttingen, 1964, pp. 24–25.

49. Ibid., p. 37.

50. Blumenberg, "Epochenschwelle und Rezeption," *Philosophische Rundschau*, vol. VI, no. 1/2 (1958), p. 94.

51. Kracauer, *Theory of Film: The Redemption of Physical Reality*, New York, 1960, pp. 200–201.

52. Quoted by Gadamer, *Wahrheit und Methode*, p. 192, from Ranke, *Weltgeschichte*, IX, p. xiii f.

53. See Croce, *History: Its Theory and Practice*, New York, 1960, *passim*.

54. Ibid., Part II, pp. 165–314.

55. See Jauss, *Zeit und Erinnerung in Marcel Proust's "A la recherche dut temps perdu,"* Heidelberg, 1955, passim. I have greatly benefited from this remarkable monograph, a model of concise and comprehensive analysis. Cf. also Poulet, "Proust," in *Studies in Human Time*, New York, 1959 (a Harper Torchbook), pp. 291–322.

56. Jauss, op. cit., p. 87.

CHAPTER 7

1. Mandelbaum, "The History of Ideas, Intellectual History, and the History of Philosophy," *History and Theory, Beiheft 5 (The Hague, 1965)*, p. 42.

2. See Hale, "Introduction," in Hale, ed., *The Evolution of British Historiography from Bacon to Namier* (a Meridian Book), Cleveland and New York, 1964, p. 59; and Hexter, *Reappraisals in History*, Evanston, Ill., 1961, p. 195.

3. Mandelbaum, op. cit., p. 44.

4. Pirenne, *A History of Europe* . . . , New York, 1955, p. 40.

5. Hexter, op. cit., p. 213.

6. Nilsson, *Geschichte der griechischen Religion*, vol. II, München, 1961, p. 324. In connection with this passage, compare Marrou's general comment in *Comment comprendre le métier d'historien*, in Samaran, ed., *L'histoire et ses méthodes*, pp. 1530–31: "How many theorists of civilization have not accepted as something to be taken for granted an organicist scheme, com-

paring the historic phenomenon, which is so complex, to a living being that is born, grows, declines, and dies. . . . As for reducing a whole civilization to one single idea, if that should be the philosopher's dream, as we are told it is, the historian must regard it as nothing but a mirage full of dangers."

7. Wendland, *Die hellenistisch-roemische Kultur* . . . (Handbuch zum Neuen Testament, 1. Bd.: 2. und 3. Teil), Tübingen, 1912, p. 152.

8. Dodds, *The Greeks and the Irrational* (a Beacon paperback), Boston, 1957, pp. 252–55.

9. Marc Bloch, *Feudal Society* (a Phoenix Book), vol. I, Chicago, 1964, pp. 41–42.

10. Ranke, *Deutsche Geschichte im Zeitalter der Reformation*, Köln, Phaidon-Verlag, n.d., pp. 128–30.

11. See Ranke, *Die roemischen Paepste in den letzten vier Jahrhunderten*, Agrippina-Verlag, Köln, n.d., pp. 193–204, *passim*. About Palestrina's music Ranke, p. 203, says: "It is as if nature had been given tone and voice, as if the elements spoke and the sounds of all life devoted themselves to worshipping in free harmony, now heaving like the sea, now ascending to heaven in jubilation and joy."

12. Cf. Kaegi, *Jacob Burckhardt: Eine Biographie*, Bd. II, Basel, 1950, p. 71.

13. Lietzmann, *A History of the Early Church* (a Meridian Book), Book II, Cleveland, Ohio, 1961, p. 32.

14. Wendland, op. cit., p. 49.

15. Ibid., p. 62.

16. Graves, *I, Claudius* (a Vintage Book), New York, 1934 and 1961, pp. 108–9.

17. Cf. Bury, *The Ancient Greek Historians* (a Dover paperback), New York, 1958, pp. 81, 91, 106, 112, 118–19.

18. Cf. for instance, Gooch, *History and Historians in the Nineteenth Century* (a Beacon paperback), Boston, 1959, p. 175 and *passim*. In his old-fashioned way, Gooch seems to endorse a fusion of scholarly and artistic intentions; thus he extols the "artistic and historic unity" of Michelet's history of the French Revolution.

19. Cf. Gershoy, "Some Problems of a Working Historian," in Hook, ed., *Philosophy and History* . . . New York, 1963, p. 75, where he speaks of the "dual nature" of history "as art and science, personal involvement and objective inquiry . . . "

20. See Meinecke, "Historicism and Its Problems," in Stern, ed., *The Varieties of History* . . . (a Meridian Book), New York, 1956, pp. 270, 272, 283.
21. Marc Bloch, *The Historian's Craft*, New York, 1959, pp. 26–7.
22. Namier, "History," in Namier, *Avenues of History*, London, 1952, p. 8.
23. Max Burckhardt, sel. & ed., *Jacob Burckhardt: Briefe*, Bremen, 1965, p. 165.
24. Taubmann, "History as Literature," *New York Times*, March 30, 1966.
25. Kaegi, *Jacob Burckhardt: Eine Biographie*, Bd. III, Basel, 1956, p. 691.
26. Croce, *History: Its Theory and Practice*, New York, 1960, p. 35.
27. Nilsson, op. cit., vol. II, pp. 324–25.
28. Pirenne, op. cit., pp. 310–11.
29. Ibid., p. 489.
30. Cf. Kracauer, *Theory of Film* . . . , New York, 1960, p. 220.
31. Rostovtzeff, *Rome* (a Galaxy Book), New York, 1960, p. 120.
32. Proust, *Remembrance of Things Past*, 2 vols., New York, 1932 and 1934, *passim*; see, for instance, vol. I, pp. 15, 656.
33. Auerbach, *Mimesis* . . . , Princeton, 1953, p. 548.
34. White, "The Burden of History," *History and Theory* (Middletown, Conn., 1966), vol. V, no. 2, corroborates this view to the extent that he emphasizes the discrepancy between modern aesthetic conceptions and the rather outdated stylistic preferences of a majority of historians. Thus he declares (p. 126) that many historians who speak of the "art" of history "seem to have in mind a conception of art that would admit little more than the nineteenth-century novel as a paradigm." For the rest, his approach considerably differs from mine.
35. Valéry, *History and Politics*, New York, 1962, pp. 515–16. The passage is drawn from his letter to André Lebey, dated September 1906. For the original text, see Valéry, *Oeuvres II* (Pléiade), Paris, 1960, p. 1543. It reads: ". . . j'ai tiré du fruit de la lecture, çà et là, d'histoires particulières de l'architecture, de la géométrie, de la navigation, de l'économie politique, de la tactique. Dans chacun de ces domaines, les choses sont filles visibles les unes des autres," whereas in "l'histoire générale chaque enfant semble avoir mille pères et réciproquement."
36. Cf. Bloch, *The Historian's Craft* (see n. 21), p. 32, where he says: "In any study seeking the origins of a human activity,

there lurks the . . . danger of confusing ancestry with explanation."

37. See Hexter, op. cit., pp. 39, 202, 213.

38. See again Laslett, "Commentary," in Crombie, ed., *Scientific Change* . . . , London, 1963, pp. 861–5; see esp. p. 864. Cf. also Laslett, "Foreword," in Hexter, op. cit., pp. xi–xiv; esp. p. xiii.

39. Cf. Jauss, "Ursprung und Bedeutung der Fortschrittsidee in der 'Querelle des Anciens et des Modernes'," in Kuhn & Wiedmann, ed., *Die Philosophie und die Frage nach dem Fortschritt*, München, 1964, pp. 51–72, *passim*.

40. See Blumenberg, " 'Saekularisation', Kritik einer Kategorie historischer Illegitimitaet," in Kuhn & Wiedmann, ed., op. cit., pp. 240–65, *passim*. See also, above, Chapter 6, p. 155 and n. 50.

41. Mehta, "The Flight of Crook-Taloned Birds," *The New Yorker*, Dec. 15, 1962, quotes comments of A. J. P. Taylor (p. 70) and Herbert Butterfield (p. 111) on this peculiarity of Namier's work.

42. Burckhardt, *Griechische Kulturgeschichte* (Kroeners Taschenausgabe, Baende 58, 59, 60), Leipzig, vol. I, p. 175 [1929].

43. Ibid., pp. 271–72.

44. Cf. Burckhardt, *Weltgeschichtliche Betrachtungen* (Gesamtausgabe, Bd. VII), Stuttgart, Berlin und Leipzig, 1929, pp. 192–208.

45. Berlin, "History and Theory . . . ," *History and Theory* (The Hague, 1960), vol. I, no. 1: 31.

46. Hexter, op. cit., pp. 22–23.

47. Merton, *On the Shoulders of Giants* . . . , New York, 1965, pp. 163–64.

48. Sterne, *The Life and Opinions of Tristram Shandy* . . . (an Odyssee paperback), New York, 1940, pp. 36–37.

49. There is a striking family likeness between the historian proceeding in Tristram fashion and the film artist, as I have described him elsewhere. To quote myself, the "true film artist may be imagined as a man who sets out to tell a story but, in shooting it, is so overwhelmed by his innate desire to cover all of physical reality—and also by a feeling that he must cover it in order to tell the story, any story, in cinematic terms—that he ventures ever deeper into the jungle of material phenomena in which he risks becoming irretrievably lost if he does not, by virtue of great efforts, get back to the highway he has left." (See Kracauer, op. cit., p. 255.)

CHAPTER 8

1. Kracauer, op. cit., New York, 1960, *passim.*
2. Marcel, "Possibilités et limites de l'art cinématographique," *Revue Internationale de filmologie,* vol. V, nos. 18–19 (July–December 1954), p. 164.
3. Dilthey, *Abhandlungen zur Grundlegung der Geisteswissenschaften (Die geistige Welt. Einleitung in die Philosophie des Lebens,* Part I), in *Gesammelte Schriften,* vol. V, Stuttgart and Göttingen, 1957, p. 365.
4. For a more recent discussion, see Mink, "The Autonomy of Historical Understanding," *History and Theory,* vol. V, no. 1 (1966); especially pp. 24–27.
5. Jaeger, *Paideia: The Ideals of Greek Culture,* vol. II, New York, 1944, p. 36.
   Marrou, *De la connaissance historique,* 4th ed., Paris, 1962, characterizes the contrast of speculative philosophers of history to professional historians (*"historiens de métier"*) by saying that they propose "that total and unified explanation which flatters the mind and satisfies its secret wants;" which means that they substitute "a scheme that has no validity for authentic history." Marrou adds, "what, in fact, is the good of history if philosophy tells us in advance what, so far as the essential is concerned, its content should be!" loc. cit., pp. 198–99.) Similarly Froude, as quoted by Hale, ed., *The Evolution of British Historiography* (Cleveland and New York, 1963 (a Meridian book)), p. 52. In a lecture he declared: "I object to all historical theories. I object to them as calculated to vitiate the observation of facts."
6. As in *La Jeunesse de Proudhon,* Paris, 1913; also, *Charles Péguy et les Cahiers de la Quinzaine,* Paris, 1918; *Vie de Frédéric Nietzsche,* Paris, 1909 and *Nietzsche,* Paris, 1944; and *Le mariage de Proudhon,* Paris, 1955.
7. Bury, *The Idea of Progress,* New York, 1955 (a Dover Book).
8. Cf. Kracauer, "Katholizismus und Relativismus," *Frankfurter Zeitung,* Nov. 19, 1921; reprinted in Kracauer, *Das Ornament der Masse,* Frankfurt am Main, 1963, pp. 187–96.
9. Cf. Rickert, *Der Historismus und seine Probleme,* Heidelberg, 1924. Rickert believes that historicism must end in nihilism and complete relativism: "As a world view, it makes lack of principle the principle and must therefore be fought with uttermost deter-

mination both by the philosophy of history and by philosophy."
(loc. cit., p. 130). Accordingly, as the idealistic philosopher
he is, Rickert emphasizes the need for objective philosophy
of history and universal history, which he would base on
"a culture psychology . . . which explores and systematically
explicates the whole of general cultural values, and by that will
also provide a system of the principles of the events of history."
(ibid., p. 116).

10. In *Der Historismus und seine Probleme* (Aalen, 1961, p. 174
ff.), Troeltsch as quoted by Mandelbaum, *The Problem of Historical Knowledge*, New York, 1938, pp. 160–61), argues as
follows: "The empirical historian will find his task in the knowledge and presentation of . . . individual developments. . . .
But he himself will not escape putting his own present and
future into these connections and recognizing behind and under
them a deeper movement. . . . He will work towards a universal conception of development, energetically drawing it out
of the thin and fragile continuities which exist between the
empirically given spheres of development in order that he may
link it to his own situation. . . . But in the end he needs for
this a metaphysical faith which will carry him high above
empirical ascertainments and characteristics . . ."

11. Meinecke's concept of "world history" betrays his great indebtedness to German idealism. This idealistic concept of world
history mingles with a theological conception which also an-
nexes to itself the idea of secular progress. Cf., for instance,
"Historicism and Its Problems" (in Stern, ed., *The Varieties of
History*, New York, 1956 (a Meridian Book)): "Culture and
nature, we might say God and nature, are undoubtedly a unity,
but a unity divided in itself. God struggles loose from nature in
agony and pain, laden with sin, and in danger, therefore, of
sinking back at any moment. For the ruthless and honest observer, this is the final word—and yet it cannot be accepted as
the final word. Only a faith which, however, has become ever
more universal in its content and must struggle endlessly with
doubt, holds out the solace of a transcendental solution to the
problem, insoluble for us, of life and culture." (loc. cit., p. 282).

12. For instance, cf. *Einleitung in die Geisteswissenschaften, Gesammelte Schriften*, vol. I, Stuttgart and Göttingen, 1959, p. 403;
and *Der Aufbau der geschichtlichen Welt in den Geisteswis-*

senschaften, *Gesammelte Schriften*, vol. VII, Stuttgart and Göttingen, 1958, pp. 105, 116, and 262.

13. *Der Aufbau der geschichtlichen Welt in den Geisteswissenschaften*, p. 290. Also cf. Gerhard Bauer, *Geschichtlichkeit*, Berlin, 1963, pp. 39–72, especially 70–71; and Gadamer, *Wahrheit und Methode*, Tübingen, 1960, p. 250 ff.

14. *Der Aufbau der geschichtlichen Welt in den Geisteswissenschaften*, p. 262.

15. *Die geistige Welt*, Part I, p. 406.

16. Jonas, *The Phenomenon of Life*, New York, 1966, p. 258.

17. Mannheim, "Historismus," *Archiv fuer Sozialwissenschaft und Sozialpolitik*, vol. 52, no. 1 (1924); see especially pp. 12, 13, 25 ff., 40–41, 43, 44, 46–47, and 54–60.

18. See n. 12.

19. For an explication of these concepts, cf. especially *Der Aufbau der geschichtlichen Welt*, pp. 137–38. See also *ibid.*, p. 165, where Dilthey says that the *Wirkungszusammenhang*, as it appears "in the greatest events of history, the origin of Christianity, the Reformation, the French Revolution, and the national wars of liberation . . . is revealed as the forming of a total force which, with unified direction, overturns every resistance."

20. Hegel, *Saemtliche Werke. (Vorrede zur Rechtsphilosophie)*. Stuttgart, 1955.

21. On Kafka, compare p. 224.

22. Compare the end of Jonas's paper, "Heidegger and Theology," where he admonishes the Heideggerean theologians not to dissolve all objective symbols, since "On pain of immanentism, . . . the understanding of God is not to be reduced to the self-understanding of man." See Jonas, op. cit., p. 261.

23. Cf. Loewith, *Gesammelte Abhandlungen*, Stuttgart, 1960. On p. 177, Lowith's argument runs: "But who tells us that the world is devised towards man and his history and that it could not also exist without us, but not man without the world."

24. The conception of dialectics here discussed was set forth especially in Adorno, *Negative Dialektik*, Frankfurt am Main, 1966, *passim*.

25. An example of a passage affirming progress is the following, in *Der Aufbau der geschichtlichen Welt*, p. 272: "Two events have removed the barriers which held back the concept of a total development encompassing all fields which had been waiting for

a long time at the threshold of historical consciousness; namely, the North American War of Independence, and two decades later, the French Revolution. A progress beyond anything that had occurred in the past had taken place in a new and most important area of the mind, that of the realization of the ideas in economy, law, and the state. Mankind became aware of its inner strength."

26. See, for example, *Die geistige Welt*, Part I, p. 404, where Dilthey says of the two basic types of *Weltanschauungen* which he distinguishes, namely, that comprising materialism, naturalism, positivism as against that which comprises objective idealism and "idealism of freedom," that "each of them has power of attraction and a potential of consistent development from the fact that it comprehends in thought the manifoldness of life from one of our typical attitudes, and according to the law inherent in that attitude."

27. Blumenberg, " 'Säkularisation.' Kritik einer Kategorie historischer Illegitimität," in Kuhn and Wiedmann, eds., *Die Philosophie und die Frage nach dem Fortschritt*, Munich, 1964, p. 249.

28. Quoted from Erich Meuthen, "Nikolaus von Kues und die Einheit," *Neue Zürcher Zeitung*, Aug. 9, 1964.

29. Kracauer, *Soziologie als Wissenschaft. Eine erkenntnistheoretische Untersuchung*, Dresden, 1922. See especially the chapter "Problematik der Soziologie," which discusses the difficulties of returning from "formal" or "pure" sociology to a "material sociology" which "strives for mastering in knowledge the reality of immediately experienced life." (loc. cit., p. 133).

30. E.g., *Einleitung in die Geisteswissenschaften*, p. 96: "These presumptuous general concepts of the philosophy of history are but the *notiones universales* of whose natural origin and fateful effects on scientific thought Spinoza gave such a masterly description.—These abstractions, intended to express the course of history, . . . of course never do more than to isolate one aspect of it, each philosophy excising from this grand reality a slightly different abstraction."

31. Quoted from Gardiner, ed., *Theories of History*, Glencoe, Ill., 1959, p. 33.

32. Ibid.

33. Wittram, *Das Interesse an der Geschichte*, Göttingen, 1963, p. 128.

34. J. P. Marquand, *Point of No Return*, Boston, 1949.

35. Cf. Heimpel, *Zwei Historiker*, Göttingen, 1962, pp. 37–39.
36. E.g., in his argument on the social effect of the defeat of Arianism in *Historische Fragmente:* "Then the whole orthodox Middle Ages kept the Jews down and periodically persecuted them; in other words, it tried to destroy them. If the Western European Arianism had won out, the Jews would within one or two centuries have become the masters of all property, and would already then have made the Germanic and Romanic people work for them." (Translated from Burckhardt, *Gesamtausgabe*, vol. 7, Stuttgart, Berlin, Leipzig, 1929, p. 264.)
37. In *Weltgeschichtliche Betrachtungen, loc. cit.*, p. 125, Burckhardt defends "good" wars as follows: "War . . . has an enormous moral superiority over the mere brutal egoism of the individual; it develops human strengths and abilities in the service of something general, in fact of the very highest general, and under a discipline which yet at the same time conduces to the unfolding of the highest heroic virtue. Indeed, only war shows to man the grand sight and vision of a general subordination under something general. Furthermore, since only real power can guarantee a lasting peace and security, and since it is war that founds real power, such a war carries in itself the future peace. But if possible it should be a just and honorable war, as for instance a war of defense . . . "
38. Burckhardt, *Briefe*, Bremen, 1965, p. 237.
39. *Weltgeschichtliche Betrachtungen*, p. 13.
40. But commenting on Plato's remark that great evil springs out of a fullness of nature rather than from weak natures capable neither of very great good nor of very great evil, Wind, with some cause, observes that "It is obvious from this remark that Plato was spared the kind of experience that moved Jacob Burckhardt to define mediocrity as the one diabolical force in the world." *Art and Anarchy*, London, 1963, p. 5.
41. Cf. Kaegi, *Jacob Burckhardt*, vol. III, Basel, 1956, p. 290.
42. *Weltgeschichtliche Betrachtungen*, p. 192.
43. *Historische Fragmente*, p. 251.
44. *Weltgeschichtliche Betrachtungen*, p. 3.
45. *Historische Fragmente*, p. 225.
46. *Weltgeschichtliche Betrachtungen*, p. 1.
47. *Ibid.*, p. 2.
48. A typical passage is the following, from *Weltgeschichtliche Betrachtungen*, p. 67: "The question at issue here is not whether

world monarchies are desirable institutions, but whether the Roman Empire actually fulfilled its own purpose." This purpose is said to be the great equalization of contrasts among the ancient cultures, "and to spread Christianity, the only institution by which their main elements could be saved from destruction by the Teutons." (Quoted after Burckhardt, *Force and Freedom*, Boston, 1964, p. 175.)

49. Quoted from Wind, *op. cit.*, p. 109.
50. Quoted from Kaegi, *Historische Meditationen*, Zürich, n.d., p. 28.
51. Huizinga, "The Task of Cultural History," in *Men and Ideas*, New York, 1959 (a Meridian Book), pp. 54–55. The quote from Taine is in English: "History means almost to see the men of another time."
52. *Ibid.*, p. 55.
53. See Kracauer, "The Challenge of Qualitative Content Analysis," in *The Public Opinion Quarterly*, vol. 16, no. 4 (Winter 1952–53), pp. 631–42.
54. See my article "Die Gruppe als Ideenträger," *Archiv für Sozialwissenschaft und Sozialpolitik*, vol. 49, no. 3 (1922), pp. 594–622; reprinted in Kracauer, *Das Ornament der Masse*, pp. 123–56.
55. Blumenberg, "Melanchthons Einspruch gegen Kopernikus," *Studium Generale*, vol. 13, no. 3 (1960), p. 174. The quote in this passage from Blumenberg's article is from Basil Willey, *The Seventeenth-Century Background*, London, 1953, p. 22.
56. Private communication by Alfred Schmidt.
57. Brod, *Franz Kafka*, Frankfurt am Main and Hamburg, 1963 (Fischer-Bücherei), p. 54.
58. See Loewith, *Jacob Burckhardt*, Luzern, 1936, p. 20.
59. *Ibid.*, p. 78.
60. Kafka, *Beim Bau der chinesischen Mauer*, Berlin, 1931, p. 38. Translation quoted from Kafka, *Parables and Paradoxes*, New York (a Schocken-Paperback), 1966, p. 179.
61. An English translation of Kierkegaard's passage was inserted from *The Journals of Kierkegaard*, ed. by Alexander Dru, New York, 1959 (a Harper Torchbook), p. 247, except for two small changes which were made for conformity to the German of Kafka's diary entry, as quoted by Brod. Indebtedness to Professor Hermann Schweppenhaeuser for having located the quotation in Kierkegaard's work.

Bibliography

Acton, Lord John Emerich, *Cambridge Modern History,* Cambridge, 1934.

Adorno, Theodor W., *Negative Dialektik, Frankfurt* a.M., 1966.

Aron, Raymond, *Dimensions de la conscience historique,* Paris, 1961 (Recherches en Sciences humaines, 16).

Auerbach, Erich, *Mimesis: The Representation of Reality in Western Literature,* Princeton, 1953.

Aydelotte, William O., "Notes on the problem of historical generalization," in Gottschalk, Louis, ed., *Generalization in the Writing of History, Chicago,* 1963, pp. 145–77.

Bacon, Sir Francis, "Advancement of learning," quoted in "Introduction" by J. R. Hale in Hale, J. R., ed., *The Evolution of British Historiography from Bacon to Namier,* Cleveland and New York, 1964, p. 17 (A Meridian Book).

Bagby, Philip, *Culture and History: Prolegomena to the Comparative Study of Civilizations,* Berkeley and Los Angeles, 1959.

Bailyn, Bernard, "The problems of the working historian: a comment," in Hook, Sidney, ed., *Philosophy and History,* New York, 1963, pp. 92–101.

Bark, William Carroll, *Origins of the Medieval World,* Garden City, New York, 1960 (A Doubleday Anchor Book).

Bauer, Gerhard, *Geschichtlichkeit,* Berlin, 1963.

Becker, Carl L., "What are historical facts?," in Meyerhoff, ed., *The Philosophy of History in Our Time,* pp. 121–37. [Written in 1926]. Garden City, New York, 1959 (A Doubleday Anchor Book).

Benjamin, Walter, "Geschichtsphilosophische Thesen," in Benjamin, Walter, *Schriften*, vol. I, pp. 494–506. Frankfurt a.M., 1955.

———, *Schriften*, 2 vols., Frankfurt a.M., 1955.

———, "Ursprung des deutschen Trauerspiels," in Benjamin, Walter, *Schriften*, vol. I, pp. 141–365, Frankfurt a.M., 1955.

Berlin, Isaiah, *The Hedgehog and the Fox: An Essay on Tolstoy's View of History*, New York, 1953.

———, "*History and theory*: the concept of scientific history," in *History and Theory* (The Hague, 1960), vol. I, no. 1, pp. 1–31.

———, *Karl Marx: His Life and Environment*, New York, 1959 (A Galaxy Book). [First published, 1939.]

Besson, Waldemar, ed., *Geschichte, Frankfurt* a.M., 1961 (Das Fischer Lexikon).

Bloch, Marc, *The Historian's Craft*, New York, 1959. Original title: *Apologie pour l'histoire ou métier d'historien*, Paris, 1950, 1964 (Cahiers des Annales, 3).

———, *Feudal Society*, vol. I, II. Chicago, 1964 (A Phoenix Book). Original title: *La Société Féodale*, Paris, 1949.

Blumenberg, Hans, "Epochenschwelle und Rezeption," in *Philosophische Rundschau* (Tuebingen, 1958), 6. Jahrg., Heft 1-2: 94–120.

———, "Das Fernrohr und die Ohnmacht der Wahrheit," in Galileo Galilei, *Sidereus Nuncius*, Frankfurt a.M., 1965.

———, Lebenswelt und Technisierung unter Aspekten der Phaenomenologie, in *Sguardi su la Filosofia Contemporanea*, vol. LI, Torino, 1963.

———, "Melanchtons Einspruch gegen Kopernikus," in *Studium Generale* (Berlin, Goettingen, Heidelberg, 1960), 13. Jahrg., Heft 3: 174–82.

———, *Paradigmen zu einer Metaphorologie*, Bonn, 1960.

———, "Saekularisation, Kritik einer Kategorie historischer Illegitimitaet," in Helmut Kuhn und Franz Wiedmann, eds., *Die Philosophie und die Frage nach dem Fortschritt*, Muenchen, 1964, pp. 240–65.

————, *Die Kopernikanische Wende*, Frankfurt, a.M., 1965.

Bock, Kenneth E., *The Acceptance of Histories: Toward a Perspective for Social Science*, Berkeley and Los Angeles, 1956.

Brod, Max, *Franz Kafka: Eine Biographie*, Frankfurt a.M., 1963, (Fischer Buecherei).

Brodbeck, May, "Methodological individualisms: definition and reduction," in Dray, William H., ed., *Philosophical Analysis and History*, New York, 1966, pp. 297–329.

Brooke, John, "Namier and Namierism," in *History and Theory* (The Hague, 1964), vol. III, no. 3: 331–47.

Buckle, Henry Thomas, *History of Civilization in England*, London, 1901.

Bullock, Alan, "The historian's purpose: history and metahistory," in Meyerhoff, Hans, ed., *The Philosophy of History in our Time*, pp. 292–99. Garden City, N.Y., 1959 (A Doubleday Anchor Book). [In *History Today*, (Feb. 1951), vol. 7, pp. 5–11].

Bultmann, Rudolf, *History and Eschatology: The Presence of Eternity*, New York, 1962 (A Harper Torchbook). [Originally published New York, 1957].

Burckhardt, Jacob, *Briefe*, select., ed., by Burckhardt, Max, Bremen, 1965.

————, *Griechische Kulturgeschichte*, Leipzig, (Vorwort 1929) Kroeners Taschenausgabe, Baende 58, 59, 60.

————, "Historische Fragmente aus dem Nachlass," in *Jacob Burckhardt-Gesamtausgabe*, Bd. VII, Stuttgart, Berlin, Leipzig, 1929, pp. 225–466. [English transl., *On History and Historians*, New York, 1965. A Harper Torchbook].

————, *Die Kultur der Renaissance in Italien*, Phaidon Verlag, Wien, no date.

————, "Weltgeschichtliche Betrachtungen," in *Jacob Burckhardt-Gesamtausgabe*, Bd. VII, Stuttgart, Berlin, Leipzig, 1929, pp. 1–208. [English transl., *Force and Freedom: Reflections on History*, Boston, 1964. A Beacon Paperback].

————, "Die Zeit Constantins des Grossen," in *Jacob Burckhardt-Gesamtausgabe*, Bd. II, Stuttgart, Berlin, Leipzig, 1929.

Burckhardt, Max, sel. & ed., *Jacob Burckhardt: Briefe*, Bremen, 1965.

Bury, John Bagnell, *The Ancient Greek Historians*, New York, 1958 (A Dover Paperback).

———, *The Idea of Progress: An Inquiry Into Its Origin and Growth*, New York, 1955 (A Dover Paperback).

———, "The science of history," in Stern, Fritz, ed., *The Varieties of History, From Voltaire to the Present*, New York, 1956, pp. 210–23 (A Meridian Book). [In Temperley, ed., *Selected Essays of J. B. Bury*, Cambridge, 1930, pp. 3–22.]

Butterfield, Herbert, *Christianity and History*, New York, 1949, 1950.

———, *George III and the Historians*, New York, 1959.

———, *Man on His Past: The Study of the History of Historical Scholarship*, Boston, 1960 (A Beacon Paperback). [First published in 1955.]

———, "Moral Judgments in History," in Meyerhoff, Hans, ed., *The Philosophy of History in Our Time*, Garden City, N. Y. 1959, pp. 228–49. [In *History and Human Relations*, London, 1931, pp. 101–30.]

Caillois, Roland, "Le Cinéma, le meurtre et la tragédie," in *Revue internationale de filmologie* (Paris, n.d.), vol. II, no. 5, pp. 87–91.

Carlyle, Thomas, [Letter] to John Stuart Mill, quoted in "Introduction," in Hale, J. R. ed., *The Evolution of British Historiography from Bacon to Namier*, Cleveland and New York, 1964, p. 42 (A Meridian Book).

Carr, Edward Hallett, *What Is History?* New York, 1962.

Collingwood, R. G., *The Idea of History*, New York, 1956 (A Galaxy Book). [First published in 1946.]

Comte, Auguste, The three stages of human progress, in *The Positive Philosophy of Auguste Comte*, transl. H. Martineau, London, 1896. [*Cours de philosophie positive*, Paris, 1877.]

Conversations-Lexikon der Gegenwart, Brockhaus, Leipzig, 1840, Bd. 4. Article: "Raumer, Friedrich von." (Author's initials unidentifiable.)

Croce, Benedetto, *History: Its Theory and Practice*, New York, 1960. Transl. by Douglas Ainslie. [Original title: *Teoria e storia della storiografia*, Bari, 1917.]

Curtius, Ernst Robert, *European Literature and the Latin Middle*

Ages, New York, 1953. Transl. by Willard R. Trask. [Original title: *Europaeische Literatur und Lateinisches Mittelalter,* Bern, 1948.]

Dilthey, Wilhelm, *Gesammelte Schriften,* Stuttgart, Goettingen.

————, Einleitung in die Geisteswissenschaften, *Gesammelte Schriften,* vol. I, 1959, 1962.

————, Die geistige Welt, *Gesammelte Schriften,* vol. V, 1957, 1961; vol. VI, 1958, 1962.

————, Der Aufbau der geschichtlichen Welt in den Geisteswissenschaften, *Gesammelte Schriften,* vol. VII, 1958, 1961.

Dodds, E. R., *The Greeks and the Irrational,* Boston, 1957 (A Beacon Paperback). [First published in 1951.]

Dray, William H., ed., *Philosophical Analysis and History,* New York, 1966.

Droysen, Johann Gustav, *Historik: Vorlesungen ueber Enzyklopaedie und Methodologie der Geschichte,* Muenchen, 1960.

Edelstein, Ludwig, "The Greco-Roman concept of scientific progress," *Ithaca,* 26 VIII -2 IX, 1962, Paris, pp. 47–61.

Eder, Josef Maria, *History of Photography,* New York, 1945.

Feininger, Andreas, "Photographic control processes," in *The Complete Photographer* (New York, 1942), vol. 8, issue 43, pp. 2795–2804.

Ferguson, Wallace K., in his Introduction to the Torchbook Edition of Alfred von Martin, *Sociology of the Renaissance,* New York, 1963, pp. v–xiii (A Harper Torchbook).

Festugière, A.-J., *La Révélation d'Hermès Trismégiste.* vol. I: *L'Astrologie et les sciences occultes,* Paris, 1944.

Finley, John H. Jr., *Thucydides,* University of Michigan Press, 1963 (An Ann Arbor Paperback).

Focillon, Henri, *The Life of Forms in Art,* New York, 1963. [Translated from *Vie des formes* by Charles Beecher Hogan and George Kubler.]

Frankfort, Henri, "The Dying God" [part of article, "Three Lectures by Henri Frankfort, 1897–1954."] *Journal of the Warburg and Courtauld Institutes* (London, 1958), vol. XXI, nos. 3–4, pp. 141–51.

————, *The Birth of Civilization in the Near East,* Garden City, N.Y., 1950 (A Doubleday Anchor Book).

Freund, Gisèle, *La Photographie en France au dix-neuvième siècle*, Paris, 1936. p. 92. Quoted in Kracauer, Siegfried, *Theory of Film*, New York, 1960.

Froude, James Anthony, quoted in Introduction in Hale, J. R. ed., *The Evolution of British Historiography from Bacon to Namier*, Cleveland and New York, 1964, p. 52 (A Meridian Book).

———, "The science of history, scientific method as applied to history, lectures," in *Short Studies on Great Subjects*. vol. 1: **2**, London, 1898.

Gadamer, Hans-Georg, *Wahrheit und Methode*, Tuebingen, 1960.

Gallie, W. B., "The historical understanding," in *History and Theory* (The Hague, 1964) vol. III, no. 2, pp. 149–202.

Gardiner, Patrick, ed., *Theories of History*, Glencoe, Ill., 1959.

Gershoy, Leo, "Some problems of a working historian," in Hook, Sidney, ed., *Philosophy and History*, New York, 1963, pp. 59–75.

Geyl, Pieter, *Debates With Historians*, New York, 1958 (A Meridian Paperback).

———, "Huizinga as Accuser of His Age," in *History and Theory* (The Hague, 1963), vol. II, no. 3, pp. 231–62.

Gooch, George Peabody, *History and Historians in the Nineteenth Century*, Boston, 1959 (A Beacon Paperback). [First published in 1913.]

Gottschalk, Louis, ed., *Generalization in the Writing of History*, Chicago, 1963 (A Report of the Committee on Historical Analysis of the Social Science Research Council).

Graves, Robert, *I, Claudius*, New York, 1934 and 1961 (A Vintage Book).

———, *The Greek Myths*, Baltimore, Maryland, 1955, 2 vols. (Penguin Books).

Guizot, François, *L'Histoire de la révolution d'Angleterre*, Bruxelles, 1850.

———, *L'Histoire de la civilisation en Europe et en France*, Paris, 1882.

Guthrie, W. K. C., "People and traditions," in Guthrie, W. K. C., and B. A. Van Groningen, *Tradition and Personal Achievement in Classical Antiquity*, London, 1960, pp. 7–22.

Hale, J. R., ed., *The Evolution of British Historiography from Bacon to Namier*, Cleveland and New York, 1964 (A Meridian Book).

Halévy, Daniel, *La Jeunesse de Proudhon*, Paris, 1913.

―――― *Charles Péguy et les cahiers de la quinzaine*, Paris, 1918.

La Vie de Frédéric Nietzsche, Paris, 1909.

―――― *Nietzsche*, Paris, 1944.

―――― *Le Mariage de Proudhon*, Paris, 1955.

Harnack, Adolph, *History of Dogma*, New York, 1961, vols. 1–7, bound as four. [Translated from the 3rd German edition by Neil Buchanan.]

Hegel, Georg Wilhelm Friedrich, *Saemtliche Werke*. (*Vorrede zur Rechtsphilosophie*). Stuttgart, 1955.

Hegel, Georg Wilhelm Friedrich, *The Philosophy of History*, New York, 1956 (A Dover Paperback).

Heimpel, Hermann, *Zwei Historiker*, Goettingen, 1962.

Heine, Heinrich, "Lutezia," in *Saemtliche Werke*, Bd. 9, Leipzig, 1910.

Hempel, Carl G., "Explanation in science and in history," in Dray, William H., ed., *Philosophical Analysis and History*, New York and London, 1966, pp. 95–126.

Herder, Johann Gottfried, "Metakritik" in *Saemmtliche Werke*, Stuttgart, Tuebingen, 1830.

Hexter, J. H., "The education of the aristocracy in the Renaissance," in Hexter, J. H., *Reappraisals in History*, Evanston, Ill., 1961, pp. 45–70.

―――― *Reappraisals in History*, Evanston, Ill., 1961.

History and Theory. Studies in the Philosophy of History (Middletown, Conn., and The Hague), vol. 1, no. 1, 1960 ff.

Hook, Sidney, ed., *Philosophy and History: A Symposium*, New York, 1963.

Huizinga, Johan, *Im Bann der Geschichte: Betrachtungen und Gestaltungen*, Basel, 1943.

―――― "The Problem of the Renaissance," in Huizinga, Johan, *Men and Ideas*, New York, 1959, pp. 243–87 (A Meridian Book). [First published in *De Gids*, LXXXIV, 1920, part 4, pp. 107–33, 231–55.]

―――― "The Task of Cultural History," in Huizinga, *Men and*

Ideas, New York, 1959, pp. 17–76 (A Meridian Book). [First published in Huizinga, J., *Cultuurhistorische verkenningen,* Haarlem, 1929.]

——, "Renaissance and realism," in *Men and Ideas,* New York, 1959, pp. 288–309 (A Meridian Book). [First published in Huizinga, J., *Cultuurhistorische verkenningen,* Haarlem, 1929.]

——, *The Waning of the Middle Ages,* Garden City, N.Y., 1954 (A Doubleday Anchor Book).

Husserl, Edmund, *Die Krisis der europaeischen Wissenschaften und die transzendentale Phaenomenologie.* Husserliana, Bd. VI, Den Haag, 1962.

Ivens, Joris, "Borinage—A documentary experience," *Film Culture* (New York, 1956), vol. II, no. 1, pp. 6–9.

Jauss, Hans Robert, "Ursprung und Bedeutung der Fortschrittsidee in der 'Querelle des Anciens et des Modernes'," in Kuhn, Helmut, and Wiedmann, Franz, eds., *Die Philosophie und die Frage nach dem Fortschritt,* Muenchen, 1964, pp. 51–72.

Jauss, Hans Robert, *Zeit und Erinnerung in Marcel Proust's "A la recherche du temps perdu"* [*Heidelberger Forschungen,* vol. 3], Heidelberg, 1955.

Jaeger, Werner, *Paideia: The Ideals of Greek Culture,* vols. I, II, III, New York, 1939–45. [Translated by Gilbert Highet.]

Jedin, Hubert, *Bischoefliches Konzil oder Kirchenparlament?: Ein Beitrag zur Ekklesiologie der Konzilien von Konstanz und Basel.* [Vortraege der Aeneas Silvius Stiftung an der Universitaet Basel, II], Basel and Stuttgart. 1963.

Jonas, Hans, *Gnosis und spaetantiker Geist,* vol. I (3. verbesserte und vermehrte Auflage), Goettingen, 1964, vol. II, Teil 1, Goettingen, 1954.

——, *The Phenomenon of Life.* New York, 1966.

Kaegi, Werner, *Jacob Burckhardt: Eine Biographie;* 3 vols., Basel, 1947, 1950, 1956.

——, *Historische Meditationen,* Zurich, no date.

Kafka, Franz, "Die Wahrheit ueber Sancho Pansa," in *Beim Bau der chinesischen Mauer,* Berlin, 1931, p. 38.

Kant, Immanuel, *Idea of a Universal History from a Cosmopolitan Point of View,* in Gardiner, Patrick, ed., *Theories of History,* Glencoe, Ill., 1959. p. 22–34. [Original title: *Idee zu einer allgemeinen Geschichte in weltbuergerlicher Absicht.*]

Kierkegaard, Soeren, *The Journals of Kierkegaard,* select, transl., ed., by Alexander Dru, New York, 1959 (A Harper Torchbook). [A German edition: *Soeren Kierkegaard: Tagebuecher. Eine Auswahl,* Wiesbaden (1947).]

Klapper, Joseph T., *The Effects of Mass Communication,* Glencoe, Ill., 1960.

Kolko, Gabriel, "Max Weber on America: Theory and Evidence," in *History and Theory* (The Hague, 1961), vol. I, no. 3, pp. 243–60.

Kracauer, Siegfried, "The Challenge of Qualitative Content Analysis," in *The Public Opinion Quarterly* (Princeton, N.J.), vol. 16, no. 4, Winter 1952–53.

———, "Die Gruppe als Ideentraeger," in *Das Ornament der Masse,* Frankfurt, a.M., 1963, pp. 123–56. Reprinted from *Archiv fuer Sozialwissenschaft und Sozialpolitik* (Tuebingen, August 1922), vol. 49, no. 3, pp. 594–622.

———, "Katholizismus und Relativismus," *Frankfurter Zeitung,* Nov. 19, 1921; [Reprinted in Kracauer, Siegfried, *Das Ornament der Masse,* Frankfurt a.M., 1963, pp. 187–96.]

———, *Das Ornament der Masse,* Frankfurt a.M., 1963.

———, *Soziologie als Wissenschaft. Eine erkenntnistheoretische Untersuchung.* Dresden, 1922.

———, *Theory of Film: The Redemption of Physical Reality,* New York, 1960.

Kristeller, Paul Oskar, "Some problems of historical knowledge," in *The Journal of Philosophy* (February 16, 1961, New York), vol. LVIII, no. 4, pp. 85–110.

———, "The moral thought of Renaissance humanism," in *Chapters in Western Civilization,* 3rd edition, New York, 1961, vol. 1, pp. 289–335. [Reprinted in Kristeller, Paul Oskar, *Renaissance Thought II,* New York, Evanston and London, 1965, pp. 20–68.]

———, "Changing views of the intellectual history of the Renaissance since Jacob Burckhardt," in Helton, Tinsley, ed., *The Renaissance* (Madison, Wis.), 1961, pp. 27–52.

Kubler, George, *The Shape of Time: Remarks on the History of Things*, New Haven and London, 1962.

Laslett, Peter, "Commentary (on part nine: 'Problems in the Historiography of Science')," in Crombie, A. C., ed., *Scientific Change . . .* , London, 1963, pp. 861–65.

———, "Foreword," in Hexter, J. H., *Reappraisals in History*, Evanston, Ill., 1961, pp. xi–xix.

Léger, Fernand, "A propos du cinéma," in L'Herbier, Marcel, ed., *Intelligence du cinématographe*, Paris, 1946, pp. 337–40. [First published in 1931.]

Lévi-Strauss, Claude, *La Pensée sauvage*, Paris, 1962.

Leyden W. von, "History and the concept of relative time," in *History and Theory* (The Hague, 1963), vol. II, no. 3, pp. 279–80. [Quoting Herder's Metakritik]

Lichtenberg, Georg Christoph, *Aphorismen, Briefe, Schriften*, Stuttgart, 1953. [Kroeners Taschenausgabe, Bd. 154.]

Lietzmann, Hans, *A History of the Early Church*, Cleveland, Ohio, 1961 (A Meridian Book). [Book I: vols. 1 & 2, Book II: vols. 3 & 4. Translated by Bertram Lee Woolf.]

Loewith, Karl, *Gesammelte Abhandlungen: Zur Kritik der geschichtlichen Existenz*, Stuttgart, 1960.

———, *Jacob Burckhardt: Der Mensch inmitten der Geschichte*, Luzern, 1936.

———, "Mensch und Geschichte," in *Gesammelte Abhandlungen: Zur Kritik der geschichtlichen Existenz*, Stuttgart, 1960, pp. 152–78.

Lovejoy, Arthur O., *Essays in the History of Ideas*, New York, 1960 (A Capricorn Book). [First published in 1948.]

———, "Present standpoints and past history," in Meyerhoff, Hans, ed., *The Philosophy of History in Our Time*, Garden City, N.Y. 1959. [In *The Journal of Philosophy* (Aug. 31, 1939), vol. XXXVI, no. 18, pp. 477–89.]

Lowe, Adolph, *On Economic Knowledge*, New York, 1965.

McPhee, William N., *Formal Theories of Mass Behavior*, Glencoe, Ill., 1963.

Macaulay, Thomas Babington, *History of England from the Acces-*

sion of James II (published in 1849–61, 5 vols.). Passage from Chapter 3, in Hale, J. R., ed., *The Evolution of British Historiography from Bacon to Namier*, Cleveland and New York, 1964, pp. 222–40 (A Meridian Book).

MacDonald, Philip, *Murder Gone Mad*, New York, 1965 (An Avon Book).

Maitland, Frederic William, *History of English law before the time of Edward I*. (1895). Quoted in Hexter, J. H., *Reappraisals in History*, Evanston, Ill., 1961, p. 195.

Malinowski, Bronislaw, *Magic, Science and Religion*, Garden City, N.Y., 1954 (A Doubleday Anchor Book).

Mandelbaum, Maurice, "The History of Ideas, Intellectual History, and the History of Philosophy," in *History and Theory*, Beiheft 5: *"The Historiography of the History of Philosophy* (The Hague, 1965), pp. 33–66.

———, *The Problem of Historical Knowledge; An Answer to Relativism*, New York, 1938. [New York, Evanston, and London, 1967 (A Harper Torchbook.)]

———, "Societal Laws," in Dray, William H., ed., *Philosophical Analysis and History*, New York, 1966, pp. 330–46.

Mannheim, Karl, "Historismus," in *Archiv fuer Sozialwissenschaft und Sozialpolitik*, vol. 52, no. 1, 1924. pp. 1–60.

Marcel, Gabriel, "Possibilités et limites de l'art cinématographique," in *Revue internationale de filmologie* (Paris, July–Dec. 1954), vols. V, nos. 18–19, pp. 163–76.

Marquand, John P., *Point of No Return*, Boston, 1949.

Marrou, Henri Irénée, "Comment comprendre le métier d'historien," in Samaran, Charles, ed., *L'Histoire et ses méthodes*, Paris, 1961, pp. 1467–1540.

———, "Das Janusantlitz der Historischen Zeit bei Augustin," in Andresen, Carl ed., *Zum Augustin-Gespraech der Gegenwart*. Darmstadt. 1962, pp. 349–80.

———, *De la connaissance historique*, Paris, 1962. [Fourth revised Printing.]

Mehta, Ved, "The flight of crook-taloned birds," *The New Yorker*, Part I, Dec. 8, 1962, pp. 59–147; Part II, Dec. 15, 1962, pp. 47–129.

Meinecke, Friedrich, "Historicism and its problems," in Stern, Fritz, ed., *The Varieties of History*, New York, 1956, pp. 267–88 (A Meridian Book). [Translated by Julian H. Franklin. First published under the title "Kausalitaeten und Werte in der Geschichte," in *Staat und Persoenlichkeit*, Berlin, 1933, pp. 29–53.]

Merton, Robert K., *On the Shoulders of Giants: A Shandean Postscript*, New York, 1965.

Meuthen, Erich, "Nikolaus von Kues und die Einheit," in *Neue Zuercher Zeitung*, August 9, 1964.

Meyerhoff, Hans, ed., *The Philosophy of History in Our Time*, Garden City, N.Y. 1959 (A Doubleday Anchor Book).

Mills, Wright C., *The Sociological Imagination*, New York, 1959.

Mink, Louis O., "The Autonomy of Historical Understanding," in *History and Theory* (Middletown, Conn., 1966), vol. V, no. 1, pp. 24–47.

Mommsen, Hans, "Historische Methode," in Besson, Waldemar, ed., *Geschichte, Frankfurt* a.M., 1961, pp. 78–91.

Murray, Gilbert, *Five Stages of Greek Religion*, Garden City, N. Y., no date (A Doubleday Anchor Book). [Third edition, 1951; first published in 1912.]

Nagel, Ernest, "Determinism in History," in Dray, William H., ed., *Philosophical Analysis and History*, New York, 1966, pp. 347–82.

Namier, Sir Lewis B., "History" in Namier, *Avenues of History*, London, 1952, pp. 1–10.

———, *Avenues of History*, London, 1952.

———, "Human nature in politics," in Stern, Fritz, ed., *The Varieties of History*. New York, 1956, pp. 381–86. (A Meridian Book). [Originally published in Namier, Sir Lewis B., *Personalities and Powers*, 1955.]

Newhall, Beaumont, *The History of Photography from 1893 to the Present Day*, New York, 1949.

Niebuhr, Reinhold, "The Diversity and Unity of History," in Meyerhoff, Hans, ed., *The Philosophy of History in Our Time*, Garden City, N.Y., 1959, pp. 313–31. [In Niebuhr, ed., *The Nature and Destiny of Man*, New York, 1953, II, pp. 301–21.]

Nietzsche, Friedrich," Vom Nutzen und Nachteil der Historie fuer das Leben," [Unzeitgemaesse Betrachtungen, Zweites Stueck], in Friedrich Nietzsche, *Werke,* erster Band, Leipzig, 1930, pp. 95–195.

Nilsson, Martin P., *Geschichte der griechischen Religion,* vol. I, 1955; vol. II, 1961. [Zweite durchgesehene und ergaenzte Ausgabe.]

Novikoff, Alex B., "The concept of integrative levels and biology," in *Science* (Lancaster, Pa.,) March 2, 1945, vol. 101, no. 2618, pp. 209–15.

Panofsky, Erwin, *Renaissance and Renascences in Western Art,* Stockholm, 1960.

Plato, *Republic,* Oxford, 1894, Cambridge, 1966.

Pirenne, Henri, *A History of Europe: From the Invasions to the XVI Century,* New York, 1955. [First published in 1938.]

———, "What are historians trying to do?," in Meyerhoff, Hans, ed., *The Philosophy of History in Our Time,* Garden City, N.Y., 1959, pp. 87–99. [In Stuart A. Rice, ed., *Methods in Social Science,* Chicago, 1931, pp. 435–45.]

Poulet, Georges, "Proust," in Poulet, Georges, *Studies in Human Time,* New York, 1959, pp. 291–322. [A Harper Torchbook.]

Proust, Marcel, *Contre Sainte-Beuve,* Paris, 1954.

———, *Remembrance of Things Past,* New York, 1932 and 1934, 2 vols., Translated by C. K. Scott Moncrieff, except for the last part, "The Past Recaptured," which has been translated by Frederick A. Blossom. [Original title: *A la recherche du temps perdu,* Paris, 1954, vols. 1–3. Bibliothèque de la Pléiade.]

Rand, Edward Kennard, *Founders of the Middle Ages,* New York, 1957 (A Dover Book). [First published in 1928.]

Ranke, Leopold von, *Deutsche Geschichte im Zeitalter der Reformation,* Koeln, no date.

———, *Die roemischen Paepste in den letzten vier Jahrhunderten,* Koeln, no date.

———, "The Ideal of Universal History," in Stern, Fritz, ed., *The Varieties of History,* New York, 1956, p. 57 [A Meridian Book].

————, "Universal history: the oldest historical group of nations and the Greeks," London, 1884, pp. xi–xiv and 2, quoted by Butterfield, Herbert, *Man on His Past*, Boston, 1960, p. 124.

————, *Weltgeschichte*, Leipzig, 1883–88.

Ratner, Sidney, "History as Inquiry," in Hook, Sidney, ed., *Philosophy and History*, New York, 1963, pp. 325–38.

"Raumer, Friedrich von" (article about him, author's initials unidentifiable), in *Conversations-Lexikon der Gegenwart*, Brockhaus, Leipzig, 1840, Bd. 4.

Rickert, Heinrich, *Die Probleme der Geschichtsphilosophie: Eine Einfuehrung*, Heidelberg, 1924. (Dritte, umgearbeitete Auflage).

Ritter, Gerhard, "Scientific history, contemporary history and political history," in *History and Theory* (Middletown, Conn. and The Hague, 1961), vol. I, no. 3, pp. 261–79.

Rostovtzeff, Michael Ivanovich, *Greece*, New York, 1963 (A Galaxy Book).

————, *The Social and Economic History of the Roman Empire*, 2 vols., Oxford, 1926.

————, *Rome*, New York, 1960. Translated by J. D. Duff. (A Galaxy Book). [First published in 1927.]

Sadoul, Georges, *L'Invention du cinéma 1832–1897*, Paris, 1946 (Historie générale du cinéma, I).

Sainte-Beuve, Charles-Augustin, *Causeries du lundi*, Paris, 1881.

Samaran, Charles, ed., *L'Histoire et ses méthodes*, Paris, 1961. Encyclopédie de la Pléiade.

Schapiro, Meyer, "Style," in Kroeber, ed., *Anthropology Today*, Chicago, 1953, pp. 287–312.

Schlesinger, Arthur Meier Jr., *The Age of Jackson*, Boston, 1945.

Schmidt, Alfred, *Der Begriff der Natur in der Lehre von Marx*, Frankfurt a.M., 1962. (Frankfurter Beitraege zur Soziologie, Bd. 11).

————, "Zum Verhaeltnis von Geschichte und Natur im dialektischen Materialismus," in *Existentialismus und Marxismus: Eine Kontroverse zwischen Sartre, Garaudy, Hyppolite, Vigier und Orcel*, Frankfurt a.M., 1965, pp. 103–55 (edition Suhrkamp, 116).

Schopenhauer, Arthur, "Die Welt als Wille und Vorstellung," in *Saemtliche Werke*, Wiesbaden, 1949, vol. 2.

Schuetz, Alfred, "The Stranger," in *The American Journal of Sociology*, May 1944, vol. XLIX, no. 6, pp. 499–507.

Sève, Lucien, "Cinéma et méthode," in *Revue internationale de filmologie* (Paris, July–Aug. 1947), vol. I, no. 1, p. 45; see also pp. 30–31.

Snow, Charles Percy, *The Two Cultures and a Second Look: An Expanded Version of the Two Cultures and the Scientific Revolution.* Cambridge, Eng., 1964.

Spengler, Oswald, "The world-as-history", in Gardiner, Patrick, ed., *Theories of History*, Glencoe, Ill., 1959. pp. 188–200. [Reprinted from *The Decline of the West*, 1926, from vol. I, Ch. 1 & 3 Original title, *Der Untergang des Abendlandes.*]

Stern, Fritz, ed., *The Varieties of History from Voltaire to the Present.* New York, 1956 (A Meridian Book).

——, "Introduction," in Stern, F., ed., *The Varieties of History* . . . pp. 11–32. New York, 1956 (A Meridian Book).

Sterne, Laurence, *The Life and Opinions of Tristram Shandy, Gentleman.* Edited by James Aiken Work, New York, 1940 (An Odyssey Paperback).

Strand, Paul, "The Photographer's Problem . . ." in *Seven Arts*, 1917, vol. 2, pp. 524–25. Quoted by Newhall, Beaumont, in *The History of Photography from 1839 to the Present Day.* New York, 1949, p. 150.

Strauss, Leo, "On Collingwood's philosophy of history," in *The Review of Metaphysics* (Montreal, June 1952), vol. V, no. 4, pp. 559–86.

Stubbs, William. *The Constitutional History of England,* Oxford, 1929. [Originally published 1874–78.] Quoted in "Introduction" in Hale, J. R., *The Eevolution of British Historiography from Bacon to Namier,* Cleveland and New York, 1964, p. 59 (A Meridian Book).

Talmon, J. L., "The ordeal of Sir Lewis Namier: the man, the historian, the Jew," in *Commentary* (New York, March 1962), vol. 33, no. 3, pp. 237–46.

Taubmann, Howard, "History as Literature," *New York Times,* March 30, 1966.

Tennant, John A., "Review of a New York Stieglitz exhibition," in *Photo-Miniature,* no. 183, 1921, pp. 138–39. Quoted by Newhall, Beaumont, in *The History of Photography . . .* New York, 1949. p. 144.

Tilly, Charles, "The Analysis of a counter-revolution," in *History and Theory* (The Hague, 1963), vol. III, no. 1, pp. 30–58. [This study has been expanded into a book, *The Vendée,* Cambridge, Mass., 1964.]

———, *The Vendée,* Cambridge, Mass., 1964.

Toqueville, Alexis de, *Souvenirs de Alexis de Tocqueville,* Paris, 1893, 1944. [English Translation, *The Recollections of Alexis de Tocqueville,* New York, 1959. A Meridian Book.]

Tolstoi, Leo Nikolaevich, *Anna Karenina,* Muenchen, no date.

Tolstoy, Leo Nikolaevich, *War and Peace,* Baltimore, 1957, 2 vols., translated by Rosemary Edmonds. (Penguin Books). [German edition, *Krieg und Frieden,* 2 vols., Bern, 1942.]

Toynbee, Arnold J., ed. and transl., *Greek Historical Thought,* New York, 1952 (A Mentor Book).

———, *Reconsiderations. A Study of History,* vol. XII. London, New York, Toronto, 1961 (A Galaxy Book, 1964).

Troeltsch, Ernst, *Der Historismus und seine Probleme,* Aalen 1961, quoted by Mandelbaum, Maurice, *The Problem of Historical Knowledge: An Answer to Relativism,* New York, Evanston, London 1967, pp. 155–65 (A Harper Torchbook).

Valéry, Paul, *History and Politics,* New York, 1962, *Collected Works,* Vol. 10. (Bollingen Series, XLV). [Original title, Valéry, Paul, *Oeuvres,* vols., 1, 2. Paris 1957, 1960. Bibliothèque de la Pléiade.]

Vico, Giambattista, *Scienza Nuova,* First edition 1725. English Edition, *New Science,* from the 3rd ed., 1744, Ithaca, 1948.

Vidal-Naquet, Pierre, "Temps des dieux et temps des hommes," in *Revue de l'histoire des religions,* vol. CLVII, no. 1 (Jan.–March 1960), pp. 55–80.

Vossler, Otto, *Geist und Geschichte: Von der Reformation bis zur Gegenwart, Gesammelte Aufsaetze,* Muenchen, 1964.

————, "Rankes historisches Problem," in Vossler, Otto, *Geist und Geschichte* . . . Muenchen, 1964, pp. 184–214.

Weizsaecker, Carl Friedrich von, *Die Geschichte der Natur,* Goettingen, 1958. [Kleine Vandenhoeck-Reihe, 1.]

Wendland, Paul, *Die hellenistisch-roemische Kultur in ihren Beziehungen zu Judentum und Christentum.* [Handbuch zum Neuen Testament, Bd. 1, Teil 2 & 3.] Tuebingen, 1912.

White, Hayden V., "The Burden of History," in *History and Theory* (Middletown, Conn., 1966), vol. V, no. 2, pp. 111–34.

Willey, Basil, *The Seventeenth Century Background,* Garden City, N.Y., 1953. (A Doubleday Anchor Book.) [First published in London, 1934.]

Wind, Edgar, *Art and Anarchy,* London, 1963.

Wittram, Reinhard, *Das Interesse an der Geschichte,* Goettingen, 1963.

A SELECTION OF BOOKS BY SIEGFRIED KRACAUER

Ginster, a novel, Berlin 1928
Die Angestellten, Frankfurt 1930
Jacques Offenbach und das Paris seiner Zeit, Amsterdam 1937
Propaganda and the Nazi War Film, New York 1942
The Conquest of Europe on the Screen. The Nazi Newsreel 1939-1940, Washington 1943
From Caligari to Hitler, Princeton 1947
Satellite Mentality: Political Attitudes and Propaganda Susceptibilies of Non-Communists in Hungary, Poland and Czechoslovakia, New York 1956 (with Paul Berkman)
Theory of Film: The Redemption of Physical Reality, New York 1960
Das Ornament der Masse: Essays, Frankfurt 1963
Dr. Kracauer's many articles, essays, and reviews have appeared in such newspapers and magazines as Harper's, Commentary, Partisan Review, Saturday Review, The New Republic, Theatre Arts, The New York Times Book Review, Frankfurter Zeitung, Neue Züricher Zeitung, National Zeitung, Basel, Mercure de France, Revue internationale de filmologie, and the English Film Quarterly.

A SELECTION OF BOOKS BY PAUL OSKAR KRISTELLER

The Classics and Renaissance Thought, Cambridge 1955
Studies in Renaissance Thought and Letters, Rome 1956
Latin Manuscript Books before 1600, New York 1960
Renaissance Thought: Vol. I: The Classic, Scholastic and Humanistic Strains, New York 1961. Vol. II: Papers on Humanism and the Arts, 1965
Renaissance Thought and the Arts, Princeton 1980 (revised edition of 1965)
Eight Philosophers of the Italian Renaissance, Stanford 1964
Iter Italicum: A Finding List of Uncatalogued or Incompletely Catalogued Humanistic Manuscripts of the Renaissance in Italian and Other Libraries, London and Leiden, Vol. I 1963, Vol. II 1967, Vol. III 1991, Vol. IV 1992, Vol. V 1993, Vol. VI 1992
Greek Philosophers of the Hellenistic Age, New York 1993
Studies in Renaissance Thought and Letters, Rome 1993
In addition, Paul Oskar Kristeller has published several hundred articles in academic journals, contributions to scholarly works, lectures and reviews. Since 1975, six Festschriften have been published in honor of Paul Oskar Kristeller.